AFTER
KHOMEINI

AFTER
KHOMEINI

Iran Under His Successors

SAÏD AMIR ARJOMAND

OXFORD
UNIVERSITY PRESS

OXFORD
UNIVERSITY PRESS

Oxford University Press, Inc., publishes works that further
Oxford University's objective of excellence
in research, scholarship, and education.

Oxford New York
Auckland   Cape Town   Dar es Salaam   Hong Kong   Karachi
Kuala Lumpur   Madrid   Melbourne   Mexico City   Nairobi
New Delhi   Shanghai   Taipei   Toronto

With offices in
Argentina   Austria   Brazil   Chile   Czech Republic   France   Greece
Guatemala   Hungary   Italy   Japan   Poland   Portugal   Singapore
South Korea   Switzerland   Thailand   Turkey   Ukraine   Vietnam

Published by Oxford University Press, Inc.
198 Madison Avenue, New York, New York 10016
www.oup.com

First issued as an Oxford University Press paperback, 2012

Oxford is a registered trademark of Oxford University Press

Library of Congress Cataloging-in-Publication Data
Arjomand, Said Amir.
After Khomeini : Iran under his successors / Saïd Amir Arjomand.
p.   cm.
Includes bibliographical references and index.
ISBN 978-0-19-539179-4 (hardcover); 978-0-19-989194-8 (paperback)
1. Iran—History—1979–1997.
2. Iran—History—1997–
3. Iran—Politics and government—1979–1997.
4. Iran—Politics and government—1997–
5. Iran—History—Revolution, 1979—Influence.   I. Title.
DS318.9.A74 2009
955.05'43—dc22   2009012266

1 3 5 7 9 8 6 4 2

Printed in the United States of America
on acid-free paper

For Kathryn

هرگز نمیرد آنکه دلش زنده شد به عشق

ثبت است بر جریده عالم دوام ما

CONTENTS

ACKNOWLEDGMENTS AND
TRANSLITERATION

I have closely followed the developments in Iran since my first book on contemporary Iran, *The Turban for the Crown: The Islamic Revolution in Iran* (Oxford University Press, 1988), was published over 20 years ago. I have many people and institutions to thank for being able to follow these developments, but will mention only the Ford Foundation for a 1987–1988 grant for a comparative study of revolutions, Gary Sick, who was then at the Ford Foundation and read and commented on a draft of Chapters 7 and 10 much more recently, the United States Institute for Peace for a 1992–1994 grant on linkages between domestic politics and the foreign policy of Iran, and the Carnegie Corporation for a 2006–2008 scholarship that enabled me to complete the writing of this book. I have adopted the simplest system for the transliteration of Persian words, that of the *Journal of Persianate Studies*. In the text (though not in the bibliography) diacritical marks have been omitted for proper names, however. The conventional spelling of the *New York Times* has been followed for such terms as Shi'ism and well-known names, such as Khomeini, Khamenei, and Ahmadinejad.

AFTER
KHOMEINI

Introduction

IRAN HAS NOT CEASED TO SURPRISE THE WORLD since the American ambassador's famous "thinking the unthinkable" 1978 cable about the imminent fall of the Shah and the coming of the Islamic revolution. The apparent sequence of moderate government under President Akbar Hashemi-Rafsanjani (1989–1997) and democratic reform under President Mohammad Khatami (1997–2005) was followed by a spectacular reversal no one foresaw. The hardliners returned to capture the Majles (Iranian parliament) in the national elections of 2004, and one of their leaders, Mahmoud Ahmadinejad, beat a former President (Hashemi-Rafsanjani) and two much better known reformist candidates in the presidential elections of 2005. President Ahmadinejad (2005–2009) has revived the revolutionary populism of old, now coupled with an aggressive foreign policy, including a nuclear program. Iran's political regime has proved remarkably resilient through all these changes, despite the disaffection of the younger half of the population. And the regime has become all the more robust and defiant internationally, partly as a result of the Bush administration's ill-advised bluff about regime change from 2002 onward.

The greatest misunderstanding concerning Iran after the revolution stems from the assumption that the revolution was over, either with the victory of pragmatism and Hashemi-Rafsanjani's program of economic reconstruction in 1989, following the Iran–Iraq war, or with the rise of the reform movement under Khatami in 1997. The truth is that the death of Ayatollah Ruhollah

3

Khomeini as the Imam and charismatic leader of the Islamic revolution in June 1989 did not mean the end of the revolution, but only the beginning of a prolonged struggle among the children of the revolution over his heritage. The raucous struggle to define, structure, and control the new Islamic political order set up by Khomeini among different factions of his followers has a logic that can be understood as the consequence of the revolution. The unique political regime produced by this struggle for Khomeini's heritage also defies understanding in generic terms, being neither a democracy nor a dictatorship. It can be easily understood, however, with reference to the distinctive and contradictory goals of the Islamic revolution.

This book draws on the sociology of revolution with a view to its long-term consequences to offer an explanation of the political development of Iran over the past two decades. Not only the vicissitudes of Iran's domestic politics, but also the shifts in its foreign policy will be shown to fit the pattern typical of the great revolutions. The unique and distinctive features of the Islamic Republic of Iran as a political regime, on the other hand, can be understood only as intended consequences of a particular revolution, the Islamic revolution of 1979, and in terms of the constitutional politics of the creation of the post-revolutionary Islamic order in Iran in the past two decades. Constitutional politics refers to the struggle for the definition of social and political order, and takes place among groups and organizations aligned behind different principles of order by their material and ideal interests. In the process of constitutional politics, the contending groups and organizations are forced to reconcile the respective logics of their principles through compromise, concession, and reinterpretation in order to translate them, more or less adequately, into an institutional order sustained by effective force.[1] The parameters for this struggle for the definition of the new political order—or the constitutional politics of Iran since 1989—will be shown to be those set at the beginning by Khomeini's mixture of theocratic, republican, and populist elements in the ideology of the Islamic revolution.

The two revolutions that shook the world in the first and last quarters of the twentieth century were the Bolshevik revolution in Russia and the Islamic revolution in Iran. The former began in October 1917 and the latter in February 1979. But when did they respectively end? This question is much harder to answer because of the indeterminate nature of the consequences that can plausibly be attributed to each revolution. Although everyone agrees that the Bolshevik revolution did not end with the death of its charismatic leader, Lenin, there is no such consensus with respect to the Islamic revolution after the death of Ayatollah Ruhollah Khomeini in June 1989.

On the contrary, it will be argued that the broad lack of comprehension of the post-Khomeini revolutionary power struggle to define, structure, and control the new order he set up is partly due to the general assumption that the revolution has ended. The great enthusiasm for the movement for reform and democratization under President Khatami was also based on that assumption. This book argues that the Islamic revolution did not end with Khomeini's death and that there was no return to "normalcy" the day after. Massive revolutionary violence abated while the revolution continued. Post-revolutionary reconstruction is very much a part of the revolution. The definition of the new political order remained incomplete and was still being contested when Khomeini died in 1989, thus setting the parameters for Iran's power struggle and constitutional politics in the two decades that followed.

Like all other revolutions, the Islamic revolution of 1979 in Iran had historical and structural causes and preconditions, as well as more immediate sociopolitical triggers.[2] Such causes can help us understand only why a revolution was likely and in fact occurred in 1979. The same kind of reasoning could also explain why the revolution was destined to be an Islamic revolution, even though there were other revolutionary groups with different aims. But we need a completely different analytical framework for understanding the direction of post-revolutionary change, particularly post-revolutionary institution building and construction of a new political order. Such institution building and political reconstruction can be analyzed as the intended consequences of the revolution as they were vaguely prefigured in the ideology of the winners but realized subsequently as the result of the post-revolutionary power struggle and constitutional politics.

To shift the focus from the causes to the consequences of the revolution requires linking the conception of revolutionary processes to the long-term constitutional politics of post-revolutionary institution building. The vision of the Islamic revolution held by its leader, Khomeini, only very gradually found embodiment in the institutional and political structure of the regime it created, the Islamic Republic of Iran (IRI). The process involved was a struggle for the definition of the new political order, and was a much longer process that the winning of the revolutionary power struggle against those groups in the original revolutionary coalition that subsequently defected, or were rejected and eliminated. The revolutionary power struggle was over by 1983, but that was almost the beginning of Khomeini's effort to translate his charisma into lasting institutions.

Institution building after the revolution and post-revolutionary developments are to a great extent determined by the subsequent transformation of
the charismatic authority of the revolutionary leader. Despite the undeniable significance of charismatic leaders in the Russian, Chinese, Cuban, and
Iranian revolutions, their role in the process of revolutionary transformation
is largely ignored in the current theories of revolution. We therefore need
to turn elsewhere in our search for an explanation. Max Weber was aware
of the importance of revolutionary charismatic leadership, seeing "a highly
emotional type of devotion to and trust in the leader" as "a natural basis for
the utopian component which is found in all revolutions."[3] To describe the
return to a new pattern of normalcy after a radical historical interruption
by a charismatic leader, Weber developed the idea of the routinization of
charisma. Routinization was defined as the transformation of extraordinary,
personal charisma at times of crisis into ordinary, lasting political institutions. From our point of view, it could be said that the failure of routinization
would mean an end to the personal leadership of the revolution and abrupt
shifts and reversals in post-revolutionary change. Successful routinization,
on the other hand, would result in the replacement of a personal system of
authority by an impersonal one, thus setting the direction of continuous post-
revolutionary transformation of the political order. Successful routinization of
charisma in twentieth-century revolutions has typically been a process of transition to collective rule. Khomeini as the Imam and leader of the revolution
exercised his charismatic authority in the following decade to shape various
revolutionary structures and institutions of the theocratic IRI, and to mini-
mize their dissonance. In doing so, he created the present system of collective
rule by clerical councils, thereby setting the parameters of Iran's subsequent
constitutional politics down to the present.

The most important parameters were set by the Constitution of 1979 and
its amendment in 1989, as ordered by Khomeini shortly before his death.
Constitutions can become the subject of intense public debate at the time of
their promulgation or subsequent crises, and thus create a frame of reference
for a variety of political groups, thereby structuring politics in ways that tran-
scend their texts or legal effect, as has been the case in the Islamic Republic
of Iran. I shall argue that the tension and contradictions among the three
main principles of the 1979 Constitution—namely, theocratic government,
participatory democracy, and populist social justice—account for the main
features of the constitutional politics of Iran under Khomeini's successors in
their struggle over his purported revolutionary legacy.

This book accordingly begins, in chapter 1, with a sketch of Imam Khomeini's career and his leadership of Iran's Islamic revolution, and examines the attempts to institutionalize his charismatic authority as the leader of the Islamic revolution from the making of the Constitution of 1979 to his death in 1989. The regime set up by Khomeini as the Islamic Republic of Iran had a constitution crafted to Islamicize through and through its original model, the French Constitution of 1958. As a result, it came to consist of three disparate elements: theocratic or clericalist, republican or democratic, and populist on the basis of social justice. Khomeini had to solve the historically unprecedented constitutional problems of establishing a modern theocracy, and his clerical successors as Iran's ruling elite embarked on the consolidation of its novel clerical institutions and councils before all else. This important aspect of the constitutional development of the Islamic regime since 1989 is treated in chapter 2, tracing the transition from the traditional Shi'ite system of hierocratic authority to that of the new state as a theocratic republic. The emergence of the system of collective rule by clerical councils and its consolidation after Khomeini's death described in that chapter account for the most distinctive feature of the IRI and represent the institutional translation of the revolutionary vision of an Islamic polity guided by the Imam himself.

Chapter 3 describes the peaceful succession to Khomeini and the transition to dual leadership by two men who were officially designated as the Leader and the President of the IRI. Sayyad 'Ali Khamenei was elected leader by the Assembly of Leadership Experts, and Hashemi-Rafsanjani elected president. President Hashemi-Rafsanjani's attempt to centralize the revolutionary power structures and to rationalize them into a "developmental state" that revived the goals of economic development and modernization is examined, as are the limits to effective centralization. This examination of Hashemi-Rafsanjani's policy offers us an opportunity to revisit the sociology of revolution. The fact that the post-revolutionary routinization of charisma occurs within the inherited modern bureaucratic state and its legal framework has a paradoxical result. The revolutionaries aim at destroying the state but the revolution paradoxically makes the state all the stronger and increases its centralization. The paradox was first highlighted by Alexis de Tocqueville with regard to the further centralization of power in the French state by Napoleon after the great revolution of 1789. Accordingly, I call the ideal-type of revolution that captures the post-revolutionary centralization of power Tocquevillian.[4]

This model, however, ignores the typical emergence of post-revolutionary regimes of collective rule by councils and politbureaus. In Iran, we find this emergence of collective rule, as well as other deviations from the unimpeded centralization highlighted in the Tocquevillian ideal-type. The distinctive features of the IRI resulted from the arrested post-revolutionary centralization of power initiated by Hashemi-Rafsanjani in the early 1990s. The typical trends toward concentration of power, both personal and institutional, were very much at work in post-revolutionary Iran, but with a distinctive inflection due to the unique constitutional position of the Supreme Jurist tailored for Imam Khomeini, on the one hand, and the reorganization of the armed forces and mobilizational militia after the war with Iraq that ended in 1988, on the other. Yet another centrifugal post-revolutionary trend, in tension with the process of centralization of power, was the emergence of economic baronies and military-foreign policy cartels that enjoy de facto semi-autonomy. These centrifugal tendencies account for the hydra-headed character of many post-revolutionary regimes, including that of the IRI.

The presidency of Hashemi-Rafsanjani also requires us to examine the consequences of revolution systematically. Two questions need to be reexamined: the transmutations of revolutionary radicalism and the very conception of the process of revolution. I have mentioned the widely held view that the Islamic revolution ended either in the early 1980s or in the latter part of the 1990s. The presumption that the revolution had ended was largely due to an influential but misleading model of revolutionary process called the "anatomy of revolution."[5] The terminology we have available for describing different types of revolutionary groups derives from that paradigm, and is problematic because of its unaltered reference to the French revolution. More seriously misleading is the conception of the revolutionary process as a sudden convulsion in the body politic, likened to a passing fever that breaks with a return to normalcy. This conception is too restrictive to account for post-revolutionary institution building and cannot explain the relation between the revolutionary power struggle and the post-revolutionary constitutional politics.[6] In this paradigm, the revolution was given an extremely short life-span of 5 years, and was said to begin with the prominence of the moderates in 1789, continue with the rise of the radicals and the reign of terror, and end with the return of the moderates in Thermidor/July 1794. The sequence identified by the anatomical metaphor has been loosely applied to the coming to power of the "moderates" in Iran at the beginning of the revolution, and again with the ascendancy of Hashemi-Rafsanjani. The Islamic revolution in Iran was seen to go through the typical cycle of the rule of the moderates (1979–1980), a subsequent takeover by the "radicals" (1981–1988), and finally a "Thermidorian" return to more moderate rule and consolidation of the revolution at the end of the war with Iraq.[7]

This typical sequence, however, even in the extended and more rigorously formalized pattern,[8] does not allow for the examination of the institutional consequences of revolutions. The construction of a new political order, I have argued, is a longer term process and involves constitutional politics. The case of the Islamic revolution in Iran suggests that the revolutionary power struggle merges with constitutional politics and is a process that is much more drawn out, requiring a long-term perspective. Furthermore, the anatomical model obscures the identities of the historical revolutionary actors. The restorers of Thermidorian moderation are not the same persons or group as the "moderates" of the initial phase of the revolution. In this book, I will call them the "pragmatists," best exemplified by the former President Akbar Hashemi-Rafsanjani. As distinct from the original 1979 "moderates," they are transformed radicals. The transformation of the radicals can take different directions and proceed in different sequences. Some radicals become pragmatists, and some radicals and some pragmatists can turn to reformism as an evolution of pragmatism. The best example of the radicals becoming reformists through pragmatism is another former President, Mohammad Khatami, and the intellectuals 'Abdolkarim Sorush and Akbar Ganji can be mentioned as examples of radicals becoming reformists directly.[9] There is also a further possible stage in the long-term revolutionary process: the return of revolutionary radicalism and an emergent and fairly distinct group associated with it. This possibility is fully realized in Iran under the current President, Mahmud Ahmadinejad, and with the recent rise of the group I call the "hardliners." The hardliners are defined by their loyalty to the martyrs of the revolution and the advocacy of return to revolutionary radicalism.

Moderates, pragmatists, and hardliners in this alternative terminology can be differentiated on the basis of two criteria: the revolutionary justification of violence and the importance of ideology as a factor in revolutionary solidarity. The identities of revolutionary groups are, furthermore, not fixed but changing. As revolutions proceed, some radicals renounce the legitimacy or utility of violence and become pragmatists or reformers. Others persist in the revolutionary justification of violence and its use and become hardliners. During the June 2009 presidential election campaign, a woman confronted Mohammad 'Atrianfar, aide to the reformist candidate and former Prime Minister Mir-Hossein Musavi, with the accusation that five thousand innocent people were executed when the latter was in power in the 1980s. Atrianfar replied, "My friend, at the beginning of the Islamic revolution we were all like Ahmadinejad, but we changed our path and our way."[10]

The grip of ideology on the revolutionaries may also be loosened and gradually cease to serve as the basis of revolutionary solidarity. At the beginning of the revolution, ideology unifies and motivates groups with little shared life experience. As the revolution proceeds, and is complemented by war in many cases, as in Iran, the revolutionary career and life experience of the winners become the basis of their group solidarity and identity. Some renounce ideology altogether and become pragmatists or reformists, while others assign it a secondary place as just a symbol for revolutionary solidarity, which is more solidly based on the shared life experience of revolutionary careers. This latter group of revolutionaries insists on the categorical and uncompromising loyalty to the revolution and the members become hardliners.[11]

The consideration of ideology in relation to shifts in group identity raises the question of the persistence and transformation of the revolutionary solidarity that has held together the IRI since its birth. The analysis, by the great Muslim historian 'Abd al-Rahman ibn Khaldun (d. 1406), of what we would call revolutions can help us understand the persistence and change in revolutionary solidarity better than the modern theories of revolution. Ibn Khaldun discussed the emergence, persistence, and transformation of a distinct type of revolutionary solidarity among the revolutionaries who form the dominant strata of the post-revolutionary regime. The prototypical solidarity for Ibn Khaldun was the solidarity of a power group on the ascendant, which he called 'asabiyya. This solidarity of a rising power group has an inbuilt tendency toward domination and the formation or takeover of the state by a new dynasty. When reinforced by religion (and by extension, ideology), which reinforces solidarity by instilling inner faith in the militant power group, 'asabiyya could act as the decisive factor in political mobilization and would result in what he called great changes of dynasty and we would call revolution.[12] The new dynasty and its ruling class, established by revolution, remain in power for a long time, but its solidarity, produced by the crude conditions of the tribal periphery, is weakened generation after generation by civilized life. Something like this process is at work with an important segment of the first generation of Khomeini's followers who made the Islamic revolution in Iran. As revolutionary leaders emerged from the harsh conditions of clandestine cells, revolutionary committees, and militias engaged in the war with Iraq to become the ruling elite of new regime, many of them acquired power and wealth and developed a more open and pragmatic attitude.

Ibn Khaldun, however, conceived of group solidarity too narrowly as tribal solidarity based on genealogy and was primarily interested in its transformation into royal domination. His interest in revolution was incidental, and he did not examine how the original revolutionary solidarity can persist and undergo a transformation, which makes the original sense of religious mission or adherence to ideology secondary but without weakening revolutionary radicalism. In the 1940s and 1950s, Edwards Shils noted that community experience in cohesive army units in the Nazi and Soviet armies generated the intense primary group solidarity that held these armies together, whereas ideological symbols and values were effective to the extent that they were reinforced by primary group solidarity.[13] The Islamic revolution generated its own primary group solidarity among the Revolutionary Guards and its mobilizational arm, the Basij, and their formative experience of revolution and war with Iraq created a strong bond of loyalty and trust that sustained the present-day hardliners as they made their bid for the take-over of all non-clerical political institutions of the IRI in 2004.

As ideology receded in importance for both the pragmatists and the hardliners, it became a mere ancillary to two kinds of solidarity born of two different kinds of formative life experience. As the life experiences of the clerical ruling elite and the lay second stratum in revolutionary Iran differed significantly, the character of their solidarity evolves in different directions. The clerical solidarity of the ruling elite was the preexisting *esprit de corps* of the religious professionals produced in the *madrasa*s and only later seasoned by the revolutionary struggle under their charismatic teacher, Khomeini. The revolutionary solidarity of the agitprops that formed the lay second stratum of the IRI had no comparably uniform preexisting educational and professional basis, but was steeled by the decisive experience of the decade of revolution and war into an insider, or to use the expressive Persian adjective, *khodi* (one-of-us) solidarity.

Chapters 3 and 8 discuss how the radicals and the hardliners are distinguished from the pragmatists by their firmer commitment to violence. So too are the radicals distinguishable from the pragmatists and the hardliners by a more rigid ideological commitment. The moderates, represented in the revolutionary coalition by the Provisional Prime Minister Mehdi Bazargan in 1979, never reappear as a significant force in post-Khomeini Iran and are mentioned only incidentally in this book. The Islamic radicals of 1979 changed in two divergent directions, splitting into the pragmatists and the hardliners of the post-revolutionary period of consolidation. Finally, those radical children of the revolution who discarded their ideological outlook two decades later, either through a pragmatic stage or directly and suddenly, will be analyzed as "reformists" in chapters 4 and 5.

One of the most interesting features of Iran's post-revolutionary development is the swift transformation, within a generation, of the ideology of the Islamic revolution into an anti-ideological, reformist intellectual movement. Chapter 4 traces the emergence of reformism as a cultural rather than a political phenomenon. The reform movement was remarkable for rejecting the revolutionary idea of Islam as an ideology. Islam was said to be richer than ideology and supportive of an alternative social and political vision, conceived as civil society and democracy and variously referred to as reformism, republicanism, and even post-Islamism. This spontaneous contestation of the clericalist official Islam that had shaped the novel institutions of the IRI caused a serious erosion of the legitimacy of the regime.

The attempt to develop the republican or democratic elements of Khomeini's constitutional heritage was not made until nearly a decade after his death. Generally it ended in failure, except for the creation of the local and municipal councils. Chapter 5 will describe this attempt by President Mohammad Khatami (1997–2005) and the reform movement led by him. The rise and fall of Khatami and the reform movement are analyzed as a phase of post-revolutionary power struggle against the Leader or Supreme Jurist and clerical hardliners by the former radicals turned reformists. The post-revolutionary power struggle took place at two connected levels. On one level, it was a struggle between two factions among the children of the Islamic revolution, only recently divided into reformers and hardliners. At the same time, it was a struggle for the definition of the political order—and thus primarily an instance of constitutional politics. Constitutional politics involves vested and evolving institutional interests, and is thus a power struggle at the institutional level. As chapter 5 shows, the political control and protection of the regime as the gatekeeper to all elected offices thus became the most important function of the Guardian Council during the Khatami presidency, eclipsing its constitutionally defined responsibilities. During the Ahmadinejad presidency, the Basij organization has similarly assumed the new function of delivering votes as the political machine of the IRI, as described in chapter 8.

The unintended consequences of revolution are as important as those prefigured in the ideas and projects of the revolutionaries, and fundamentally affect the structure of the political community and its social base. Khomeini's overthrow of the Shah set in motion an integrative social revolution that continues to unfold, quietly and hidden from the public eye, which is fixed on the political turmoil and power struggle among his successors.

The closed character of the ruling class as a cause of revolutions and its opening as their consequence were highlighted by Aristotle among the ancients and Vilfredo Pareto among modern social scientists.[14] Pareto also discussed the phenomenon of the replacement of one ruling class by another through revolution, which makes history the graveyard of aristocracies, and called it "circulation of elites." A more precise conception of the circulation of elites can be found in another Italian thinker, Gaetono Mosca, who saw revolutions as a starting point of the formation of a new political class. Mosca also considered the successful institutionalization of what he called the "political formula" (Max Weber would call it "principles of legitimacy") crucial for the consolidation and legitimation of a ruling class, and made an important distinction between the ruling class itself and the "second stratum" that serves the ruling class by running the state.[15] By opening and broadening the social base of the political society, furthermore, the revolution can unleash processes such as urbanization and spread of education that greatly accelerate social change and social and geographic mobility. As the enlargement of the political community goes hand in hand with greater social mobility and reintegration of dislocated social groups, I call the ideal-type of revolution that captures it "integrative revolution." Integrative revolution enlarges the political community and broadens the franchise and/or other political rights, notably access to power, and generates a new political class on the basis of the new principles of legitimacy established by the revolution.

Chapter 6 describes the demographic, social, and political consequences of the Islamic revolution of 1979 as an integrative revolution. The enlargement of the political community, social integration, and the acceleration of the processes of social change are analyzed as unintended structural consequences of the Islamic revolution. The integrative dimension of the Islamic revolution consists in greatly increased social mobility, the considerable increase in the urban population relative to the rural and the outstripping of the number of men in the universities by women. These changes make the Iran of 2008 a very different country from that of 1979. More central to our explanation of the consequences of the Islamic revolution in Iran is the evidence for the formation of a new political class discussed in chapter 6. An interesting pattern emerges from this discussion of the post-revolutionary circulation of elites and changes in the social stratification: although the change of the ruling elite happens only once with the revolution for a whole generation, the post-revolutionary circulation within the second stratum in the higher ranks of the state bureaucracy and in the Majles has been continuous. It is important to note, however, that the circulation of the second stratum is confined to the generation I have called the children of the Islamic revolution, and it has not been easy for the younger generation to break into it any more than it has been for the outsider (non-*khodi*) groups from the same generation, which cannot prove their Islamic revolutionary credentials.[16]

Chapter 8 presents the military-security personnel and those who man the higher ranks of the state bureaucracy as the second stratum of the IRI as the representatives of Iran's new political class, a class that is seeking to shape its outlook and articulate its aspiration to political domination. To secure a modicum of independence from the Leader and especially from the clerical ruling elite, Ahmadinejad and the military-security elements of the second stratum turned politicians have sought to appropriate the last element of Khomeini's constitutional heritage, one that had not been claimed by either the clerical ruling elite or the reformers. Claiming to follow the "line of Imam," they took what was left—namely populism and social justice—and championed it as proof of their unflinching loyalty as the children of the Islamic revolution of 1979. The chapter deals with the most recent trend in the politics of the IRI and the toughest to understand, namely the ascendancy of the hardliners in 2004 and their defeat of the moderates and the reformists in 2005. The misunderstanding of this trend is best illustrated by the reference to Ahmadinejad and his supporters as "conservatives" in the media and by many analysts, which is very misleading. Our revisionist sociology of revolution shows that the return of the hardliners is not as anomalous as it seems, and suggests that the group is much more accurately described as (revolutionary) "hardliners," as they purport to recover the original purity of the Islamic revolution.[17]

I have argued that the case of the Islamic revolution in Iran suggests, as with the Russian and the Mexican revolutions, that the revolutionary power struggle is much longer than the revolutionary process analyzed in the works on the anatomy of revolution.[18] It is much more drawn out because it merges with the constitutional politics of succession to the charismatic leadership of the revolution and therefore requires a long-term perspective.[19] A long-term perspective on the process of revolution is equally important for the light it sheds on the foreign policy of the IRI. Chapters 8 and 10 analyze the foreign policy of the IRI. After the failure of the policy of export of revolution in the early 1980s, the most aggressive phase of Iran's foreign policy occurred with the ascendancy of the hardliners among the Revolutionary Guards under Ahmadinejad nearly three decades after the Islamic revolution of 1979. This is roughly the same time span that separated the hardliners' ascendancy and peak of Soviet expansionism in Stalin's worldwide export of the Marxist–Leninist revolution from the Bolshevik revolution of 1917. The increased involvement of the Revolutionary Guards and its special Qods Force in Iraq in particular, but also in Lebanon and Afghanistan, and Ahmadinejad's placing of nuclear development at the center of the public arena to mobilize public opinion are proof of the shift from pragmatism to an expansionist foreign policy that accompanies the rise of the hardliners.

Chapter 9 finally looks at Khomeini's actual successor to the position of the Leader and the Supreme Jurist, Ayatollah Sayyed 'Ali Khamenei. It uncovers a very different process of concentration of power in the hands of the Leader, and examines his relationship with the ruling stratum of the IRI, namely the clerical elite participating in collective government through the clerical councils, as well as his role in the promotion of the hardliners with a military-security background, including President Ahmadinejad, into leading positions within the administration. The chapter also examines his unique function as the spiritual guide of the IRI, especially his attempt to thwart what he considers the cultural invasion of the West by assuming the moral leadership of the Muslims of the world. It concludes with reflections on the general characteristics of the Islamic regime in Iran, which is increasingly described by Iranian dissidents as a clerical monarchy.

The far-reaching changes caused by the Islamic revolution in Iran are not denied, but nor are they understood. This book should make the consequences of the Islamic revolution intelligible to two groups of readers. Outsider readers, who see Iran through the lens of the newspaper headlines and find the developments covered in this book strange and foreign, may be surprised to find it as part and parcel of a global pattern of the revolutionary process. The book's theoretical bird's eye view should, furthermore, elicit instant recognition from insider readers, immersed in details of current Iranian politics but unable to make sense of the overall pattern.

I

Khomeini and the Islamic Revolution

AS THE UNDISPUTED LEADER OF THE ISLAMIC REVOLUTION and the founder and charismatic leader of the Islamic Republic of Iran (IRI) from 1979 to 1989, Ayatollah Ruhollah Khomeini set the direction of post-revolutionary developments in the two decades after his death. Iran has remained firmly in the hands of Khomeini's followers, the children of the Islamic revolution, and his successors who inherited the IRI have continued along one of the several paths he broke or adumbrated.

Leadership of the Revolution

When Khomeini overthrew the monarchy in 1979, he was already an old man. His Islamic revolutionary rhetoric was of course directed against Mohammad Reza Shah and the United States, but his formation predated the advent of both the last Shah and the United States on the Iranian scene, as did the preoccupations that made him a revolutionary when he was already an aging Grand Ayatollah (Sign of God).[1] Shi'ism had by the beginning of the nineteenth century developed an independent hierocracy (religious institution) that constituted one of the two powers in Iran's authority structure, the other power being the monarchy—the state under the Shah. This was in marked contrast to Sunni Islam and also to the first two and a half centuries of Shi'ism in Iran under the Safavid dynasty (1501–1722). In the twentieth century, state-building, secularization, and modernization greatly weakened the Shi'ite hierocracy but did not impair its independence from the state. What Khomeini succeeded in doing in the 1970s was mobilizing the militant elements within the beleaguered hierocracy for revolution against monarchy. Unlike the younger generation, Khomeini was not motivated by any obsession with the United States, even though he inimitably expressed the view of younger Iranians during the revolution by referring to it as the Great Satan. He was moved first to protest in the early 1960s and then to revolutionary action in the 1970s to preserve the Shi'ite tradition, which had nourished him and which he now saw as threatened with extinction. What Khomeini was taking on was thus no less than the whole twentieth-century idea of modernization that had become entrenched in the political culture of Iran since the Constitutional Revolution (1906–1911).

Born in 1902, Khomeini was an orphan raised by his mother, who died when he was in his teens, his uncle and an older brother during Iran's Constitutional Revolution. Shi'ite religious leaders appeared in the forefront of the first popular protests in 1905 and 1906 but were quickly divided during that revolution. One of them, Shaykh Fazlollah Nuri, propounded the idea of "*shari'a*-based constitutionalism" (*mashruta-ye mashru'a*) and led a traditionalist movement against the Majles (Iranian parliament) in 1907–1908. When interviewing the Grand Ayatollahs for my Ph.D. dissertation in 1977, I was startled to discover their view of the Constitutional Revolution, which has since become common in Iran due to the revisionist historiography of the Islamic revolution in its search for a genealogy. The Grand Ayatollah Musavi Shirazi, who came closest to Khomeini in intransigence if not power during the revolutionary crisis, told me: "In reality, the Constitutional Revolution was only a game, and the foreign powers launched it to bring about the separation of the spiritual powers and government. The cause of all the calamities in this country is this very constitutionalism (*mashrutiyyat*)."[2] On the eve of the revolution, the Ayatollahs thought the intellectuals and reformist bureaucrats in the first decade of the twentieth century had taken unfair advantage of their predecessors—the Shi'ite leaders who mobilized the masses and forced the Shah to grant a constitution, but were then excluded from power after their victory and the establishment of a constitutional government. Khomeini undoubtedly shared this view. When I interviewed him in January 1979, just before he returned to Iran, he was unqualified in his endorsement of Shaykh Fazlollah Nuri, who was to be lionized after the Islamic revolution as the far-sighted champion of Islam against the West.[3] The bitter memory of Iran's first revolution did not die after the Islamic revolution. It was evoked positively by the "liberal" nationalists within the Islamic revolutionary coalition, such as Bazargan and Bani-Sadr during the 1979–1981 period, but also by the hardliners with great apprehension. Even as late as 1997, less than two months before the election of President Khatami, the conservative Ayatollah Mahdavi-Kani would react to the reformist claim that political legitimacy stems from the will and allegiance of the people by asserting that "I fear that the episode of constitutional revolution might be repeated."[4]

The policies of centralization and secularization under the builder of Iran's modern state, Reza Khan, Minister of War and Prime Minister since 1921, and thereafter Reza Shah Pahlavi (1925–1941), were opposed by a few clerics in the 1920s and 1930s, but this opposition remained ineffective. The reign of Reza Shah encompassed Khomeini's formative years. Khomeini was atypical in his studies and chose to specialize in mystical philosophy, which was highly suspect in the legalistic scholarly community of Qom. While teaching mystical philosophy to a small number of students, he also began teaching courses in ethics for a much larger audience in the 1930s. The popularity of these lectures made the police apprehensive.[5] Khomeini never forgot the loss of clerical power that resulted from secularization and the modernization of the state and the humiliation of clerics by Reza Shah; he transferred his visceral hostility to the latter's son, Mohammad Reza Shah (1941–1979), whom he contemptuously referred to as "the son of Reza Khan" throughout the revolutionary struggle.

State building and secularization undermined the power and institutional interests of the hierocracy. It was, however, by no means the only menace to the Shi'ite tradition that alarmed Khomeini, nor the one that first prompted him into action in the public sphere. The threat that made him a public intellectual long before he became a revolutionary was not political but cultural. Although he knew and was sympathetic to the clerical activists opposed to Reza Shah in the 1920s and 1930s, Khomeini's entry into the public arena began a few years after Reza Shah's departure from Iran. In 1944, when he was in his early forties, Khomeini anonymously published a book attacking the advocates of Islamic reform. Writing on behalf of the religious leaders of Qom, whose authority was challenged by the proponents of the reform of Shi'ism, he offered an extensive and point-by-point refutation, in ten times as many pages, of an anticlerical, modernist pamphlet by a journalist, 'Ali Akbar Hakamizadeh, and indirectly of the teachings of the latter's mentor, Rezaqoli Shari'at-Sangalaji, a clerical advocate of reform of Shi'ism whose followers called him "the Great Reformer" (*mosleh-e kabir*). Khomeini also attacked the views of the historian and reformist Ahmad Kasravi, without naming him explicitly.[6] Kasravi was later assassinated because of those views by the first band of Islamic terrorists, the Devotees (*fedā'iyān*) of Islam, who enjoyed Khomeini's support.

Khomeini's book, *Revelation of Secrets* (*Kashf al-asrār*), has not received the attention it deserves despite its ready availability since the revolution. What is striking about this book is the staunch traditionalism of Khomeini's vigorous defense of the Shi'ite hierocracy and its practices against the criticism of the modernists, who are derided as Wahhabis and imitators of the heretical Baha'is. Foremost among the traditional Shi'ite practices attacked by the reformists and defended by Khomeini was "imitation" (*taqlid*)—that is, the imitation of the clerical jurist by laymen, which is the foundation of clerical authority and the hierocracy in Shi'ism.[7] Khomeini saw the reformist attack as part of the imperialist plot to destroy the Shi'ite hierocracy and thereby Islam, which would have no guardians and be left to the compliant interpretation of feckless laymen. He countered by accusing the critics, who pretend to liberate themselves from imitation, of aping the enemies of Shi'ism: "at times, they imitate Ibn Taymiyya and the savages of Najd [i.e., the Wahhabis], at times the Babis and the Baha'i Abu'l-Fazl Golpaygani."[8] Among the Shi'ite traditional practices attacked by the reformists and defended by Khomeini were supplication of the dead for granting of wishes, intercession (*shafā'at*), miracles of the prophets, and holding religious gatherings to commemorate the martyrdom of Imam Hossein and his family (*rawzakhāni*).[9]

Having defended the authority and prerogatives of the religious elite as clerical jurists and guardians of the Shi'ite tradition, Khomeini proceeded to refute his opponents' ideas of government (*hokumat*) and the law (*qānun*).[10] Here, he lumped reformists together with modern middle-class intellectuals, and offered a robustly traditionalist cultural critique of modernization under Reza Shah, ridiculing the modernist intellectuals who were "fooled and lured by naked women in streets and swimming pools"[11] and condemning mixed schools for boys and girls, cinema, the removal of the veil, and the borrowing of foreign hats as well as foreign laws, all of which were said to be forbidden by the law of Islam or divine law. Khomeini's political ideas were just as traditionalist as his cultural critique. He displayed his erudition in discussing the conditional justification of working for the government by medieval Shi'ite jurists, even when it is in the hands of tyrants—a subject he never mentioned again when he began developing his own political theory in the

1960s.[12] He also showed his familiarity with the more recent political views of the Shi'ite jurists during the Constitutional Revolution, implicitly siding with the traditionalist Shaykh Fazlollah Nuri and against the constitutionalist Mirza Hossein Na'ini, whose view was dismissed with an incidental remark: "deceiving appearance notwithstanding, there is no fundamental distinction among constitutional, despotic, dictatorial, democratic... and communist regimes."[13]

On the other hand, Khomeini reiterated Nuri's idea of "*shari'a*-based constitutionalism," with an added and sharply invidious contrast between secular laws "emanating from the syphilitic brains of a senseless bunch" and "the law of Islam, which God has sent down for eternity and all of humankind." The only form of government acceptable to reason is God's government. "No religious jurist has said or written in any book that we are kings and sovereignty is our right." Nevertheless, "the laws of parliament must be the explication of the very divine law.... As we have said earlier, we do not say government must devolve on the jurist (*faqih*). We say, however, that the government must observe the divine law... and this is not possible without the supervision of the clergy."[14]

With the advent of modern mass politics, the conditions of clerical domination change. As Max Weber observed, "Hierocracy had no choice but to establish a party organization and to use demagogic means, just like all other parties."[15] Thus, in the early 1960s, Khomeini set out to create, in contradistinction to the nationalist and the socialist political parties, a traditionalist political movement which was to be led by the hierocracy as the guardians of the Shi'ite tradition. Khomeini first appeared on the national political scene in 1963 as an outspoken critic of the Shah and his reform program. He was imprisoned, and after violent suppression of demonstrations by his supporters, exiled to Turkey, and then moved on to the Shi'ite holy city of Najaf in Iraq. It was during the decade and a half of exile in Iraq that Khomeini began to prepare a beleaguered Shi'ite hierarchy for the takeover of a hostile, secularizing state of the Shah. The first organized group Khomeini put together in 1963 was destined for a long clandestine life before the revolution and an equally long public life after the revolution. It was a mixed group of his lay and clerical supporters that called itself, grandly if awkwardly, the Coalition of Islamic Societies (*hey'athā-ye mo'talefa-ye eslāmi*; henceforth Mo'talefa) that succeeded in assassinating Prime Minister Hasan-'Ali Mansur in 1966. As the number of its clerical members, who were originally to guide and supervise the laymen, grew disproportionately in the 1970s, they formed their own organization in 1977 in preparation for revolution and called it the Society of Militant Clergy (*jāme'a-ye ruhāniyun-e mobārez*, JRM).[16]

By that time, Khomeini had enlisted many of the ablest and most energetic Shi'ite clerics. The militant clerics rallied in opposition to the corrupting influence of Western cultural domination and to the Shah's policies, which they considered a threat to the existence of religious institutions. Khomeini had trained a large number of clerics in his long teaching career, first in Qom and later in exile in the Shi'ite centers of learning in Iraq. The official historian of the Islamic revolution, in a work written in the mid-1970s, claimed that Khomeini had trained 500 *mojtaheds,* or Shi'ite jurists, throughout his long teaching career, and that 12,000 students took his courses in the years immediately preceding his exile.[17] The militant clerics began calling him Imam—a title reserved for the 12 holy Imams and not used by anyone else for over a thousand years. The leading clerics, who were later to occupy the highest positions of power in the Islamic Republic, were, with rare exceptions, Khomeini's former students, or his collaborators in the agitations of the 1960s. They tended to be from the traditional urban background typical of the Shi'ite clergy in the preceding century. Keenly aware of the dispossession of the Shi'ite hierocracy by the Pahlavi regime, they sought to recover lost historical privileges. The younger clerics, on the other hand, were heavily drawn from humbler rural and small-town backgrounds. For them, the Islamic revolution would create avenues of rapid upward social mobility. However, the ideological weapon for the recovery of their lost privileges by the ranking militant Ayatollahs, and for ensuring the rapid social ascent of the younger clerics from humbler backgrounds, was supplied by Khomeini in the form of his theory of theocratic government or *velāyat-e faqih.*

In his 1944 book, Khomeini had maintained that *mojtaheds* had the authority to supervise parliamentary legislation and the deeds of the monarch. In the following decade, he took a radical position in a tract on independent law-finding (*ejtehād*), which he had apparently written in the early 1950s but not published until 1964–1965. He used the term *hākem* not only in the Arabic, technical sense of (religious) judge, but also in the Persian everyday sense of governor, to extend the judicial authority of the *mojtahed* to the political sphere as the right to rule.[18] While in exile in Najaf, Khomeini developed this idea further into his theory of *velāyat-e faqih* as the mandate of the jurist to rule,[19] both in a series of lectures in Persian that were published in Beirut in 1970 under the title of *Velāyat-e faqih,* and in a work of jurisprudence on transactions, published in the second volume of his treatise *Kitāb al-bay'* in

1971. According to the traditional Shi'ite theory, the political authority of the infallible Imams fell into abeyance after the disappearance of the Twelfth Imam, the Mahdi, in the ninth century. The authority of the Imams as teachers in religion and the Sacred Law (*shari'a[t]*), however, was transferred to the Shi'ite jurists. The scope of clerical authority gradually expanded over the centuries. Khomeini was the first Shi'ite jurist to open the discussion of "Islamic government" in a work of jurisprudence, and he took the radical step of claiming that the Imams' right to rule also devolved upon the jurists during the occultation of the Twelfth Imam. Not only did the mandate to rule devolve upon the religious jurists, but if one of them succeeded in setting up a government, it was the duty of the other jurists to follow him.[20]

This last step, contrasting sharply with the traditional Shi'ite principle that no jurist has any authority over other jurists, radically undermined the position of the other *mojtahed*s, who were categorically independent according to the traditional Shi'ite theory, especially the preeminent jurists at the highest echelon of the Shi'ite hierarchy, the so-called *marāje'-e taqlid* (sources of imitation). As Hashemi-Rafsanjani attested in the Friday sermon following Khomeini's death, this was a revolutionary departure from the Shi'ite tradition: "The writing of *The Mandate of the Jurist* itself at that time in Najaf was a great revolution: that he should come from the jurists and write on such a topic!"[21] Neither Khomeini nor his successors were able to reconcile the old and the new principles of juristic authority, however.

With his theory of theocratic government made known in clerical circles, Khomeini began to prepare a beleaguered Shi'ite hierocracy for the takeover of a hostile, secularizing state, though without any general public discussion of the Mandate of the Jurist, for which the time was not considered ripe. The vaguer but more emotive term, "Islamic government" (*hokumat-e eslāmi*) was instead used as the main revolutionary slogan. Khomeini's clerical followers were enjoined to live up to their responsibility as the custodians of the Shi'ite tradition, and to unite to remove the danger and to preserve Islam. To do so, they had to overthrow the monarchy and set up an Islamic theocratic government. The younger militant clerics mobilized by Khomeini preached his revolutionary message in mosques and religious gatherings. It is interesting to note that Khomeini's defense of clerical authority in 1944 reflected the traditional ranking within the hierarchy, aiming primarily at the vindication of the clerical jurists while putting down the preachers or "people of the pulpit" (*ahl-e menbar*) somewhat disparagingly.[22] Now, the pulpit—politicized, modernized, and technologically amplified through the widespread use of cassettes—became Khomeini's main revolutionary platform. Other groups, too, became vocal in their opposition to the Shah when he tried to liberalize his regime in 1977, and unanimously accepted Khomeini's leadership of the revolution.

Upon the victory of the Islamic revolution, Imam Khomeini insisted that he was setting up a government based on the Sacred Law (*hokumat-e shar'iyya*) and appointing a prime minister "by the general and the sacred mandate (*velāyat-e shar'i va velāyat-e 'āmm*).[23] He treated the property confiscated from the Pahlavi family and other industrialists of the old regime as war booty according to religious law, and consolidated them into a number of foundations, most notably the Foundation for the Disinherited (*bonyād-e mostaz'afin*). Most of the foundations were put under the direction of clerics. Khomeini as the charismatic leader of the Islamic revolution issued many of the early revolutionary decrees as the "Deputy of the [Hidden] Imam"[24] (and not as a jurist). In that capacity, he also appointed Mehdi Bazargan, the leading member of the liberal and nationalist elements in the revolutionary coalition, as the prime minister of a provisional government. His mandate was also extended to the legal sphere and his manual of jurisprudence, *Tahrir al-wasila,* was declared the law of the land.[25]

In December 1979, Khomeini declared that the nation that had so overwhelmingly approved the new Constitution "wants neither East nor West but only an Islamic Republic—this being so, we have no right to say that the nation that engaged in an uprising did so in order to have democracy."[26] In the course of the ensuing power struggle of the early 1980s among the partners in the revolutionary coalition, Khomeini sanctioned the violent suppression of the leftist and secular elements. The most important group eliminated in the process in street and house-to-house fighting was the Islamic radical group, the Mojahedin-e Khalq-e Mosalman.[27] He was equally merciless toward his clerical opponents, "demoting" Grand Ayatollah Sayyed Kazem Shari'atmadari and putting other Grand Ayatollahs under house arrest, but did not authorize violence against them.[28] Once the revolutionary power struggle ended with the complete victory of his supporters and the Iranian state and the revolutionary structures were brought under clerical control, Khomeini opted for normalization and the rule of law. He declared the Persian New Year 1360 (1981–1982) the "year of the rule of law" (*sāl-e hokumat-e qānun*), maintaining that "all the Prophets since the beginning of the world have come for the establishment of the law (*qānun*); and Islam has come for the establishment of the law."[29] On December 15, 1982, he issued a decree in eight clauses guaranteeing all Iranian citizens security from arbitrary arrest and confiscation of property and promising the restoration of law and order. The revolution had ended for him, and the rule of law under the Islamic constitution had begun. In the six years that followed, Khomeini sought to maintain unity between the conservative and the radical clerics and their respective allies, and intervened whenever necessary to prevent the tilting of the balance of power in favor of the former.

Khomeini remained ruthlessly firm and resolute to his last days. He opposed the ending of the increasingly unpopular war with Iraq (1980–1988) until he finally decided to drink "the cup of poison" and accept a ceasefire with Iraq on July 18, 1988. Two days later, the Iraq-based forces of the Mojahedin-e Khalq attacked western Iran and were wiped out. In the following weeks, he ordered the execution of well over 3000 Mojahedin who had already served or were serving sentences given them by revolutionary courts.[30] Despite the vehement protest of his successor-designate, Ayatollah Montazeri, that the execution of those who had already been sentenced by the courts and committed no new offenses meant "disregard for all judicial principles," Khomeini opted for their elimination by judicial murder.[31] Khomeini issued what can in retrospect be considered a vintage "governmental ordinance" (*hokm-e hokumati*),[32] ordering clerical judges to sentence the "treacherous hypocrites" [Mojahedin] who "are waging war on God and are condemned to execution:"

> The passing of the sentence in Tehran is incumbent [as a religious duty] on the *shar'i* judge Hojjat al-Islam [Ja'far] Nayyeri, the Prosecutor [Mortaza] Eshraqi, and the representative of the Ministry of Information and Security,[33] after having agreed upon it by a majority.... [T]he sentences are to be carried out in all other prisons and provincial centers by the competent judges, prosecutors and representatives of the Ministry of Information and Security on the basis of a majority of votes.[34]

Only at the end of his long life did God finally not let Khomeini have his way. He could not overthrow Saddam Hussein the way he had the Shah. On March 16, 1988, the Iraqi army used chemical weapons to wipe out 4000 Kurds who had allied themselves with Iran, and used the same weapons to overwhelm some 5000 Iranian troops in the Fao peninsula. In mid-July 1988, Majles Speaker Hashemi-Rafsanjani, who had replaced President Khamenei as the commander-in-chief of the armed forces at the beginning of June, convinced Khomeini that the military situation had decisively turned in Iraq's favor and was hopeless.[35] The world, especially the United States, turned a blind eye to Iraq's use of chemical weapons, and on July 3, an Iran Air commercial flight was downed by a missile from the USS *Vincennes*, killing all 290 persons aboard. On July 17, Iran accepted a ceasefire on the basis of UN Security Council Resolution 598, which it had earlier rejected. The ship captain's assurance that the plane was shot down in error did little to alter Khomeini's conviction that the Great Satan was behind the Little Satan. He admitted defeat, excoriating neither evil power, but acknowledged the definitive failure to export the Islamic revolution. He considered ceasefire less bearable than death and martyrdom, but said he drank "the cup of poison" in the interest of the revolution and the Islamic order. In the little time he had left (it turned out to be less than a year), the Imam had to attend to the constitutional crisis of his Islamic order.

The incipient collapse of communism in the last year of his life renewed Khomeini's optimism, and in his New Year message of January 1, 1989, he told the Soviet leader, Mikhail Gorbachev, that he should learn about Islam as communism now belonged to the museum of history. "The Islamic Republic of Iran, as the greatest and most powerful base of the Islamic world, can easily help fill up the ideological vacuum of your system!"[36] In April 1989, he ordered the revision of the Constitution of 1979 on seven precise points to ensure that, unlike communism, the theocratic republic he had set up in Iran would survive into the next millennium.

Khomeini died on June 3, 1989. Just as millions of Iranians massed to welcome him when he returned as the Imam from exile in 1979, a million or more joined his funeral procession when he died 10 years later.

Having had the privilege of praying behind him and interviewing him in Neaphle-le-Chateau near Versailles in January 1979, I visited his mausoleum in January 1993. I was struck by the suggested prayer for visitors to the mausoleum of Imam Khomeini, which was hanging on the walls. I had heard the rumor that Khomeini's visceral hatred of Reza Shah colored his attitude toward his namesake, Imam Reza, the eighth holy Imam of the Shi'a, who was buried in Mashhad. The prayer begins in praise of the Prophet and the first seven holy Imams, but omits the eighth, Imam Reza, and the subsequent Imams, replacing them with the latter-day Imam buried in the mausoleum, the "Holy Warrior Spirit of God (*ruh Allāh al-mojāhed*),[37] Khomeini." I have not been able to confirm whether Khomeini had seen the prayer before his death, but suspect he had or would have approved of it.

The Making of Khomeini's Constitutional Order

The institutions of the theocratic Islamic Republic of Iran, shaped by Khomeini as its Imam and Leader of the Revolution, have provided the framework for Iran's constitutional politics to the present. Khomeini did not set up a government in a vacuum, however, but took over an existing one that had undergone considerable modernization in the course of the twentieth century. His project of the Islamicization of the Pahlavi state and its trans- formation into a Shi'ite theocracy required a drastic transformation of the Shi'ite legal tradition. From being what Max Weber called a "jurists' law," the Shi'ite religious law had to be transformed into the law of the modern state based on a written constitution. This required its extension beyond matters of ritual and ethics to cover public law; and the typical activity of the Shi'ite jurists—"law-finding," or setting the norms for acts of worship, ritual, and transactions—had to be supplemented, if not replaced, by legislation and codification.

As a first step in this transformation, Shi'ite jurisprudence had to come to terms with constitution making. Khomeini had carefully chosen the term "Islamic government" (*hokumat-e eslāmi*) as his revolutionary slogan, and instructed his agents not to discuss his theory of Mandate of the Jurist during the revolutionary mobilization against the Shah. He had not mentioned the word "republic" (*jomhuri*) in his writings on government, and there is reason to believe that he considered the Islamic republic the form of government for the period of transition to theocracy. This much was confirmed on the eve of the referendum on the 1979 Constitution by Ayatollah Mohammad Hosseini Beheshti,[38] a founder of the Society of Militant Clergy and member of Khomeini's inner circle: "As the first slogan, 'Islamic government' was chosen, which was very good and expressive, and when it was decided that the regime would have a President, it was called the 'Islamic Republic,' but the true and perfect name for this regime is the 'regime of the *umma* and Imamate' (*nezām-e ommat va emāmat*)."[39]

Khomeini had little or no interest in constitutional law, and had said in 1970 that "if laws are needed, Islam has established them all. There is no need for you, after establishing a government, to sit down and draw up laws, or, like rulers who worship foreigners and are infatuated with the West, run after others to borrow their laws."[40] Even after seizing power, he displayed complete innocence of its institutional and constitutional dimensions: "Don't be afraid of the Mandate of the Jurist; the jurist does not wish to compel the people with force. If a jurist wants to use force, this jurist would have no mandate. It is Islam; in Islam the law rules, and the honorable Prophet was also the follower of the law, the divine law!"[41]

Perhaps for these reasons, or because of anxiety for the future of the Islamic revolution,[42] Khomeini personally did not show much interest in the making and content of the constitution in the first two months after the revolution, but just wanted a constitution promulgated as quickly as possible. The draft constitution quickly prepared was based on the model of the 1958 Constitution of the French Fifth Republic by the Provisional Government and made no reference to his theory of theocratic government. Hasan Habibi, a member of the drafting committee, took the draft to Qom and submitted it to Khomeini, who circulated it among the Grand Ayatollahs in March 1979. Khomeini himself made some minor changes in the margins and signed it, as did a number of other Ayatollahs.[43] There was no mention of the *velāyat-e faqih* and no provisions for a supreme jurist as the Leader of the Republic in the draft constitution published on June 14, 1979, but Khomeini publicly endorsed it and recommended its speedy ratification three days later.[44] The publication of the draft constitution, however, immediately generated an intense debate among the intellectuals that alarmed Khomeini because of its secular tone, and must have brought back the memory of the intellectuals getting the better of the clerical leaders in the Constitutional Revolution at the beginning of the century. With his Islamic revolution much more secure, Khomeini decided it would be a mistake to leave constitution making to the lay intellectuals. At the end of June, he told the clerics, "This right belongs to you. It is those knowledgeable in Islam who may express an opinion on the law of Islam. The constitution of the Islamic republic means the constitution of Islam. Don't sit back while foreignized intellectuals... give their views and write what they write."[45]

At the onset of the revolution, Provisional Prime Minister Mehdi Bazargan had extracted the promise of a constituent assembly for making the constitution of the new state. Khomeini could not have liked the idea as there had been two docile constituent assemblies to amend the constitution under the monarchy. The first had proclaimed Reza Khan the new monarch in 1925, provoking Khomeini to ask the following question in 1944:

We would like to ask: is it not better, instead of a constituent assembly consisting of a number of crooks (*ma'lum al-hāl*), whose laws you blindly consider sacred, [to form] an assembly of pious *mojtaheds* who know God's commandments and are just?[46]

Whether for this or for other reasons, Khomeini had proposed to bypass the promised constituent assembly and to submit the draft directly to a referendum. But Bazargan and Bani-Sadr insisted on the election of a constituent assembly while Hashemi-Rafsanjani asked the latter, "Who do you think will be elected to a constituent assembly? A fistful of ignorant and fanatical fundamentalists who will do such damage that you will regret ever having convened them."[47] Bazargan and Bani-Sadr won their pyrrhic victory. However, Ayatollah Mahmud Taleqani proposed that the kind of assembly Khomeini had had in mind in the 1940s, an Assembly of Experts, be elected nationwide, instead of the promised constituent assembly. Khomeini agreed, and the Assembly was duly elected on August 3, 1979. Of the 73 members of this Assembly, 55 were clerics.[48] Khomeini promised not to interfere with the deliberations of the Assembly of Experts but sent it an inaugural message, instructing it that "the constitution should be based on Islam," without a single article contradicting Islamic ordinances, and should provide "for the needs of future generations in accordance with the divine laws." Referring obliquely to the clerical jurists of the proposed Guardian Council and reminding the 55 clerical members of the Assembly of their status, Khomeini also asserted that "the determination of what is consistent and what contradicts Islamic standards belongs solely to the high-ranking religious jurists." He then entrusted the constitutional translation of his idea of the Mandate of the Jurist (*velāyat-e faqih*) to his clerical lieutenants, Ayatollahs Hosyan-'Ali Montazeri and Sayyed Mohammad Hosayni Beheshti. The latter cut short the debate on the principle of the Mandate of the Jurist in the Assembly of Experts, which passed it on September 12, while the former aired it in public for the first time in his Friday sermon two days later, securing the worshippers' acclamation in their cry: "Mandate of the Jurist is the protector of our revolution!"[49] Clerical opponents of the principle within the Assembly were able to vent their frustration only later, and one of them pleaded passionately: "Do not allow our enemies to say that a bunch of mullahs sat there and wrote a constitution to justify their own rule. For God's sake, don't do this...by consigning all the power to the Jurist, do not turn the sovereignty of the people into a lion without head, tail, and body. For God's sake, don't do this."[50] But this passionate plea had no effect. From that point on, the constitutional developments in the IRI primarily consisted of a series of adjustments required for a working synthesis of the theocratic idea of the Mandate of the Jurist with the legal principles and organization of the modern Iranian nation-state.

During the three decades before the Islamic revolution, a new approach to the reception of constitutionalism in the Muslim world had developed. It had first appeared when the Muslims of India decided to have their own modern state and created Pakistan. It involved the pouring of the Qur'an and *hadith*s (sayings and deeds of the Prophet) into the framework of a systematic total ideology such as Marxism. Mawlana Abu'l-A'la Mawdudi and his Jama'at-i Islami, which successfully pushed for a declaration of God's sovereignty, had very limited impact on the content of the 1956 Constitution of the Islamic Republic of Pakistan, but generated a new and ideologically powerful idea that the state should be an "Islamic state" and its constitution should be based on the scriptural sources of Islam. This idea was the product of Islamic political ideologies in Pakistan and Egypt, and was finally imported into Iran shortly before and during the Islamic revolution of 1979. The embodiment of an Islamist ideology in a *shari'a*-based constitution became a major goal of the ideologues of the Islamic revolution in 1979, including the clerical lieutenants Khomeini put in charge of constitution making.

In an important lecture delivered on the eve of the referendum on the 1979 Constitution at the birthplace of Islamic ideology in Iran, Tehran's famous Hossaynia Ershād, its chief architect, Ayatollah Beheshti, reflected on the theoretical foundations of the proposed Constitution. He disclosed the true character of the political regime that the Constitution was designed to create as the "regime of the *umma* and Imamate." The fundamental error of Iran's first revolution, the Constitutional Revolution, he argued, was to call the new order it created "constitutional" (*mashruta*), a concept that was "borrowed and did not pertain to the Islamic culture."[51] The historic mission of the current [Islamic] revolution was to base the Constitution on a correct ideological (*maktabi*) conception of Islam and thereby to convert "the people" into the *umma* (community of believers). "From the perspective of the Islamic ideology," this *umma* inevitably needs the Imamate.[52] It follows that "the management of society deriving from the *umma* and Imamate is based on the ideological school (*maktab*)."[53] Beheshti's interpretation of Khomeini's Mandate of the Jurist as continuous (*mostamerr*) Imamate was thus constitutionalized as the core institution of the new Islamic regime.[54]

This made the 1979 Constitution of the IRI an "ideological constitution": Islam was simply put in the place of the dominant ideology in its Preamble.[55]

The *shari'a,* which had appeared in Iran's first (non-ideological) Constitution of 1906–1907 as a *limitation* to the Legislative Power, now encompassed the entire modernized state and its constitution. Thirteen verses from the Qur'an and one other scriptural citation were incorporated into the text of the Constitution, and an Appendix consisting of additional verses and Traditions of the Prophet and the holy Imams pertaining to its most important Articles served as further proof that the 1979 Constitution of the IRI was derived from the sources of the Shi'ite law. Its Article 4 declared that all laws must be based on the "Islamic standards" (*mavāzin-e eslāmi*) [i.e., norms of the *shari'a*], and any found inconsistent with them is null and void, including all the Articles of the Constitution itself.[56] The critical function of nullification of all proposed and existing laws found inconsistent with Islamic standards was given to the six clerical jurists of the Guardian Council, who were to be appointed by the Leader and thus entrusted with protecting the ideological foundations of the Constitution of the Islamic Republic of Iran.[57] Khomeini's position as the Leader in the Constitution endowed him with the extra-constitutional powers of the Supreme Jurist, and ensured his continued supremacy over the Constitution.

Khomeini was even less wedded to ideology than to constitution making, and once he had the constitution he wanted and securely won the revolutionary power struggle, he dropped his emphasis on ideology in favor of the rule of law. Although he had stressed the importance of ideological commitment (*maktabi-budan*) 37 times during the first Majles elections in 1980, the frequency of this requirement decreased to five and then to at most two during the elections of the Second and the Third Majles in 1984 and 1988, respectively.[58] The decade of the revolution and war led by Khomeini was, however, a decade of constitutional crisis and dissonant institutionalization.[59] To reduce the tension among contradictory aspects of the revolutionary regime and increase its institutional coherence, Khomeini had to intervene as the Leader and Supreme Jurist on a number of occasions.

The first constitutional crisis of the Islamic Republic of Iran did not involve Islam. Its parameters were set by the French model for the cohabitation of the President and the Prime Minister, and it immediately drew in the radical, pro-Prime Minister (Rajaee) Majles against the moderate President (Bani-Sadr). Constitutional conflict took a new form as this crisis ended with the dismissal of President Bani-Sadr in June 1981. In fact, the conflict between the Islamic Consultative Assembly (*Majles-e Shurā-ye Eslāmi*) and the Guardian Council over reconciling legislation and Islamic standards had already begun with the legislative work of the First Majles. Adhering to traditional Shi'ite principles of jurisprudence and using their power to determine the consistency of the Majles enactments with the Islamic standards, the jurists of the Guardian Council, led by the erudite Ayatollah Lotfollah Safi, the son-in-law of Grand Ayatollah Golpaygani, raised objections to over one-third of the bills passed by the Majles. They returned these bills for modification, and vetoed several bills for land distribution, nationalization of foreign trade, labor, distribution, hoarding, and other economic measures in the 1980s. These had been found to be at odds with the rules of the Sacred Law, usually on grounds of the infringement of the rights of private property and freedom of contract, although there was occasional protection of other rights, such as dismissal from government service for allegedly belonging to the Freemasonry.

In 1981, when the Guardian Council had vetoed a bill on land within the limits of cities, Majles Speaker Hashemi-Rafsanjani sought Khomeini's explicit intervention as the Supreme Jurist to overcome the veto. In a terse letter to Khomeini, Hashemi-Rafsanjani proposed a radically broadened interpretation of the Shi'ite jurisprudential principles of public expediency or interest (*maslahat*) and overriding necessity (*zarurat*).[60] Khomeini refused to intervene, but issued an order delegating his authority as the Jurist to the majority of the deputies of the Majles to determine overriding necessity and posit laws, on a temporary basis, as "secondary titles" (*'anāvin-e thānaviyya*). Khomeini's endorsement of Hashemi-Rafsanjani's innovative jurisprudence (*feqh-e puya*) in order to reconcile the Shi'ite jurists' law with the rational-legal framework of the nation-state was severely challenged by the Grand Ayatollahs. One of them, Grand Ayatollah Golpaygani, argued against Khomeini vehemently, and wrote to the latter to reject the contention that "the primary ordinances of the *shari'a* offer no solution to our current problems" and to complain that his order meant forsaking "the primary ordinances under the banner of overriding necessity. I fear the day that they [the majority of Majles deputies] find an overriding necessity to violate God's ordinances as the day that they turn what God has made permissible into forbidden, and his forbidden into permissible."[61]

The Guardian Council eventually yielded to Khomeini after requiring some amendments,[62] but persisted in vetoing other legislation. In January 1983, Hashemi-Rafsanjani tried once more to invoke Khomeini's extra-constitutional authority to solve the constitutional deadlock, but Khomeini's intervention again fell short of the explicit exercise of the legislative authority of the Supreme Jurist. Rather than using the novel category of "governmental ordinances" (*ahkām hokumati*) as deriving from the Mandate of the Jurist, he reaffirmed the authorization of the Majles, this time requiring a majority of two-thirds instead of a simple majority. Khomeini did, however, to the chagrin of the dissenting Grand Ayatollahs, take pains to reconcile deviations from the primary norms of the Sacred Law through legislation with Shi'ite jurisprudence in his own way. While expounding his notion of the rule of law in an Islamic order on the anniversary of the Islamic revolution on February 11, 1983, he explained that there was no difference between the incumbency of the "primary" and "secondary" ordinances. He arrived at this position circuitously, arguing first that "determination of the subject in secular or customary matters (*'orfiyya*)" could properly be done by the Majles deputies upon technical expert advice and with a majority of two-thirds. But then came an extraordinary zigzag: Despite their derivative character and the fact that they were now passed by a two-thirds majority of the Majles, the "secondary ordinances" (*ahkām thānaviyya*) had to be obeyed by the citizens just like these primary ones, as these were two categories of "divine ordinances" (*ahkām Allāh*).[63]

When it came to bills specifically designed to Islamicize the Iranian legal system, the Guardian Council was easier to satisfy. Important legislation to Islamicize the public law of the IRI included the new criminal law, which incorporates the penalties (*hodud*) and *qesās* provisions (*lex talionis*) of the *shari'a* and has been in effect, with periodic modifications, since 1982. Other instances of substantive Islamicization include the 1983 rent law and 1988 law of punishment for speculation and hoarding (*ehtekār*),[64] while the jurisdiction of the revolutionary courts was regulated by another law in 1983.

Early on, Khomeini had affirmed that "I and other clerics will not hold a position in the future government . . . I shall only take upon myself the responsibility of guiding the future government."[65] He restrained his politically ambitious clerical lieutenants from running for presidency, and the first two Presidents were consequently laymen. But the assassination of some prominent clerics by the Mojahedin-e Khalq and other radical Islamic groups during the revolutionary power struggle of the first two years made Khomeini change his mind. He admitted to having asked "the clergy to attend to their spiritual and guiding role after the revolution. But we made a mistake, and we should have the courage to admit our mistakes. . . . We reversed our earlier assertions and asked the clergy to run the country."[66] Hojjat al-Islam Sayyed 'Ali Khamenei thus ran for President in 1981 and was elected with a massive turnout. On the wave of a terrorist Mojahedin attack that had killed the President and the Prime Minister, Khamenei won the highest (95%) of the popular vote with a 75 percent turnout of the electorate.[67] President Khamenei and Majles Speaker Hashemi-Rafsanjani, however, had little success in turning the Islamic Republican Party into a one-party, totalitarian agency of mass mobilization by 1987 and requested its indefinite suspension, arguing that it had performed its main function of constitutionalizing the *velāyat-e faqih* and was now proving divisive. Khomeini had always suspected that political parties would sow dissension and division within the Muslim community, and acceded to their demand on June 1, 1987.[68] The party was in fact redundant as the organization of the Friday prayer-leaders, using mosques and Friday sermons to address large congregations, had by then evolved into Iran's distinctive mechanism for political mobilization under direct control of the Supreme Jurist.

The Grand Ayatollahs who opposed Khomeini and his regime did not pose a serious threat, and he was relatively restrained in dealing with them. But the problem of disciplining the younger and more radical clerics among his revolutionary followers was more serious and required an institutional response. The issue came to a head in 1986 when Sayyed Mehdi Hashemi, a relative of Ayatollah Montazeri who had assassinated a pro-Shah cleric in 1976 and had more recently formed a secret organization to export the Islamic revolution, leaked to the Lebanese media the news of Hashemi-Rafsanjani's secret arms deal with the United States through Israel (the Iran-Contra affair).[69] Hashemi-Rafsanjani had been apprehensive of Hashemi's amassing of arms and recruits and had alerted Khomeini and others.[70] This highly embarrassing disclosure forced Khomeini to act against his successor-designate's relative and protégé, and he used the occasion to make an institutional response to an endemic problem. The Special Court for Clerics was thus set up by Khomeini in June 1987 in order to try Hashemi and his associates. With Hojjat al-Eslams Fallahiyan and Razini as prosecutor and *shar'i* judge, respectively,[71] Hashemi was tried in August and executed in September 1987. The Special Court for Clerics would remain the Leader's chief instrument for disciplining the clerical elite of the Islamic Republic.

Meanwhile, the conflict between the Majles and the Guardian Council continued. In 1986–1987, legislation designed to tighten the government's grip on the private sector in its fight against "economic terrorism" was vetoed by the Guardian Council. In July 1987, Khomeini issued a *fatwā* (injunction) delegating to the government his authority as the Jurist to enable it to regulate prices and execute "governmental punishments" (*ta'zirāt-e hokumati*).[72] In January 1988, Khomeini overcame his reluctance and reprimanded

President Khamenei for saying that the authority of Islamic government could be exercised only within the framework of the ordinances of the Sacred Law (*ahkām*). Government in the form of the God-given absolute mandate (*velāyat-e motlaq*) was "the most important of the divine commandments and has priority over all derivative divine commandments.... [It is] one of the primary commandments of Islam and has priority over all derivative commandments, even over prayer, fasting and pilgrimage to Mecca." Five days later, in a letter that set the tone for a chorus of affirmations and clarifications by the ruling clerical elite, Khomeini referred to the President as a brother who supported the Absolute Mandate of the Jurist. A campaign to promote the new elaboration of Khomeini's theory immediately followed. A chastened President Khamenei not only understood the principles of the new theocratic absolutism but propounded them:

> The commandments of the ruling jurist (*vali-ye faqih*) are primary commandments and are like the commandments of God.... The regulations of the Islamic Republic are Islamic regulations, and obedience to them is incumbent.... [They are all] governmental ordinances (*ahkām-e hokumati*) of the ruling jurist.... In reality, it is because of the legitimacy of the Mandate [of the Jurist] that they all acquire legitimacy.... The Mandate of the Jurist is like the soul in the body of the regime. I will go further and say that the validity of the Constitution, which is the basis, standard and framework of all laws, is due to its acceptance and confirmation by the ruling jurist. Otherwise, what right do fifty or sixty or a hundred experts have...? What right do the majority of people have to ratify a Constitution and make it binding on all the people?

This explicit degradation of the Constitution of the Islamic Republic was indicative of a new phase in the constitutional development of Iran. On February 6, 1988, Khomeini appointed a commission, which included among its members the six jurists of the Guardian Council, the President, and the Prime Minister, to determine "governmental ordinances" in cases of disagreement between the Majles and the Guardian Council.[73] The Council for the Determination of the Interest of the Islamic Order (*majma'-e tashkhis-e maslahat-e nezām-e eslāmi*), henceforth the Maslahat Council, held its first meeting a week later, set its procedural rules, and elected President Khamenei chairman. With this final step to end the decade of constitutional crisis, to resolve the uncertain status of the novel "governmental ordinances" and the difficulties in Islamicizing the Iranian public law, "*maslahat* was declared to be the final decisive principle of legislation." Ayatollah 'Abdol-Karim Musavi-Ardabili, the President of the Supreme Judiciary Council, who was among those who had pressed Khomeini to set up the Maslahat Council, hailed its creation as "the most important of all the achievements of the revolution."[74]

It was not easy to reconcile Khomeini's final legal revolution with the Shi'ite legal tradition of the jurists' law. It led to the resignation of the Guardian Council's Secretary and ablest jurist, Ayatollah Lotfollah Safi, who insisted on remaining faithful to the Shi'ite tradition by opposing the imposition of Maslahat or public interest upon the norms of its jurisprudence. Imam Khomeini acknowledged the validity of Safi's objection but nevertheless affirmed that his revolutionary deviation was necessary. The legal logic and rationality of the modern state Khomeini had swallowed thus finally overcame the traditional logic of the Shi'ite jurists' law.

As death fast approached, Khomeini had not completed his constitutional work. To make matters worse, Khomeini forced his successor-designate, Ayatollah Montazeri, to resign on March 28, 1989. In addition to the already pressing need for working out the constitutional implications of the statements on the Absolute Mandate of the Jurist, there was an urgent need for constitutional resolution of the problem of succession. On April 18, 1988, 170 Majles deputies, and the Supreme Judiciary Council separately, urged the ailing Imam to order the revision of the Fundamental Law. He agreed within a week, assigning the task to a committee consisting of 18 clerics and two laymen, to which the Majles was invited to add five of its members. They were given two months to revise the Constitution's clauses on Leadership, centralization of authority in the Executive, centralization of authority in the Judiciary, centralization of management of the radio and television network, the number of Majles deputies and the changing of its official designation to the National Islamic Assembly, the place of the new Maslahat Council, and making provisions for subsequent constitutional amendments. The Council for the Revision of the Constitution did not assume any general constituent powers, but rather saw its scope limited strictly to these items according to the Imam's authorization.[75] The amended Constitution laid the foundation of the present regime and thus guided the post-revolutionary transition in the IRI.

2

Dual Leadership and Constitutional Developments after Khomeini

THE ASSEMBLY OF LEADERSHIP EXPERTS MET ON JUNE 4, 1989, the morning after Khomeini's death, and elected Sayyed 'Ali Khamenei as Khomeini's successor, the Leader of the Islamic Republic, by 60 out of 74 votes. Except for "Imam," all of Khomeini's political titles were transferred to Khamenei. This appears to have been in accordance with Khomeini's wish. According to Hashemi-Rafsanjani's later testimony, the day after he and Khamenei delivered the letter of dismissal as Khomeini's successor to Ayatollah Montazeri in Qom at the end of March 1989, they had a meeting with the ailing Khomeini in the company of the President and Vice-President of the Assembly of Leadership Experts, in which they reportedly tried to change Khomeini's mind on the grounds that there was no other suitable candidate for succession. They were all surprised, and Khamenei himself was "shocked," when Khomeini pointed to the latter as his successor. It is interesting to note that in the June 4, 1989, meeting of the Assembly of Experts after Khomeini's death, both Rafsanjani and Khamenei argued for a Leadership Council of three, which was still in the Constitution, but the majority decided to vote for one.[1]

The swift election of Khamenei proved the most remarkably smooth succession in the history of world revolutions. It was unconstitutional, however, as he did not have the rank of *marjaʿiyyat* (being a source of imitation) as required by Articles 107 and 109 of the 1979 Constitution, which was still in force when Khomeini died. Constitutionality is not a mark of revolution, and the spirit of the move was probably to divide Khomeini's power between his two closest lieutenants, one of whom, President Khamenei, was selected by the clerical Assembly as the Leader of the Islamic Republic; the other, Majles Speaker Akbar Hashemi-Rafsanjani, was duly elected as its President by popular vote on July 28, 1989. Dual leadership seemed quite appropriate for the emergent system of post-charismatic, collective clerical rule. Early on, the new President Hashemi-Rafsanjani, who was considered the more astute and competent of the two by many, appeared as the dominant party in the diarchy. However, the newly amended Constitution had stacked the cards heavily in favor of the Leader Khamenei, and it was hard for him not to win.

The future of the regime was in doubt after the death of its charismatic leader, with no guarantee that it would be a constitutional order. The constitutional amendments that augmented the powers of the Leader under the Absolute Mandate of the Jurists were not yet completely drafted. The Council for the Revision of the Constitution continued its work at full speed and completed it on July 8, 1989. Although most important revisions were made in the month after Khomeini's death, the Council faithfully followed his instructions. The new Leader approved it and ordered a national referendum on the amended Constitution, and according to the official figures, over 97 percent of the voters approved the referendum, held alongside the presidential elections on July 28.[2] The massive popular approval was Khomeini's posthumous charismatic gift to the regime he had blessed—both to its Constitution and its President. The late Imam's authority now seemed divided between a clerically selected Leader and a popularly elected President.

Among Khomeini's revolutionary followers, these two powerful men were very similar in age and political outlook. Both were in their fifties, were political pragmatists, and were proponents of progressive Islamic jurisprudence (*feqh-e puyā*). They began to vie for power and supremacy in the period of transition to collective rule. Despite their similarities, they took different paths of action. The political positions they took were increasingly determined by the constitutionally defined vested interest of the office they each held, rather than their personal will. The Leader won against the President in 1989–1997, just as the same Leader would win a much more intense power struggle against a very different President in 1997–2005. In both periods, the constitutional cards were stacked in favor of the Leader. Admittedly, the rules of the power struggle were not yet fully and clearly set, but the Leader turned out to be the better player in both constitutional and routine politics.

Khamenei firmly retained his control over the Revolutionary Guards, whose elite Qods (Jerusalem) Forces were directly subordinate to him, and over the Mobilizational Corps (*Basij*). He also maintained Khomeini's pervasive network of clerical commissars, not covered by the Constitution, in the government bureaucracy, military and security services, religious and mobilizational organizations, the foundations and foreign relations, as well as the provincial and municipal Friday prayer leaders (*imām jom'a*s). The Office of the Supreme Leader, meanwhile, developed special ties with the intelligence services and the Special Court for Clerics.[3] In 1992, the staunch advocate of the Mandate of the Jurist, 'Ali-Akbar Nateq-Nuri, became the Speaker of the Fifth Majles, and with the help of the Majles hardliners, Khamenei forced Hashemi-Rafsanjani to give the Interior Ministry to one of his men, Hojjat al-Islam Mohammad Besharati, and to keep another, Hojjat al-Eslam 'Ali Fallahian, as the Minister of Intelligence. He proceeded to replace Hashemi-Rafsanjani's men with his own, such as the Larijani brothers, and also to put his men, notably the clerical hardliner Gholam-Hossein Mohseni-Ezhehi, into key positions in the judiciary.

The Constitutional Amendments of 1989

To solve the problem of unsuccessful cohabitation of the President and the Prime Minister, the office of the Prime Minister was abolished, putting the cabinet directly under the President as the Head of the Executive Power. The office of the President was further strengthened by allowing him to appoint Deputy-Presidents (Article 124) and by the creation of a Supreme National Security Council (*Shurā-ye 'Ali-ye Amniyyat-e Melli*) chaired by him (Article 176). However, the President's position vis-à-vis the Leader was significantly weakened. A new Article (112) established the Council for the Determination of Interest of the Islamic Order as an organ of the state at the service of the Leader. The functions of the Maslahat Council were expanded beyond arbitration between the Majles and the Guardian Council. It was also to advise the Leader on "the determination of the general policies of the regime" (Article 110) and on any other matter he referred to it. The Supreme Judiciary Council was replaced by a single Head of the Judiciary Power to be appointed by the Leader for five years.

None of Iran's earlier constitutions had a provision for amending the constitution, though an ad hoc "constituent assembly" had been convened for that purpose under the Pahlavis. On the eve of the Islamic revolution, Khomeini had followed this precedent and promised a constituent assembly; however, he instead opted for an Assembly of Experts to write the new constitution. The Constitution of 1979 still did not provide a procedure for its amendment. A final Article (177) was added with the 1989 amendments that made provisions for the convening of an Assembly for Constitutional Review (*Shurā-ye Bāznegari-ye Qānun-e Asāsi*) by the Leader with the advice of the Maslahat Council. The approval of the Leader was required before any amendment could be put to a national referendum, and to Ayatollah Beheshti's posthumous delight,[4] the Mandate of the Jurist to rule as continued Imamate (*velāyat-e amr va emāmat-e ommat*) was declared unalterable, alongside Iran's established religion and the republican form of government.

The foremost and most difficult task had of course been the constitutional implementation of the highly problematic Absolute Mandate of the Jurist, or minimally the settlement of the Leadership issue. In accordance with Khomeini's instructions, the qualification of *marja'iyyat,* or being a source of imitation, for the Jurist was eliminated in the amended Article 109. Ayatollah Yazdi argued extensively against it during the constitutional debate, pointing out that it was irrelevant to the functions of the *mojtahed* occupying the position of the Leader that concern "governmental problems and not the explanation of the *shar'i* commandments of God."[5] The provisions for a Leadership Council to fulfill the function of the Jurist, which also mentioned *marja'iyyat,* were eliminated in the amended Articles 5 and 107.[6] While Khomeini was still alive, members of the Review Assembly came to the conclusion that having a Leadership Council had no basis in Islamic jurisprudence and was incompatible with the authority of the Jurist as the legitimate ruler (*vali-ye faqih*), and asked his permission to eliminate it. Khomeini agreed in one of his last verbal instructions.[7] Thus, the powers of Leadership were to be concentrated in a single person, as were the Executive and Judiciary Powers. The already extensive powers of the Leader in the 1979 Constitution, including Executive Power "in matters directly concerned with the Leadership" were expanded,[8] giving him the power to appoint and dismiss the head of the Iranian radio and television (Article 175), transferring to him the responsibility for coordinating the relations among the three Powers from the President (Article 57),[9] and entrusting to him "the determination of the general policies of the regime" (formerly included among the Prime Minister's responsibilities) (Article 110). Not much of substance could be done to incorporate the theoretically flawed idea of the Absolute Mandate into the Constitution. Nevertheless, despite sharp disagreements among his colleagues, the Revision Council President Ayatollah Meshkini pressed for some token acknowledgment, and in the very last session ominously succeeded in incorporating Khomeini's latter day terminology into the Constitution in Article 57 on the independence of the three Powers under "the Absolute Mandate to Rule" (*velāyat-e motlaq-e amr*).[10] Legislative Power, by contrast, became further diffused, even though in principle it emanated from the Leadership. It could be exercised by all citizens, lay and clerical, through their participation in the Majles, by the six clerical jurists of the Guardian Council, all of whom were appointed by the Leader, and by his clerically dominated new advisory body, the Maslahat Council.

The critical importance of the Assembly of Leadership Experts had been demonstrated by its swift choice of Khomeini's successor. It was given the power to dismiss the Leader not just for incapacitation but also "if it should become apparent that he had lacked one of the qualifications from the beginning" (Article 109). This new formulation appears to give the Assembly virtually unrestricted latitude in light of the fact that the qualifications include not only jurisprudential competence but also a "correct political and social perspective, administrative and managerial competence, courage and adequate power for Leadership." Furthermore, the Assembly had already established a mechanism for monitoring the conduct of the Leader. In its internal regulations passed in 1983 (Articles 1 and 19), the Assembly had set up a seven-man Investigation Committee to supervise continuously the conditions and comportment of the Leader. This Committee was further given the responsibility of "supervising the administrative organization of Leadership in coordination with the Leader."[11] With its enhanced power of dismissal and its supervisory committee, the Assembly of Leadership Experts became an influential organ in the collective conciliar clerical rule.

The Maslahat Council was recognized as the advisory arm of Leadership and was given the authority to determine major state policies. This went beyond Khomeini's original terms of institution, which had stipulated that it "should not become a power alongside the other [three] Powers" and another major clerically dominated organ of the conciliar regime. The Council was destined to become a new legislative body of some importance. The Maslahat Council includes the six clerical jurists of the Guardian Council who are *mojtahed*s. From its creation, the Maslahat Council has in fact increased the power of these jurists who have been included among its members The jurists of the Guardian Council thus wear two hats. As one of them once boasted, "I have one responsibility in the morning, another in the evening.

My responsibility in the morning is to speak according to the *shari'a* [in the Council of Guardians], my responsibility in the evening is to see to the public interest [in the Maslahat Council]!"[12]

The constitutionalization of the Maslahat Council was the culmination of the reception of the Sunni principle of *maslahat* (public interest), which had been firmly rejected by the Shi'ite tradition, and amounted to what I call "Sunnitization of Shi'ism."[13] With the traditional dualism of religious and political authority being replaced by theocratic monism, the Leader of the Islamic Republic assumes a position similar to the Ottoman Sultan as the Caliph: he legitimizes the entire apparatus of the state and all public law as Islamic and he can legislate on the basis of expediency and public interest. It can be further argued that the Leader's authority is more extensive than the Caliph's because, as the Supreme Jurist, he is entitled to issue "governmental ordinances" with implicit divine sanction. There is also another significant difference: the conciliar institutionalization of the legislative authority of the Supreme Jurist was made possible by the distinctly clericalist Shi'ite heritage and found its embodiment in the Maslahat Council and the Assembly of Leadership Experts.

Constitutional Development of Clerical Conciliarism

The constitutional politics of the first decade of the Islamic Republic had centered around two issues. First was the radical depreciation of the traditional Shi'ite institution of *marja'iyyat-e taqlid* in order to make room for the new theory of theocratic government. The other was the increasing centralization of authority in the post-revolutionary state. The transition from Khomeini's charismatic rule to a system of collective conciliar rule by the clerical elite set the parameters for the constitutional politics of the second decade in the Islamic Republic of Iran (IRI).

The conciliar institutionalization of hierocratic authority, which began under Khomeini's leadership, set the stage for the post-charismatic clerical constitutional politics of the 1990s. The first obstacle to the new conciliar rule by the clerical elite was the traditional Shi'ite hierarchy based on superiority in religious learning (*a'lamiyyat*) among the preeminent jurists. The contradiction between the novel Imamate based on the Mandate of the Jurist and the traditional *marja'iyyat* had become fully evident in the 1980s, resulting in the elimination of all explicit references to the latter principle in the amended Constitution in 1989. Nevertheless, a residue of the contradiction remained in the awkward wording of the amended Article 107 on the election of the Leader by the Assembly of Leadership Experts. Far more importantly, the contradiction between the old and the new principles was a constant source of tension between the political and the religious institutions of the IRI.

The first half of the 1990s was thus marked by the clash of the state-based newly institutionalized political authority of the clerical elite of the Islamic Republic and the traditional *madrasa*-based authority of the "sources of imitation" (*maráje'-e taqlid*). The clash had been pushed aside by Khomeini but not resolved. The incompatibility of the two forms of authority was highlighted with the deaths between August 1992 and November 1994 of three Grand Ayatollahs. The crisis produced by the deaths of these sources of imitation revealed the structural fault line of the regime.[14] The Head of the Judiciary Ayatollah Mohammad Yazdi and other clerical supporters of theocratic monarchy made a serious attempt to unify the two offices for the benefit of the Leader of the IRI as its sole occupant, but that attempt failed.[15]

This failure to achieve consistency with the traditional Shi'ite hierocratic authority did not hamper the development of the new clerical conciliar system that is the constitutional framework of post-Khomeini Iran. It has a Leader (*rahbar*) and three distinctive organs. The Leader is a clerical monarch ruling in the name of God with more extensive powers than any constitutional monarch or elected president in the world. In addition to his extensive constitutional powers, the Absolute Mandate of the Jurist entitles him to issue "governmental ordinances" (*ahkām-e hokumati*), and he has done so at some critical points. The office is generally recognized as being incompatible with democracy. Although it is theoretically an elective office because the clerics of the Assembly of Experts who elect the Leader are themselves popularly elected, a very small social group, the Mullahs, are privileged over the majority of the lay population, thus making democracy or rule by the people questionable. In addition to his extensive constitutional powers, the Leader presides over an extensive network of powerful clerical commissars who are accountable only to him. The Leader as the Ruling Jurist (*vali-ye faqih*) has representatives in the ministries, the military and security services, the revolutionary organizations, and the economic foundations. They are supervised by the Office of the Supreme Leader, which also supervises the Friday prayer leaders of the major cities and the provinces. The provincial Friday prayer leaders are counterparts to the governors of the provinces (now 30 of them) and are highly influential because, unlike the latter, they do not rotate and enjoy very long tenures at the pleasure of the Leader. The system extends beyond these councils and includes the Judiciary Power and the Special Court for Clerics directly responsible to the Leader.[16]

The Constitution of 1979 had given the Guardian Council the power to supervise the presidential and Majles elections, the result of the assimilation of the French constitutional model.[17] This incidental feature suggested the Guardian Council as an instrument of political control to Iran's ruling elite after the death of Khomeini and the end of his charismatic leadership. In 1990, in anticipation of its impending elections, the Assembly of Constitutional Experts used its special legislative prerogative to ensure the exclusion of radical clerics by stiffening the requirement of candidacy to *ejtehād,* and, more consequentially, by leaving the qualification of the candidate to the Guardian Council, except for those "explicitly or implicitly approved by the Leader."[18] In December 1991, the Guardian Council, in anticipation of serving the function of political control in the elections for the Fifth Majles by excluding same troublesome radical clerics, interpreted the supervision of elections in Article 99 of the Constitution as "approbationary" (*estesvābi*) and asserted its authority over "all stages of the electoral process, including the approval or rejection of the qualification of the candidates."[19] The formula was adopted by an amendment to the electoral law in July 1995.[20]

The Guardian Council was already used as an instrument of political control during the institutionalization of clerical domination under Khomeini,[21] taking its supervisory power to mean the vetting of the candidates for the Majles on whose qualifications the Constitution had been silent. But the proportion of Majles candidates rejected while Khomeini was alive was about 15 percent; it jumped to over 25 percent after his death.[22] The Guardian Council, under fire from Khatami and the reformists when they stood their ground and showed themselves capable of fighting hard,[23] was forced to restrain its rejection of candidates for the 2000 elections. Its Secretary, Ayatollah Ahmad Jannati, later repented for this laxity, and asked for God's forgiveness. The Council again rejected nearly a third of the candidates in 2004 and 2008. Some 88 incumbent Majles deputies were rejected in 2004, and many reformers were among the 2,250 candidates rejected out of a total of 7,597 in 2008.[24] With the arbitrary and blatant abuse of the Council's supervisory power, as one newspaper put it a few years ago, the eligibility to run for elections is "no longer a right but a privilege."[25]

A new gate-keeping function in the selection of the clerical elite was given to the clerical jurists of the Guardian Council. The constitutional amendments of 1989 explicitly added the supervision of the elections for the Assembly of

Leadership Experts to the functions of the Guardian Council (Article 99), and it took over the examination of the candidates to determine the requisite level of *ejtehād* with a law passed by the Assembly of Leadership Experts in July 1990.[26] The Council used its powers to disqualify an ever-increasing proportion of candidates. The exclusionary trend in vetting candidates is even clearer with regard to the Assembly of Experts than the Majles (table 2.1).

It can be stated categorically that the Guardian Council has made no contribution to institution building in the IRI. The main reason for this failure is the absence of a written jurisprudence remotely comparable to the jurisprudence of other constitutional courts (or the Supreme Court in the United States). Early on, when Ayatollah Safi was its Secretary (1980–1988), the Council backed its opinions by reasons and legal arguments, but this practice ceased after his resignation.[27] Despite the urging of the Leader on the occasion of its twentieth anniversary in July 2000,[28] the Guardian Council has failed to create any constitutional jurisprudence. This has gone hand in hand with the increasing politicization of judicial review, which preceded the politicization of the Judiciary and the use of courts as an instrument of political repression. The Council interpreted its function of supervising elections as the power to reject the qualification of candidates for all elected offices, including the presidency, without giving its reasons, as is also usually the case when it vetoes legislation. As a result of this overload, the Council's primary functions of judicial review and determination of conformity of legislation with Islamic standards have been overwhelmed.

TABLE 2.1   Candidates for the Assembly of Experts Rejected by the Guardian Council

Election	Number of Applicants	Number Rejected[1]	%
1982	168	22	13
1990	183	77	42
1998	396	250	63
2006	495	332	67

Sources: Buchta 2000: 60; *Agence Press France* 11/29/06; *The Times* 12/18/08.

[1]Or withdrawn.

Since 2000, the effect of the Guardian Council on institution building has been negative. It paralyzed legislation and nearly destroyed the Majles as an institution during the Khatami presidency by extending its veto on grounds of inconsistency with Islamic standards to such items of legislation as the annual government budget. In January 2002, the Council vetoed as contrary to the *shari'a* bills that were found to be at variance with the "governmental orders of the Leader, the orders of the late Imam, and even the regulations of the Supreme Council for Cultural Revolution." In January 2003, it rejected a Majles bill against torture on the grounds that it contravened the internal regulations (*ā'in-nāma*) of state prisons.[29] A year later, the Head of the Judiciary unexpectedly intervened with a statement that torture was forbidden in Islam, and the reformist Sixth Majles in its last days quickly exploited this boon by incorporating his statement into its amended bill, which then passed by the Guardian Council.[30]

The Guardian Council has shown no concern about removing abundant internal contradictions within the Constitution of the IRI. One obvious contradiction is between the *shari'a* and the principle of equality of all citizens before ordinary state laws, which is the basis for the majority of complaints by members of religious minorities to the presidential Commission for the Implementation of the Constitution.[31] Nor is this contradiction resolved through the secondary mechanism of Shi'ite jurisprudence.[32] Reconciling contradictions between Iranian law and international law is even further removed from the politicized concerns of the Guardian Council. For example, the gruesome *shar'i* punishments (*hodud*) obviously contradict the international human rights instruments that outlaw cruel and inhumane punishments.

The Maslahat Council, the other major clerically dominated organ of the regime, has outgrown even its expanded scope in the constitutional amendments of 1989, and has become a new legislative body of major importance. Unlike the Guardian Council, the Maslahat Council is under no obligation to return changed items of legislation to any other organ. It began its independent law-making by changing items of legislation other than those subject to disagreement between the Guardian Council and the Majles. In fact, such cases of disagreement amounted to only less than a third of its enactments in the first 4 years of its existence. Nevertheless, according to the Guardian Council's constitutional interpretation of October 15, 1993, "no legislative organ has the right to annul or rescind an enactment of the Maslahat Council."[33] When Hashemi-Rafsanjani knew he would retain the chairmanship of the Maslahat Council after completing his second term as President of the IRI in 1997, he reaffirmed that if it "has issued a law, the three powers cannot repeal it."[34]

Notable instances of legislation by the Maslahat Council include a December 1991 law establishing a High Disciplinary Court for Judges, the introduction of alimony in November 1992, which paved the way for amending the law of judiciary appointment to allow appointment of women as judges in April 1995, the July 1994 law of military courts, and the May 1995 law concerning governmental punishments of smuggling and foreign currency.[35] The Council's function of advising the Leader concerning the determination of major state policies also requires a mixture of constitutional interpretation and legislation. This is clear with regard to the privatization of the economy. The Council submitted its guidelines for economic policy to the Leader late in 2004, which were approved by him in May 2005 and November 2006 and given to the Executive for implementation. It involved a radical rein-terpretation of the letter and spirit of Article 44 of the Constitution, which divided the economy into three sectors, the private, the cooperative, and the public. Except for the extractive oil and gas industries, the state was ordered to gradually divest 80 percent of its ownership of economic enterprises in the public sector. The Majles had frustrated President Hashemi-Rafsanjani's attempts at privatization through legislation in the 1990s. As the chairman of the Maslahat Council, the former President was able to institute sweeping privatization with only the Leader's consent.

The Assembly of Leadership Experts has limited legislative power, which it can exercise independently of the Leader, unlike the Maslahat Council.[36] For example, the Assembly did set up an Investigation Committee to supervise the conditions and comportment of the Leader on a continuous basis. This Committee holds regular meetings throughout the year and upgraded itself to a regular advisory body to the Leader.[37] Its Secretariat has, furthermore, assumed the function of strengthening the intellectual foundations of the theocratic (velā'i) regime, and to that end began publication of a quarterly, Hokumat-e Eslāmi, in 1996.[38] In 1997, the Committee advised the Leader, Ayatollah Khamenei, to reconstitute the Maslahat Council under the retiring President Hashemi-Rafsanjani with the mandate to assume its function of offering advice on major policies of the regime and thus implement the amended Article 110 of the Constitution.[39] It is interesting to note that when the Leader and the Head of the Judiciary were vying with President Khatami for authority over plans for reform and reorganization, the Assembly of Leadership Experts passed its own four-point reform program at its 2001 general session, the first and most important being the upgrading of its capabilities to "carry out the function of investigation and supervision." The other points included greater involvement in domestic and foreign policies and the defense of the *velāyat-e faqih* as a form of "meritocracy in the Islamic political regime" against those who wish to offer "Western democracy," and "under the pretext of realizing liberalism and democratic methods, manipulate and transform religious values."[40]

The suggestion of President Hashemi-Rafsanjani as chairman of a revitalized Maslahat Council was just the beginning of a special relationship. In the 2006 elections, he entered an intense contest for the leadership of the Assembly of Leadership Experts against the hardliner Ayatollahs Mohammad Taqi Mesbāh-Yazdi (President Ahmadinejad's spiritual mentor) and Ahmad Jannati. He won impressively in Tehran and was elected its first Vice-President. The Assembly elected Hashemi-Rafsanjani its new President when its ailing first President, Ayatollah 'Ali Meshkini, died at the end of July 2007. In his election speech, Hashemi-Rafsanjani signaled his intention to increase the visibility of the Assembly by telling his fellow clerics: "If the assembly of experts wants to take responsibility for important practical duties and to interfere in the current issues of the country at the highest level and to be more active in various areas, there is no obstacle from a legal and Islamic viewpoint."[41] He was reelected the Assembly's President by a two-thirds majority in March 2009 (figure 2.1).[42]

Perhaps the most intriguing recent constitutional developments are those concerning the Judiciary. One of the aims of the constitutional revision of 1989 was to centralize Judiciary Power, and to that end, it replaced the Supreme Judiciary Council with a single Head of the Judiciary Power, a *mojtahed,* to be appointed by the Leader for five-year terms (amended Article 157) in order, among other things, to reorganize the Judiciary and implement the functions enumerated in Article 156 (amended Article 158), which included "supervision over the proper execution of laws" and "measures to prevent occurrence of crime and to reform criminals."

The Chief Justice of the Supreme Judiciary Council under Khomeini, Ayatollah Musavi-Ardabili, had sought to rationalize the chaos arising largely from the new Islamic criminal law and the verdicts of the revolutionary courts. In accordance with Article 161 of the Constitution, the Supreme Judiciary Council used the pre-revolutionary law of June 1949 on the uniformity of judicial process with its added clauses of July–August 1958 as the basis of its ruling that was binding on all the courts.[43] This modest measure of successful Islamicization of the law, however, stands in sharp contrast to the failure of effective Islamicization of the Judiciary after Khomeini's death, when Ayatollah Mohammad Yazdi held the newly created position of the

FIGURE 2.1 Leader Khamenei and President of the Assembly of Leadership Experts, Akbar Hashemi-Rafsanjani (left), meet with members of the Assembly of Leadership Experts in Tehran, February 21, 2007. (AP Photo/IRN)

Head of the Judiciary from 1989 to 1999. To combat the chronic shortage of religious jurists and a mounting backlog of cases, the June 4, 1994 Law of General and Revolutionary Courts abolished the position of prosecutors and the appeal system in an attempt to revert to the Kadi courts as prescribed in the *shari'a*. The result was generally chaotic. Ayatollah Sayyed Mahmud Hashemi-Shahrudi, who succeeded Yazdi as Head of the Judiciary in 1999, declared the Judiciary he was taking over to be a wreck (*virāneh*), 70 years behind other institutions, and promised major reforms and reorganization.[44]

The Iraqi-born Ayatollah Hashemi-Shahrudi, known in Iraq as Mahmud al-Hashemi and a disciple of the martyred reformist jurist Mohammad Baqer al-Sadr, wasted no time in asserting himself against the reformist President Khatami by claiming that reform was the concern of all the three Powers, and he had as good a claim as the President for supervising the rule of law and observance of the Constitution."[45] In an oblique response to Khatami's Commission for the Implementation of the Constitution, he set up the Special Committee to Oversee Correct Implementation of the Leader's Policies, whose real purpose seemed to be keeping the President in check. He also launched his program for "judiciary development" (*tawse'a-ye qazā'i*), insisting that it had not been inspired by the Western pattern, during a week-long gathering in the new Persian year 1380 (beginning on March 21, 2001).[46] The term "judiciary development," although clearly inspired by the United Nations' Development Program (UNDP), was predictably purported to be "a slogan arisen from the text of the pure Mohammadan Islam!"[47] Hashemi-Shahrudi's definition of "judicial development" in his opening statement at the gathering, however, had as little to do with the UNDP as it did with pure Mohammadan Islam. He innovatively defined judiciary development as "judiciary empowerment" in line with the current global expansion of judiciary power but with particular reference to Article 156 of the Iranian Constitution. Having categorically stated that "development means empowerment,"[48] Shahrudi took it to mean the growth of judicial power to the fullest extent allowed by a somewhat expansive interpretation of the Constitution. He accordingly maintained that the Judiciary Power has not one but two constitutional axes: the obvious administration of justice and the supervision of proper rule of law, which has not been so evident but, in fact, had been completely neglected. This supervisory function is taken to mean the power of judicial review to ensure the constitutionality of laws and of administrative regulations.[49] Shahrudi's hitherto uninstitutionalized claim to judicial review is unprecedented in Iran's civil law system, even after its post-revolutionary Islamicization.[50]

He also hints at the unconstitutionality of the ordinary law implementing Article 173 because of its failure to conform to Shahrudi's constitutional interpretation of the provisions for judicial empowerment.[51] In his statement on judiciary empowerment, Shahrudi notes that the Head of the Judiciary is responsible only to the clerical monarch (*vali-ye amr*) and not to the Majles or the President, and that the Majles has no power of interpellation over him or any judge or official of the Judiciary.[52]

Shahrudi put forward an expansive interpretation of the third clause of Article 156 on "measures to prevent occurrence of crime." Noting that it had no parallels in other constitutions of the world, Shahrudi nevertheless included this function of prevention of wrongdoing.[53] In October 2000, he had wanted his National Inspectorate to develop intelligence and information-gathering capabilities to fight economic corruption.[54] But the true utility of this empowering judicial interpretation was the justification of the suppression of the press by the courts, a measure intended to forestall sedition.[55] With regard to judiciary reorganization, he sought direct support of the Maslahat Council to reintroduce the division of courts into criminal (*keyfari*), family and personal status (*madani*), civil and commercial (*hoquqi*), the differentiation of the offices of judge and prosecutor, specialized courts, and an appellate system.[56] The law reestablishing the lower (*dādsarā*) and appellate courts passed the Majles in the spring of 2002.[57]

Hashemi-Shahrudi emphasized the importance of specialized consultation within the Judiciary and instituted regular sessions of expert judges in towns and provincial capitals to answer questions and requests for guidance by the courts under jurisdiction. The first set of sessions dealing with problems in criminal law arising from the new Islamic penal code and laws and regulations of revolutionary courts was held from 2000 to 2002 in district branches of the Ministry of Justice. The selection of their procedures published for the instruction of judges suggests that a bureaucratic mechanism was put in place for the rationalization of legal process.[58] He also strengthened the Legal Office (*edara-ye hoquqi*) of the Judiciary and instituted a Research Center in Jurisprudence (*markaz-e tahqiqāt-e feqhi*) to answer enquiries from the courts and provincial branches of the Ministry of Justice. The Center draws on the rulings (*fatwās*) of the seven designated "sources of imitation," including the Leader, Ayatollah Khamanei, but does so alongside the rulings of other living *marāji'* as well as those of the late Ayatollahs Khomeini and Kho'i and the classics of Shi'ite jurisprudence. This Research Center, like the Legal Office of the Ministry of Justice, follows Article 167 of the Constitution, consistently upholding the priority of ordinary laws over Shi'ite jurisprudence. The resort to the latter is thus residual, along the lines provided for by the Egyptian Civil Code of 1948 and the Afghan Constitution of 2004. Furthermore, it is usually inconclusive as the *fatwās* presented to supplement ordinary laws are often contradictory, and categorical instructions seem to be provided only when a pertinent positive law is found additionally. Indeed, the latter seems to make the *fatwās* redundant. For example, four out of five *fatwās* produced in response to the question of whether women can be judges according to the *shari'a* gave a negative answer but were overruled by the Legal Office of the Judiciary, which cited an ordinary law on the appointment of women as judges.

Ayatollah Shahrudi considers his judicial development Islamic style suitable for exportation to the rest of the Muslim world. He has appointed judiciary attachés to embassies in some Muslim countries, and signed an agreement for judiciary cooperation with Qatar in April 2008.[59] Shahrudi, however, disapproves of stoning for adultery as prescribed by the *shari'a,* and thinks the judges can and should commute it to other forms of punishment in the public interest (*maslahat*).[60] His conception of judiciary organization is a managerial one of an administrative hierarchy in which judges are subjected to the authority of the district and provincial directors (*modirān*)—a far cry from the traditional autonomy of the Kadi. In addition, he has at his disposal a High Disciplinary Court for Judges to discipline the judges, as the Leader disciplines the clerics by means of the parallel and presumably model Special Court for Clerics. Nor does Ayatollah Shahrudi fail to remind the directors of these branches of the Judiciary that they are the "representatives of the Supreme Jurist and the clerical monarch!"[61]

Finally, the clerical conciliar system required political control of the clerical class for whose disciplining Khomeini had already set up the Special Court for Clerics in 1987. Khamenei as the new Leader approved the regulations for the Special Court in August 1990. The Special Court for Clerics was organized into a court system independent of the Judiciary and under the direct control of the Leadership, and a second branch was added to it a few months later. It has its own prison and correctional facilities. Not only was the Special Prosecutor responsible solely to the Leader, but the bylaws of the Court were issued by the Leader to emphasize its total independence—not only from the Judiciary but also from the Legislative Power.[62] This Special Court disciplines members of the clerical profession not only for commission of misdeeds but also for omission to fulfill their duties, and all its prosecutors are appointed by the Leader.[63] In a 1999 report to the UN Commission on Human Rights in 1999, the UN Special Representative on Iran deemed the Special Court for Clerics an extra-constitutional judicial body and recommended its abolition.[64] Its great value as an instrument of repression and for disciplining the privileged social stratum of the Islamic Republic, however, was proven during Khamenei's decisive fight against the clerical reformists. The trials of important members of the clerical elite in 1999—Hojjat al-Eslams Mohsen Kadivar, Mohammad Musavi- Kho'ini-ha, editor of the reformist newspaper *Salām*, and finally the Interior Minister, 'Abdollah Nuri—were particularly spectacular, but the Court continues to operate as the main instrument of repression of dissidence. It has put many dissident clerics behind bars and executed a number of them.[65]

Contestation of Clerical Domination

The Special Court for Clerics could discipline dissidents only after the fact and was not fully effective in suppressing clerical dissent. As their clerical status gave them somewhat greater immunity than was enjoyed by lay intellectuals, some young clerics belonging to the reform movement dared to challenge the official doctrine of the Mandate of the Jurist. As early as 1995, Hojjat al-Islam Hasan Youssefi Eshkevari, who had been a deputy in the First Majles, put forward his proposal for "religious democratic government," denying the official claims that Islamic sources suggested a special form of government and that the form of government was a matter for religion and the Sacred Law. "Even the Imamate, as believed by the Shi'a," he asserted, "has no connection with the phenomenon of government," citing a *fatwā* issued by the great Shi'ite jurist, Akhund Khorasani, in the first decade of the twentieth century "that during the Era of Occultation, the government of the Muslims rests with the majority of the people." He concluded that "the idea of *velāyat-e faqih* was inserted into an already tested political system— that is, a 'republic' and a parliamentary system."[66] Eshkevari also tried to raise the banner of social justice in Islam: "Justice...includes the realm of legislation, and according to the Koran implementing justice is closer than anything else to piety."[67] His effort had little effect, however, because of its dissonance with both clerical dissent and the lay reformists' discovery of civil society and democracy. Social justice as the third item on Khomeini's agenda was left for the return of the hardliners under Ahmadinejad.

The broad, public reopening of the legitimacy and definition of the fundamental principle of order in the Islamic Republic of Iran, namely the Absolute

Mandate of the Jurist, was the immediate result of the election of President Khatami. In November 1997, two disgruntled senior Ayatollahs, who had been pushed aside by the present Leadership after a very long association with the regime, spoke out against the Leader. Ayatollah Montazeri and Ayatollah Azari-Qomi openly challenged the Leader and the principle of Leadership on the basis of the Mandate of the Jurist. Montazeri also published a booklet, *Popular Government and the Constitution* (*Hokumat-e mardomi va qānun-e asāsi*), in which he refuted the idea of the Absolute Mandate of the Jurist and the authority of the jurists of the Guardian Council to reject candidates for elected office. This open expression of dissent within the clerical elite enabled lay groups opposed to the principle of clerical rule to voice their opposition. When Ayatollah Montazeri was put under house arrest in March 1998, 385 dissent clerics demanded his release, and the retailers and craftsmen in his hometown of Najafabad went on strike.[68] Various organizations issued proclamations of support, and the idea that the office of the Leader be made elective and have a limited term was publicly discussed. The taboo on the discussion and questioning of the principle of theocratic government in the press was thus broken for good.

One of Montazeri's students, Hojjat al-Eslam Mohsen Kadivar, who also belonged to the reform movement and was completing a doctoral thesis in philosophy, had written a book on different approaches to government in Shi'ite jurisprudence, *Theses on the State in Shi'ite Jurisprudence* (1997). His work presented Khomeini's theory, hitherto officially considered *the* Shi'ite view of government, as one among eight recognized Shi'ite views of the state. In 1998, he took a bold step beyond Montazeri, and in *Hokumat-e velā'i* (Government based on the "absolute appointive authority of the jurists"), he offered an explicit critique of Khomeini's theory and a refutation of the legal arguments for the validity of the official doctrine of theocratic government.[69] The book traced the progressive extension of the authority of the jurists from judiciary competence to the right to rule, and from authority over special categories of persons such as the insane and orphans, as specified by the policing (*hisba*) rules of the *shari'a,* which Kadivar accepts, to authority over the people in general, as in the Absolute Mandate of the Jurist, which he rejects.[70] The book also contains a painstaking, and often abstruse, refutation of the "traditional" and "rational" bases of the official doctrine in terms of traditional Shi'ite jurisprudence. Kadivar reminds his readers that before Khomeini's ideological revolution in Shi'ism, the authoritative traditional Shi'ite interpretation of "those in authority" of the Qur'an (Verse 4.59) was that it referred to no one other than the 12 holy Imams.[71] He further points out that by the clear implication of this view of the authoritative Shi'ite commentators, "ordering absolute obedience to the fallible [as do the proponents of the Absolute Mandate of the Jurist] is reprehensible." His own position is that the authoritative traditional Shi'ite interpretation of another equally important Qur'anic verse that includes the plural of *vali* [Q 9.71,] implied "the general authority of the believer (*velāyat-e 'omumi-ye mo'menin*)," which should be "the basis for the political philosophy of Islam during the occultation of the Infallible [Imam]."[72]

Kadivar's theory remains strictly within the bounds of Shi'ite jurisprudence, and offers none of the hermeneutic questioning put forward by Mohammad Mojtahed Shabestari and 'Abolkarim Sorush, who argued that the Shi'ite jurisprudence itself was a historically contingent discipline. The fact that it does not meet this higher critical standard, however, should not blind us to its serious impact on the foundations of the legitimacy of theocratic government. Nor should it be forgotten that the reformists had avoided a frontal challenge to the Mandate of the Jurist. Before Ayatollah Montazeri spoke out, Behzad Nabavi, the pro-reform leader of the Organization of the Mojahedin of the Islamic Revolution, had prevaricated on the term "absolute," while another reformist leader, Sa'id Hajjarian, had distinguished between defending the "good" and the "bad" arguments for the Mandate of the Jurist,[73] resting his hope on the clear delineation in the Constitution of "the principles of theocracy and democracy in the Islamic regime."[74] Even after Montazeri's outburst, Hajjarian approached the issue obliquely and defensively toward the end of 1997, when rebuffing the attack on the reformists by the hardliner newspaper *Resālat,* which advocated a theocratic society in place of the reformers' "civil society."[75] Again, Hajjarian put his faith in the Constitution as "the national covenant (*mithāq-e melli*) and the guarantee of the legitimacy of the Islamic regime." Only in January 2000, in a short editorial entitled "Autocracy, hierocracy (*rabbāni-sālāri*) and democracy," did Hajjarian confront theocracy directly by taking on Ayatollah Javadi-Amoli's assertion that the Assembly of Leadership Experts in its selection of the most qualified jurist was responsible to God, not to the people.

From 2000 onward, the focus of constitutional debate shifted from the Absolute Mandate of the Jurist to the four-way contestation among the Executive, Legislative, and Judiciary Powers and the organs of clerical control. Then, in a striking interview with the Iran Students News Agency on February 1, 2005, just as he began contemplating another run for the presidency, the former President Hashemi-Rafsanjani minimized the significance of the *velāyat-e faqih,* considering it instead as an indirectly elective office deriving its legitimacy, like everything else in the IRI, from the will of the people and their oath of allegiance (*bay'at*). He thus highlighted the favorite Sunni trope of *bay'a(t)* as bestowal of sovereignty by the people on the ruler with an oath of allegiance. This amounted to an implicit rejection of the peculiarly Shi'ite claim for the legitimacy of theocratic rule as the continuation of that of the holy Imams.[76] The primary intention behind Rafsanjani's striking statement was democratization in order to win the reformist vote, but the statement also confirmed the growing Sunnitization of the political thought of the Islamic Republic.[77]

3

Thermidor at Last

Hashemi-Rafsanjani's Presidency (1989–1997) and the Economy

Economics is a matter for the donkey (*khar*). Our people made the revolution for Islam, not for the Persian melon (*kharboza*).
—Khomeini's speech in Qom on August 24, 1979

KHOMEINI KNEW WHAT HE WAS SAYING when he reminded his patiently suffering followers they had not made the revolution for more melons. The Iranian economy was still a wreck at the time of Hashemi-Rafsanjani's takeover a decade later. Despite the quadrupling of the price of oil, Iran's per capita gross national product (GNP) in 1988 was just getting back to the level it had been 21 years earlier—that is, before the massive economic growth spurt that preceded the Islamic revolution—and labor productivity had slipped almost as badly. The first step to rectify the situation, according to the new President's economic advisor, was to create the political and cultural preconditions for economic growth through liberalization and education, respectively.[1] The more obvious and specific political precondition was the smooth post-revolutionary transfer of power and political stability that would permit the transition of an amorphous revolutionary power structure into a developmental state. Rafsanjani's personal predisposition may have played a part in setting economic development as a major policy goal. When he had been sent by Khomeini to visit Islamic revolutionary groups opposing the Shah abroad in the mid-1970s, he had proven to be an avid traveler and had taken much interest in the economic development of Japan, Europe, and the United States.[2]

Hashemi-Rafsanjani called his first cabinet "the cabinet of reconstruction," and most of its 23 members were technocrats who had studied in the

TABLE 3.1   Government Employees (excluding the armed forces)

Year	Number (in thousands)	Total Population (in thousands)	As % of the Population	As % of the Households
1976	1,277	33,709	3.8	19
1987	1,434	50,681	2.8	14
1991	2,113	55,837	3.8	20
1997	2,360	61,016	3.9	19
2006	2,251	70,496	3.2	13

Source: Sālmāna-ye āmāri (Statistical Yearbook), 1371 [1992–1993], 79; 1376 [1997–1998], 113; 1385 [2006–2007], 48, 110, 153.

West. His second cabinet in 1993 included nine engineers and eight M.D.s or Ph.D.s.[3] Economic planning was revived for the purpose of reconstruction with the First Five-Year Plan (1990–1994). More fundamentally, economic reconstruction required the revamping of the developmental state. As can be seen in table 3.1, the size of the state grew considerably in absolute terms and relative to that of the population, and reached the peak of its development in the last year of Rafsanjani's presidency (1997), employing 2.36 million people—roughly the same percentage of the population but twice as many people as the Shah had employed before the revolution.

The employment in the public sector, however, indicates a completely different story. There is a massive jump in the number of persons employed in the public sector as a result of the revolutionary nationalizations and confiscations (table 3.2).

Even adjusting for the growth of jobs in the government bureaucracy, it is evident that the number of other public sector employees (mostly economic enterprises) jumps from about 400,000 before the revolution to about 2 million in 1986 and does not change significantly thereafter, though the percentage of public employees in the total number gradually drops with the growth of the private sector.

Hashemi-Rafsanjani reopened Tehran's stock market in 1989 and laid out the legal framework for privatization in the First Five-Year Development Plan. He made the stock market available for valuing and selling public enterprises and maintained a pro-market program in the Second Development Plan (1995–1999). The Majles halted the first phase of privatization in the summer

TABLE 3.2   Employment in the Public Sector

Year	Public Sector Employees (in thousands)	Total Employed (in thousands)	As % of Total
1976	1,673	8,709	19
1986	3,453	11,002	31
1996	4,258	14,572	29
2006	5,025	20,476	25

Source: Sālmāna-ye āmāri (Statistical Yearbook), 1385 [2006–2007], 148.

of 1994 amid accusations of no-bid sales and corruption, and the second phase, 1995–1997, was confined to workers and war veterans. The third phase, 1998–1999, fell under Khatami's presidency.[4] Overall, the progress of privatization was very slow, mainly because the public and nationalized enterprises were overstaffed and the staff was protected by the Labor Law; in 1996, 70 percent of the total budget still belonged to public enterprises. Iran's "market openness" improved considerably over the tightly controlled war economy of the 1981–1988 period,[5] and Rafsanjani submitted Iran's first application to join the World Trade Organization in 1996. The economy grew for the first 3 years of Hashemi-Rafsanjani's presidency from 1989 to 1992, but the fall in oil prices and serious mismanagement of the currency and economy brought economic growth to a complete halt in 1994–1995. Nevertheless, Rafsanjani maintained a relatively high ratio of development to current expenditure (about one-third, which dropped to one-quarter by the end of Khatami's term). There was a noticeable rise in economic inequality between 1990 and 1992,[6] which explains the sharpened popular perception of economic nepotism and corruption that caused great resentment after the economic growth halted.[7]

The Hydra-Headed Structure of Military and Economic Power

Foremost among the tasks of post-war reconstruction was the amalgamation and rationalization of the armed forces and mobilizational structures of the Islamic Republic of Iran (IRI). The Islamic Revolutionary Guards Corps (IRGC; sepāh-e pāsdārān-e enqelāb-e eslāmī) and the Army of Mobilization (*sepāh-e basij,* henceforth Basij; a militia or "army of twenty million") were set up by Khomeini's decrees of May 5 and November 26, 1979, respectively, and played a major role in the war with Iraq from 1980 to 1988. Although the regular army had been purged and weakened to the point that it posed no threat to the regime, the Revolutionary Guards grew into an important military force of 120,000 as a result of the war with Iraq. The Basij currently has some 740 regional battalions of 300 and 350 and many more reservists.[8]

As President, Hashemi-Rafsanjani continued the reorganization of the Revolutionary Guards he had begun as Khomeini's commander-in-chief of the armed forces. He introduced military ranks and uniforms modeled on the regular army in 1989, and sought to integrate them with the regular army by establishing the Ministry of Defense and Armed Forces Logistics. Significantly, the new minister was Akbar Torkan, a technocrat who had been the managing director of the defense industries. Although the IRGC and the Basij were not disbanded, they were given new economic functions in order to join the reconstruction effort and expand the defense industries. In June 1991, the Majles passed Hashem-Rafsanjani's bill to reorganize the revolutionary committees, the municipal police, and the rural gendarmerie into Law Enforcement Forces (*niruhā-ye entezāmi*). To integrate the revolutionary committees into the Law Enforcement Forces, Rafsanjani had to overcome fierce opposition from the radicals who feared the consequent loss of their revolutionary identity.[9] He also set up a general command office under another civilian functionary of the IRGC to further the integration of the Revolutionary Guards and the regular army in early 1992.[10] After replenishing the armament lost in the war with Iraq, annual military expenditure dropped by over one-third between the 1989–1991 period and the 1992–1996 period, and annual military imports dropped by twice as much (66%).[11] In November 1992, the hardliners in the new Fourth Majles passed the Law of Legal Protection for the Basij militiamen, enabling them to act in the same way as the Law Enforcement Forces.[12] In November 1994 the Majles passed a law allowing law enforcement personnel to shoot and kill demonstrators.[13] The IRGC and the Basij proved their utility during the urban riots of 1994–1995, which they loyally suppressed.

To expand his personal power, the Leader foiled the President's efforts at the integration of the Revolutionary Guards into the regular army after 1992. Khamenei gave the Basij a mission to be "present in all public spheres particularly to protect revolutionary-Islamic values," and in November 1992 authorized the project *Labbayk ya Khomeini* (submission to thou,

O Khomeini!), sending them to "organize and direct Hezbollahi cells in universities in order to carry out commanding good and forbidding evil."[14] The Guards resented Hashemi-Rafsanjani's ending of the war with Iraq and sought Khamenei's protection. It was offered especially to the Qods Forces, whose budget is classified and directly controlled by the Leader.[15]

Hashemi-Rafsanjani's post-war reconstruction turned the IRGC into an economic empire. As the manager of one of Iran's largest steel factories recalled years later:

> Hashemi-Rafsanjani's decision was to change the atmosphere and direct those forces' energy towards economic activities. IRGC equipment was shifted to economic and construction activities. Satellite companies connected to IRGC, the Construction Crusade [Jihad] or the Intelligence Ministry began to mushroom, allowing those with access to equipment and resources to bid for contracts.[16]

Of particular importance was the growth of the engineering arm of the IRGC, known as the Seal of the Prophets (*khātam al-anbiyā'*) Headquarters, which greatly extended the IRGC's economic empire into construction, transportation, telecommunications, finance, and the oil and gas sectors.

By 1992, the size of Iran's military-industrial-commercial complex stood at 45,000 employees, roughly as many as that of the much more populous Pakistan and almost twice as many as Indonesia.[17] In the subsequent decade, the empire of the Revolutionary Guards grew enormously and well beyond the military industries. It has become the beneficiary of regular no-bid government contracts and is involved in the whole range of economic activities, including the construction sector and Tehran's subway construction, directly or in connection with other enterprises and foundations. The IRGC flagrantly used military force to enlarge its economic clout in May 2004 by abruptly closing down Tehran's new Imam Khomeini International Airport the day after its inauguration under the pretext that its operation by a Turkish contracting consortium was a threat to Iran's "security and dignity."

If the army had two or more unintegrated components, one under the Leader and the other under the Minister of Defense, with the former also seriously competing with the Ministry of Intelligence, the integration of economic baronies was even more loosely integrated under the Leader. After the revolution, all the banks and large industrial companies were expropriated, but Khomeini did not allow the state to take them over. Rather, they were treated as booty under Islamic law and many were amalgamated into six independent foundations set up in the first years of the revolution. The largest of these, the Foundation of the Disinherited (*bonyād-e mostaz'afīn*), absorbed the Pahlavi Foundation and, despite its name, was a conglomerate of 1049 enterprises and 2786 real estate units by 1982.[18] These economic foundations, known singly as *bonyād* (the Persian word for foundation"), control an estimated 40 percent of the Iranian economy, and even though as much as 58 percent of the state budget was reportedly allocated to them in 1994, their heads are not responsible to the state but only to Ayatollah Khamenei.[19]

Rent-seeking is widespread among the *bonyād*s and various enterprises of the military-industrial-commercial complex. The foundations and their partners in the military-industrial-commercial complex are beneficiaries of "special licenses" to import various goods as well as informal arrangements with the Revolutionary Guards who control the ports. As with the no-bid construction contracts, the bazaar is cut out of these arrangements and cannot compete. By means of special licenses and grants these enterprises establish direct links with the informal sector of the economy, as well as food and other cooperatives, completely by-passing the bazaar.[20]

The *bonyād*s sustain their own network of contractors and suppliers. Clerical families and their relatives are prominent among the beneficiaries and contractors of these economic foundations and among government contractors. Nepotism is rife in the economy, as it is in the appointment to governmental positions. Indeed, the term *āqāzādehgān* (sons of masters)[21] was coined to refer to the new politico-economic elite consisting of the families of the clerical upper stratum. In close connection with the *āqāzādehgān* in government and foundation business are a larger group of former revolutionaries from the bazaar turned businessmen and some members of the second stratum from bazaari families, or with pre-revolutionary bazaar connections, who were co-opted by the regime in 1979 and the early 1980s and have made fortunes from rent derived from government concessions and licenses in the closed domestic markets of Iran.[22] It is hard to obtain data on this group, as they hardly pay income tax and are much better at hiding their wealth than the Shah's ostentatious industrialists. Economic liberalism and cultural conservatism or traditionalism under the Mandate of the Jurist constitute the distinctive outlook of this group of hardliners. The best representative of this group is the ruffian revolutionary turned monopolist, Habibollah 'Asgarawladi, who served as Minister of Commerce from 1981 to 1983. He had used the Mo'talefa, the clandestine organization he had founded in

1963, to mobilize support in the bazaar and to create a network linking it to the foundations.

Under Khatami, corruption became the subject of a public debate between the President and the Head of the Judiciary, and each claimed jurisdiction in dealing with it as one of the reform items highlighted by the Leader. The notorious corruption trial of Shahram Jaza'eri in January 2002 revealed one extensive network of corruption involving the *āqāzādehgān,* Majles deputies, and government officials.[23] Equally damaging were the revelations by a former consultant of the Majles Judiciary Investigations Committee,[24] and an unsuccessful candidate in the municipal elections on Ahmadinejad's ticket, 'Abbas Palizdar. In a talk at the University of Hamadan in June 2008, Palizdar, purporting to draw on 123 economic corruption files on which the courts were not acting, described the appropriation of public enterprises and networks of economic corruption. These involved the sons and relatives of many of the most important members of the clerical ruling elite, including Hashemi-Rafsanjani, Emami-Kashani, Mohmmad-Yazdi, Fallahian, and Vaez-Tabasi, as well as the former IRGC commander Rafiqdust and the Mo'talefa leader 'Asgarawladi.[25] Palizdar was promptly arrested.

As a result of the halt to Hashemi-Rafsanjani's centralization, the semi-independent baronies or political cartels were consolidated into a hydra-headed power structure. The emerging political cartels consisted of organizations, enterprises, and institutions that amalgamated or coordinated their activities and began to pursue their interests through the existing and developing political channels. This cartelization of interest led to the politics of compromise, log-rolling, and give-and-take among representatives of organized interests, which was facilitated by the clerical style of collective rule. In aggregating these interests, two very important institutions became arenas of special-interest politics: the Majles, in which the cartels placed or co-opted representatives, and the provincial and local networks around the institutionalized clerical power of the Leader-appointed Friday prayer leaders, the Guardian Council, and above all, the Leader himself. The election of the provincial and municipal councils may also have created a new political channel for pushing cartel interests after 1999.

Stalled Political Liberalization

Like Khatami eight years later, Hashemi-Rafsanjani lacked majority support in the Majles during his first term. The radicals, who were the majority in the Third Majles, pushed Rafsanjani, who had been the leading proponent of "innovative jurisprudence," into the conservative camp as he was forced to rely on his alliance with Khamenei and became dependent on help from the hardliner, traditionalist jurists of the Guardian Council. In preparation for the 1992 Majles elections, the Guardian Council fully assumed the new function of political control through disqualification of candidates, notably Rafsanjani's radical opponents. The Council's heavy hand in disqualifying radicals delivered the Fourth Majles (1992–1996) to a hardliner majority. Hashemi-Rafsanjani made a comfortable adjustment to the right, which seemed to work well for a year or two, but by the end of 1993, his increased dependence on the hardliners proved just as frustrating as the earlier obstruction from the radicals for his program for economic reconstruction, which had to move very slowly. The situation improved in his last year in office with the Fifth Majles (1996–2000). Although the radical clerics boycotted the 1996 elections in anticipation of yet another round of broad disqualification by the Guardian Council, Rafsanjani's Servants of Construction gained 80 seats, and he reached out to the emergent group of reformists associated with the Organization of the Mojahedin of the Islamic Revolution in the Majles. He sheltered some of the reformers within the interstices of the developmental state, notably the Center for Strategic Studies he had established as a foreign policy think tank in 1990.[26]

The Majles, first under the radicals and then under the hardliners, frustrated Hashemi-Rafsanjani's program for economic liberalization, but this effect should not be exaggerated. The President had great power vis-à-vis the Majles. The abolition of the office of prime minister in the constitutional amendments of 1989 gave the President more power as the head of the executive branch of government than his predecessor. Furthermore, he took advantage of his prerogative to appoint more than one deputy-president, multiplied the number of deputy-presidents, and appointed advisors opposed or rejected by the Majles. When the hardliners in the new Majles refused to confirm his favorite Minister of the Economy, Mohsen Nurbakhsh, in 1992, Rafsanjani promptly appointed him his Deputy-President for Economic Affairs. The failure of the economic liberalization and privatization programs must therefore be largely attributed to the structure of economic interests and Rafsanjani's lack of political will to challenge them seriously.

Following his economic advisors, Hashemi-Rafsanjani considered the repair and expansion of higher education a key precondition of economic development. Two-thirds of the teaching cadres of the universities had been purged during the Cultural Revolution. Hashemi-Rafsanjani in effect ended the Cultural Revolution by making the incoming students sign a promissory note undertaking not to challenge the professors' authority.[27] The number of students in institutions of higher education tripled from the 1986–1987 to the 1991–1992 academic year, surpassing the pre-revolutionary level as a percentage of the population, and doubled yet again to over 1,200,000 in 1996–1997. The massive expansion of the open university, the Islamic Free University, under Hashemi-Rafsanjani was the most important feature of the revamping of the educational system. By the end of Rafsanjani's second term, the Free University, which had branches in small towns, had slightly more students than the regular universities.[28]

As for the other precondition of economic development, namely political liberalization, Hashemi-Rafsanjani's main agent was his Minister of Culture and Islamic Guidance, Mohammad Khatami. Khatami removed some of the restrictions on the press, and in 1990 he set up the press jury somewhat incidentally provided for in the Press Law of 1985.[29] He also removed some restrictions on music and greatly encouraged film-making. The number of newspapers and journals rose from 102 in 1988 to 369 in 1992. *Kiān* began publishing in 1991, and soon became the leading reformist periodical until its closure in 2001.[30] Rafsanjani also established several organizations for women, notably the Women's Social-Cultural Council, and established a special bureau for women's affairs in 1991.[31]

Elements of civil society also grew within Rafsanjani's developmental state. He appointed Gholam-Hossein Karbaschi, a former seminarian who had tried his hand at urban planning in Isfahan, as mayor of Tehran in 1989 to fix the city ravaged by revolution and war. By the end of Hashemi-Rafsanjani's presidency, Karbaschi had set up some 138 cultural complexes and 27 sport centers, *shahrvand* (citizen) department stores, shopping malls, and the municipality's daily newpaper, *Hamshahri* (Fellow-citizen), with a circulation of around a million.[32] He also set in motion a construction boom by selling Tehran's skyline through the issuing of licenses for high rises far exceeding the height allowed by city regulations and building codes. The decisive defeat of Hashemi-Rafsanjani was in his struggle against the Leader, not the Majles. It came toward the end of his second term in September 1996, when one of his several deputy-presidents, 'Attaollah Mohajerani, aired the idea that Article 114 of the Constitution be amended by the Maslahat Council to allow him to run for another term.[33] The idea was vetoed by the Supreme Leader, who was occasionally being called Imam and was increasingly less inclined to share power. This marked the definite end of the post-Khomeini dual leadership. Hashemi-Rafsanjani's only revenge as outgoing President was to teach the Leader a lesson by preventing the rigging of the elections in favor of the Leader's candidate, Nateq-Nuri, and by having his men help Khatami organize his electoral campaign and be elected President. At that point, however, the clerical elite was mindful to avoid any rift between the Leader and the President that would weaken the system of collective clerical rule, and acted behind the scene. The Assembly of Leadership Experts put some pressure on the Leader, through its commission for monitoring the conditions of Leadership, to revitalize the Maslahat Council in the spring of 1997 in order to provide a suitable job to ease Hashemi-Rafsanjani out of the presidency.

Revolutionary Power Struggle: The Emergence of the Hardliner and the Reformist Factions

Factionalism, a notable feature of the politics of the IRI, is explained by the absence of political parties. After the unhappy experience of the Islamic Republican Party (IRP) and its closure in May 1987, Khomeini's followers were left with the Society of the Militant Clergy (*jāme'a-ye ruhāniyyat-e mobārez;* JRM), which had been formed at the onset of revolutionary mobilization in 1977. But the division that destroyed the IRP immediately resurfaced within the JRM. In the spring of 1988, Khomeini approved the decision of a group of radical clerics to split from the JRM and form their own political association, the Association of Militant Clerics (*majma'-e ruhāniyun-e mobārez;* MRM), and the parent Society increasingly drifted to conservatism. Although the IRI Constitution allows the formation of political parties, alongside political "groups and associations (*anjomanhā*)," very few political organizations have been allowed to register as "parties." The objections to political parties range from the clerical paternalism of the long-time JRM Secretary, Ayatollah Mahdavi-Kani, who declared, "I am against party formation among the clergy because the cleric is the father of the people;" to the fascistic view of the Mo'talefa that parties sow dissension and destroy the sacred unity of the community.[34] With rare exceptions such as the pro-Khatami Solidarity Party (*hezb-e hambastegi*), even those political groups that advocated participation through political parties in the 1990s, such as the Organization of the Mojahedin of the Islamic Revolution and the Islamic Participation Front, did not register themselves as parties.

The formation of the hardliner traditionalist clerical faction in opposition to Hashemi-Rafsanjani and the pragmatists occurred in the Fifth Majles

(1992–1996) under the Majles Speaker Nateq-Nuri. The emerging hardliners displayed a continued commitment to violence, exemplified by the leader of the original Hezbollah, Hadi Ghaffari, who gathered the club-wielding mobs who attacked the opponents of the Mandate of the Jurist. Mas'ud Dehna-maki similarly organized and led the Helpers of the Party of God (*ansār-e hezbollāh*), as the group was called from 1993 onward, while its sibling, Sisters of the Helpers of God (*khāhrān-e ansārollāh*), embarked on vigilantism among women.[35] Clerics such as Ayatollah Mesbah-Yazdi encouraged them to do so, as did the Guardian Council Secretary Ayatollah Jannati, who set up a headquarters for the Revival of Commanding the Good and Forbidding the Evil (*setād-e ehyā'-e amr-e be-ma'ruf va nahy az monkar*). The hardliners were also distinguished by diminishing ideology as a motive force and replacing it with loyalism and group solidarity stemming from revolutionary fellowship and life experience. Ideology still served a purpose, but only instrumentally to cudgel opponents.

Already in 1991, before becoming the Majles Speaker, Nateq-Nuri had sought to condense the Islamic revolutionary ideology into a single neo-tradi-tionalist clericalist tenet: "During the occultation [of the Hidden Imam], the Supreme Jurist (*vali-ye faqih*) enjoys the same rights and powers as those of the Imams and the Prophet, and his wishes are the commands and duty for all."[36] 'Asgarawladi brought the Mo'talefa faction into the fold by subscribing to the Mandate of the Jurist as the principle of legitimacy of government, which can be God's only government for the only acceptable party, the party of God (*hezbollāh*).[37] Islamic vigilante groups, which had their own press and recruited heavily among the Basij militia and the poor, put mobilizational vigilantism under the umbrella of the Mandate of the Jurist, and acted as the executive arm of the hardliners. This was done by declaring the Mandate of the Jurist the fundamental principle of the Islamic Republic, but adding to obedience to the jurist the fundamental religious obligation of "commanding the good and forbidding the evil."[38]

To organize counter-mobilization against liberalization, the ideologues of the hardliner faction formulated their ideas in direct opposition to Hashemi-Rafsanjani's pragmatism. One of their organs describes its goal as "guarding the principles of the revolution and spreading principal-orientedness or what I shall call Fundamentalism (*osulgarā'i*), and to fight deviation." This meant that "preserving revolutionary values and principles is vital and should not be sacrificed for the sake of freedom and development." And further, "political and economic openness in Iran will cause the collapse of the revolution."[39]

The hardliners further stated that "Democracy is nothing but the dictatorship of capital, consumerism and selfishness. Democracy is reactionary; it is a return to *jāheliyya* (age of ignorance), paganism and disbelief ..."[40] Adherence to true Islam, "the pure (*nāb*) Islam of Mohammad," was equated with "being melted in the Mandate of the Jurist." Their obligation to unleash violence against the internal enemies of Islam became critical after the reformists came to power under Khatami. As one of their magazines declared in September/ October 1997 to the recruits from the Basij militia, "Brothers, the war has not ended, it has just begun!"[41] Notable among the semi-clandestine groups that decided to take the law into their own hands in 1998–1999 in order to punish the reformers—"the corrupt enemies and thousand-faced hypocrites who have made divine government and the pure Islam of Mohammad the field of their savage depredation—" was one calling itself the Devotees of the Pure Islam of Mohammad (Peace be upon Him).[42]

In June 1995, another organization, the Group for the Defense of the Values of the Islamic Revolution, was formed by Hojjat al-Islam Mohammad Rayshahri and a group of other clerical hardliners. It was clearly a reactionary formation against Rafsanjani's pragmatism, deploring its creeping liberalism, rumors of separation of religion and politics, and compromise with world-eating imperialism.[43] The organization proved ephemeral and its members did not even vote for Rayshahri in the 1997 presidential elections.

In making the Mandate of the Jurist the focal point of the hardliner faction, JRM Secretary and Majles Speaker Nateq-Nuri staked its field, leaving the other two elements of the IRI constitutional mixture to other factions. The JRM heavy guns followed suit: "the Mandate of the Jurist is not a matter for elections; it is a matter of recognition" (Mahdavi-Kani); "In Islam, the issue is the selection of the more pious (*aslah*), and not electoral competition in the Western style" (Movahedi-Kermani); "Under no circumstances does the Mandate take its legitimacy from the people, and the agreement or disagreement of the people has no effect on the principle of the Mandate of the Jurist" (Ostadi).[44]

Hardliner counter-mobilization intensified after Khatami's election. During the student unrest in July 1999, some 400 vigilantes belonging to different groups attacked the University of Tehran dormitories, savagely beating some 800 students and killing one of them. A member of one vigilante group revealed that the hardliner Ayatollahs Mesbah-Yazdi, Mahdavi-Kani, and Jannati had authorized the attack. The reformist cleric and lawyer who defended the victims, Mohsen Rohami, was jailed for conspiracy to defame the Ayatollahs.[45] Counter-reformist violence in opposition to Khatami was predictably accompanied by the affirmation of the Mandate of the Jurist at the discursive level. In March 2001, Ayatollah Mesbah-Yazdi would declare the Mandate of the Jurist to be "the continuation of divine rule. Opposing it would be equal to apostasy and negation of Islam." A Friday prayer leader would ask in July 2002, "If the Leader is able to appoint the Head of the Judiciary, why [should he] not dismiss the President? Why not dissolve Parliament?"[46]

The transformation of the radicals into reformists began at the same time as the hardliner counter-mobilization and partly in reaction to it. The radicals in the Third Majles (1988–1992) increasingly coalesced around the MRM to form a faction until after the 1992 elections, when its members were massively disqualified by the Guardian Council. The Association decided to suspend its activities, which were resumed only in October 1995, although its newspaper, *Salām* (Peace), was already leading the transition from radicalism to reformism. The clerics of the JRM sought to put national sovereignty and republicanism above the Mandate of the Jurist. In 1992, they affirmed that "all pillars of the regime, even the Mandate of the Jurist, draw [legitimacy] from republicanism. . . . In the constitution, the primary role of managing the country is relegated to the people."[47] Or as one of its leading members put it in 1997, "The acts of the just Supreme Jurist are legitimate (only) when the people accept his Mandate."[48]

The critical event that marks the onset of rethinking among the Islamic radicals was their massive disqualification by the Guardian Council and its supervisory committees for running in the 1992 Majles elections. A total of 141 incumbent MPs lost their seats, including Majles Speaker Karrubi. When Behzad Nabavi and others asked the Guardian Council why they were disqualified, the following general answer was given on its behalf by Ayatollah Khaz'ali: "So long as we have the power, we will not allow such morons (*'avazi*) to enter the Majles and we will spray them with DDT!"[49] Sitting in the cold outside the Fourth Majles, the radicals began rethinking and reinventing themselves. In October 1991, shortly before MRM suspended its activities, Nabavi reconstituted the Organization of the Mojahedin of the Islamic Revolution, which had originally been formed out of seven tiny radical groups in April 1979 as the armed pro-Khomeini counterpart of the Mohahedin-e Khalq. They followed the line of the Imam unflinchingly, considering "the *velāyat-e faqih* as the continuation of the movement of the Prophets," to quote the title of a booklet it published in 1981.[50] The group was nevertheless later dissolved by Khomeini on the advice of the clerical mentor he had appointed to oversee it. The Organization filled the vacuum created by MRM as a new nucleus for the clustering of the much reduced radical faction in the Fourth Majles (1992–1996), while publishing the periodical, *'Asr-e mā* (Our age), which acted as a major influence in the transition from Islamic radicalism to reformism. *'Asr-e mā* saw its task as defending the republican features of the Islamic constitutional order against the clerical hardliners who were bent on obliterating them: "People's participation is the cornerstone of the Islamic Republic"; indeed, "the Islamicity of the regime emanates from its republicanism."[51] Therefore, "if the regime is not republican, it would not remain Islamic either. Any attempt to delete the republicanism of the regime...is a reactionary and counter-revolutionary act." Furthermore, "the left believes in elective Mandate of the Jurist and considers the popular vote and election the basis of Islamic government. According to this view, during the age of occultation [of the Twelfth Imam], the hand of God comes out of the people's sleeve."[52] The drift to reformism and advocacy of democratization was not accompanied by any openness toward groups whose orientation was not Islamic. When criticizing the Guardian Council's exclusionary gate-keeping in the announcements preceding the 1996 elections, for instance, the Organization stated no general principles but protested only against the exclusion of the children of revolution whose commitment and revolutionary credentials were impeccable.[53]

When the universities reopened after the purges and Islamicization known as the Cultural Revolution in 1983, only the Islamic student associations were allowed to operate under an Office of Consolidation and Unity (*daftar-e tahkim va vahdat*), whose leaders acted very much like officials of a revolutionary government and should be considered part of the revolutionary elite. By the early 1990s, however, these Islamic student leaders found themselves completely deserted by the fast growing and politically apathetic student body and began reinventing themselves. By 1995, they were joining the radicals who were turning reformist and their emergent reformist press, notably *Salām*, *'Asr-e mā,* and the monthly *Kiān*. They talked about democracy, placed the law above the Supreme Jurist, who was to be accountable and elected, and thus coalesced with the reformist faction.[54]

Within Rafsanjani's developmental state, the Center for Strategic Studies became a nucleus for the growth of reformism. Sa'id Hajjarian shifted its focus to political development, gathered the future leaders of the reform movement around him, and built bridges to the emergent reformist press, writing regularly for *'Asr-e mā* until he launched his own *Sohb-e Emruz* (Today's dawn). With the new Majles elected in 1996, Hajjarian sought to define a reformist position, or in his words, "the identity of the Islamic left," within the existing constitutional frame but in contradistinction to the "traditionalist right" (*rāst-e sonnati*). Against the latter's exclusivism or monopolism and constant "thinning of national sovereignty and the regime's republicanism," he shifted the emphasis onto the republicanism of the Islamic constitutional order, which entailed popular participation.[55] He was optimistic that this could be done, and wanted the children of the revolution to do it alone and without building any bridges to the disenfranchised groups and constituencies. He was, in fact, suspicious of reaching out for international help in creating pressure for democratization, believing it would "result in liberalizing the political atmosphere to the advantage of the supporters of the West."[56]

Hashemi-Rafsanjani remained in the JRM after the radical clerics had split to form the MRM, but the former increasingly drifted toward conservatism and opposed his liberalization. He proposed to put his supporters on the JRM list for the 1996 elections, but his proposal was rejected by JRM's new Secretary, Majles Speaker Nateq-Nuri. Rafsanjani's pragmatic technocrats then formed their own political party under Tehran's mayor Karbaschi in anticipation of the 1996 Majles elections and called themselves "Constructionists" or "Servants of Construction" (*kārgozārān-e sāzandegi*), and made a coalition with a number of Islamic radicals turned reformist, such as Mortaza Alviri. The hardliner MPs were alarmed by this coalition and their leader, Nateq-Nuri, was moved to declare: "Liberalism is a real threat for the country and it must be eradicated. . . . The building of a few roads and bridges and the completion of some development projects is not tantamount to upholding revolutionary values."[57]

The Servants of Construction included Hashemi-Rafsanjani's brother, 'Ali Hashemi, his daughter, Fa'eza Hashemi, and his deputy-presidents, Mohajerani and Nurbakhsh. They launched a weekly, *Bahman,* advocating the rule of law and renounced "illegal and violent methods for elimination of [political] rivals." They also advocated economic reconstruction and growth and development, and declared underdevelopment a danger that threatened the revolution and the regime.[58] Development, based on science and technology, was seen as the means to the "revival of Islamic culture" and political liberalism was seen as a prerequisite of development. Political liberalism was taken to mean pluralism and competition among political parties, and freedom of the press and association within the limits set by the law.[59]

The final stimulus to the unification of the Islamic radicals under the umbrella of reformism came from the firm gate-keeping of the Guardian Council, which repeated the disqualification and exclusion of many of them from the Fifth Majles. In the summer of 1995, the Majles had passed a law that further expanded the supervisory power of the Guardian Council to be "unequivocal throughout the duration of the election and with regard to all matters." On the eve of the 1996 elections and in response to Hajjarian's sarcastic criticism, the Council's Speaker, Ayatollah Emami-Kashani, defended the law by saying, "The blade of 'unequivocal supervision' of the Guardian Council is the blade of due process of law." He also declared, "The basis of the approval or rejection of candidates would be their total and true allegiance to Islam, the regime, and the Mandate of the Jurist."[60] With the Fifth Majles in the hands of the hardliners, the reformists pinned their hope on the 1997 presidential election. The MRM put forward Mohammad Khatami as its candidate. During his electoral campaign, Khatami affirmed that "the constructive path of Mr. Rafsanjani must continue." In another speech he emphasized that "economic development must be accompanied by political development." Khatami did not fail to reassure his senior clerical colleagues that their fear was baseless and "the Constitutional Revolution will not be repeated. . . . Anyone who has accepted the Republic has also accepted republicanism, Islamicity, and the Mandate of the Jurist."[61]

Although the reformist discourse developed during the last years of Hashemi-Rafsanjani's presidency, it cannot be said to have become predominant. To appreciate the suddenness of the dramatic shift in hegemonic discourse in 1997, it is worth remembering that as late as June 1996, when pro-Rafsanjani pragmatists and the radical deputies belonging to Behzad Nabavi's Organization of Mojahedin of the Islamic Revolution formed a parliamentary coalition, it was called the "Hezbollah Association (*majma'*) of the Majles." Their rhetorical appropriation of the Islamic revolutionary term, *hezbollāh,* was immediately contested by an opposing hardliner coalition, which called itself the "Hezbollah of the Majles," and yet a third parliamentary coalition of the "Independent Deputies (*nemāyandeg ān-e mostaqell*) of the Hezbollah"![62] The discarding of the slogan of Hezbollah for civil society in 1997 had the suddenness of a meteor.

4

Revolutionary Ideology and Its Transformation into Islamic Reformism

KHOMEINI'S SENSE OF MORAL OUTRAGE AGAINST MODERNIZATION as westernization was widely shared by an important section of the younger generation of
intellectuals who enjoyed neither his lofty position in the Shi'ite hierocracy nor
his deep and fortifying roots in the Shi'ite tradition. This common sentiment
of moral indignation found a variety of expressions in the search for cultural
roots and authenticity in pre-revolution Iran. Islam was gradually highlighted
as the predominant element in the native cultural heritage. The confluence of
discordant attempts in search of cultural authenticity by writers obsessed with
the West and seeking to construct a new collective identity vis-à-vis the West
acquired greater coherence with the importation of the Islamic ideology, in part
through translations of the Pakistani Islamic ideologue, Maulana Abu'l-A'la
Mawdudi. Mawdudi's central idea was that Islam had to be reshaped into a
modern ideology by defining Islamic political, economic, and cultural systems
if it were to bring about an Islamic revival against Western cultural and political
domination. Marxism was the model ideology, to be emulated and superseded
by an Islamic ideology. This notion of Islamic ideology gained currency in the
political literature of the late 1960s and early 1970s in Iran, and took an increasingly revolutionary turn. Its triumph was marked by Khomeini's theocratic
redefinition of Shi'ism in the months following the revolution, and culminated
in his final constitutionalization of the theocratic government as the Absolute
Mandate of the [supreme religious] Jurist by the time of his death.

An entirely different moral sense of modernity and tradition emerged in the 1990s, discarding the notion of ideology and offering an anti-ideological appraisal of Islam and democracy as the core elements of political modernization. This chapter examines this cultural trend; the following chapter deals with its impact on the constitutional politics of the Islamic Republic of Iran (IRI).

Nativism and the Ideology of the Islamic Revolution

Moral indignation against westernization in Iran predated the outbreak of revolution in 1979 by a few decades. It began as a series of nativistic protests, which gradually cohered in the shape of an Islamic ideology. The mythical construction of the West was the counterpart of native myth-making, and it was not exclusively or primarily a religious affair. It was rather a fairly general indigenous response to Western cultural domination in which Islam played a varied and fluctuating role before becoming dominant in the revolutionary crescendo of the late 1970s and early 1980s. This cultural nativism has been characterized as "Orientalism in reverse" and "Occidentalism."[1] Although Khomeini's own publicistic career had a modest beginning in the 1940s and a few other Shi'ite clerics turned to the public sphere, the indigenous response to Western domination in the two decades after World War II was formulated by another group: lay intellectuals with a clerical background and upbringing. The most notable members of this group were Sayyed Fakhr al-Din Shadman, Sayyed Jalal Al-e Ahmad, and 'Ali Shari'ati.[2]

Al-e Ahmad, the modernist writer who initiated the process of the reception of this Islamic ideology in Iran, set the direction of future development in two steps: first by characterizing the Iranian cultural malaise as "Westoxification" (*gharbzadegi*), a term he adopted from Sayyed Ahmad Fardid, a philosophy professor at the University of Tehran in search of authenticity and inspired by the German philosopher Martin Heidegger. Like his mentor, Fardid, Al-e Ahmad turned to the Islam of his childhood and clerical family for a cure for this disease toward the end of his career. Al-e Ahmad's Westoxification proved definitive as the diagnosis of the age,[3] and constituted what sociologists call "the definition of the situation" for a whole generation. He was followed by the Sorbonne-educated sociologist 'Ali Shari'ati, who is the best known of the Islamic ideologues before the revolution. It is interesting to note that Shari'ati, too, came from a clerical family; his father was a former cleric who had become an Islamic publicist in civic associations and public gatherings.

With Shari'ati, the process of the ideologization of Islam gathered full momentum. When asked what his greatest achievement had been, Shari'ati replied: "in one sentence: the transformation of Islam from a culture to an ideology."[4] Both Al-e Ahmad and Shari'ati had been Marxists for a significant period. Shari'ati, in particular, adopted what was a Western instrument of protest—namely, ideology—as a weapon for combating the pernicious cultural domination of the West. He further identified the belief in the return of the Hidden Imam as the Mahdi with the modern myth of revolution: it really meant the redemption of Herbert Marcuse's one-dimensional man by the coming revolution.[5] Even the mild-mannered and liberal Mehdi Bazargan was not able to resist the modernist charm of ideology and had published *Divine Election and Ideology (Be'that va ideolozhy)* in 1966. It was, however, left to Shari'ati to formulate and promote a compelling notion of Islamic ideology in his search for a reinvigorated collective conscience through the reform of Shi'ite Islam.[6] The great irony of Al-e Ahmad's life, as well as Shari'ati's, was that "the Islamic ideology" is "the deepest, most effective form of Westoxification ever."[7] In the end, the pouring of Islam into the ideological framework borrowed from Marxism amounted to a "colossal redefinition of Islam." For Al-e Ahmad and Shari'ati, "the West" was the projected civilizational other, the point of reference toward which they "painted themselves into a corner of a revolutionary self-definition."[8]

The clerics, however, did not leave the ideological field to laymen for long. Al-e Ahmad's cousin, Ayatollah Sayyed Mahmud Taleqani, was closest among the emerging clerical ideologues to the Marxist camp and absorbed its terminology into his writings on Islamic economics.[9] Ayatollah Mohammad Hosayn Tabataba'i, who shared Khomeini's atypical interest in philosophy, turned to combating Marxist and Western materialism in the public sphere. Khomeini's students in religious law and philosophy such as Ayatollahs Mortaza Motahhari, Mohammad Hosseini Beheshti, and Hossein-'Ali Montazeri, who became his main lieutenants in the revolutionary struggle, also turned to publicistic activity to combat Western materialism. These clerics turned ideologues helped redefine Shi'ite Islam in a revolutionary direction. This redefinition and revolutionary transformation culminated in Khomeini's construction of an ascetic revolutionary political ethic and, above all, in his new theory of theocratic government. The critical link between revolutionary Islamic ideology and charismatic clericalism was provided by Shari'ati's Islamicization of the fashionable Leftist ideas of revolutionary leadership, such as "guided democracy" and "democratic centralism" in *Ommat va emāmat* (The community of believers and leadership/Imamate), which was published in 1970.[10] Imamate was necessary as the leadership in the period of transition from liberation to self-government and realization of the true Islamic consciousness in the fully emancipated society or *umma*.[11] The key role in the clericalist modification of Shariʿati's Islamic ideology and his idea of revolutionary leadership, and in their subordination to Khomeini's theory of theocratic government on the basis of the Mandate of the Jurist, was played by Ayatollah Beheshti. Beheshti, who had been the director of the Islamic Center in Hamburg before the revolution, incorporated Khomeini's theory into the 1979 Constitution of the IRI. Other clerical publicists, too, avidly took over Shariʿati's notion of Islamic ideology and reshaped it to their liking. Mohammad Taqi Mesbah-Yazdi, for instance, published his *Guarding the Ideological Trenches* (*Pāsdāri az sangarhā-ye ideolozhik*) in 1981. With the creation of the Islamic revolutionary ideology and its clericalist constitutionalization by Beheshti, what we might call Shiʿite Jacobinism dominated revolutionary Iran under Khomeini's charismatic leadership without any serious challenge for a full decade.

The obsessive concern of the secular intellectuals with the West was not necessarily shared by Khomeini and his clerical colleagues who led the revolutionary movement against the Shah in order to restore and preserve a Shiʿite tradition they saw as gravely threatened by modernization and westernization. The clerical ideologues were not particularly tormented by ambivalence toward the West and were much more securely grounded in the Shiʿite tradition they wanted to save. This much was already clear from Khomeini's traditionalist rebuttal of Shiʿite modernism in the 1940s.[12] For this reason, the Islamic revolution was undoubtedly a traditionalist revolution in its motivation.[13] However, the restoration of a tradition in practice always entails its transformation. Despite Khomeini's intention, shared by most of his clerical followers, the traditionalist revolution of 1979 brought about a revolution in Shiʿism. As early as December 1984, in an outburst against the recalcitrant traditionalists who considered taxation at variance with the Sacred Law (*shariʿat*), the Majles Speaker (later President) Hashemi-Rafsanjani reminded his opponents that they were sitting in Parliament—something that had no precedent in Islamic history, any more than having a president, cabinet of ministers, prime minister, and the like—and affirmed that there was no legal precedent or ruling "in Islam for 80 per cent of the things on which we base Islamic government today."[14] In fact, the Islamic revolution in Iran resulted in both the traditionalization of a modernizing nation-state and the modernization of the Shi'ite tradition. The profound transformation continued after Khomeini's death in two radically different directions by his feuding heirs.

This paradoxical result was the consequence of Khomeini's choice of revolution as the means for the preservation of the Shi'ite tradition. Revolution resulted in the takeover of the state, which in turn set in motion the unexpected constitutional developments and the post-revolutionary power politics previously discussed. The unexpected, eleventh-hour victory of Sayyed Mohammad Khatami on a platform of political reform in the presidential elections of May 1997 opened a new phase in the history of the IRI. President Khatami's landslide victory in 1997 can be regarded as the political edge of a deep cultural movement for the Shi'ite reformation that was well underway in the 1990s before his election gave it a major boost. This cultural movement was one in which the dialectics of tradition and modernity, set in motion by Khomeini, played out under his successors.

From the Islamic Ideology to the Reform of Islam

The movement for the reform of Islam was very much a product of the children of the Islamic revolution, and can be presented as one of the revolution's long-term, unintended consequences. The movement's leading figure since the early 1990s, 'Abdolkarim Sorush, is a philosopher of science who was trained in pharmacology in London and was appointed a member of the Commission for Cultural Revolution in 1980 by Imam Khomeini after the closure of the universities. The most forceful theorist of the religious reform movement in the late 1990s and early 2000s, Mohammad Mojtahed-Shabestari, similarly, is a Shi'ite cleric who had been Ayatollah Beheshti's colleague at the Islamic Center in Hamburg in the 1970s and was elected to the First Majles after the revolution in 1980. Hojjat al-Islam Mohsen Kadivar, who wrote a detailed work in Shi'ite jurisprudence refuting Khomeini's theory of theocratic government in 1998 and was imprisoned in 1999, was a student of electrical engineering at the time of the revolution and switched to the seminaries of Qom as an enthusiastic Islamic revolutionary. Last but not least, President Khatami himself had succeeded Beheshti at the Islamic Center in Hamburg, when the latter returned to Iran to take a leading position in the Islamic revolutionary movement in 1978. He was elected to the First Majles with Mojtahed-Shabestari in 1980 and served as the revolutionary Minister of Culture and Islamic Guidance from 1982 to 1986, and again from 1989 until his forced resignation in July 1992. In addition to being fellow-revolutionaries, what these clerical reform-ists shared with the lay intellectual Sorush was a keen interest in philosophy and rational theology which they used as a tool for the reconstruction of religious thought.

Sorush had begun to distance himself from Islamic revolutionary thought in a series of articles on the expansion and contraction of the Sacred Law published between 1988 and 1990. In 1992 he made a radical break with the revolutionary characterization of Islam as an ideology. Bazargan had paved the way for this break, on the anniversary of Mohammad's divine election in January of that year, by decoupling ideology and divine election and declaring that God had sent his Prophets to prepare humankind for the hereafter and "not to tell them how to conduct their politics and run their affairs in this world."[15] In a critique of 'Ali Shari'ati a few months later, Sorush argued that Islam as a world religion is "richer than (farbehtar) ideology" because it allows for a variety of different interpretations.[16] In his memorial speech after Bazargan's death in January 1995, Sorush bluntly stated: "Bazargan was once infatuated with religious ideology, but his death has put an end to that idea. His death is a symbol of the death of that idea."[17] An ideological society (idealized as a monistic [tawhidi] society by Shari'ati and his followers) would, in fact, allow no room for intellectual inquiry, criticism, or a multiplicity of ideas.[18] In his contributions to the debate on tradition and modernism in 1994 and 1995 in Kiān, the new reformist periodical, Sorush offered a devastating critique of Al-e Ahmad's Occidentalism. He also deplored the ideologization of knowledge and modern political ideas, pointing out that "Islamic rights" make no more sense than "Islamic water."[19] Sorush's lectures and publica-tions were enormously popular. By the end of 1995, he had become enough of a problem for the regime for Foreign Minister Velayati to call him an enemy of the nation who had weakened "the foundations of national inde-pendence and cohesion as well as damaging the stature of the government."[20] Soroush's classes were interrupted, and he was beaten by intruding ruffians but continued with his reconstruction of Islamic thought.

The intellectual formation of 'Abdolkarim Sorush differed considerably from that of Al-e Ahmad and Shari'ati. He had not been a Marxist, and his antipathy to ideology was probably influenced by Karl Popper's Open Society and Its Enemies (1945) and reinforced by his interest in Popper's philosophy of science during his stay in London in the 1970s. By contrast, he shared with Ayatollahs Khomeini, Tabataba'i, and Motahhari a keen interest in the seventeenth-century philosopher Molla Sadra, the leading figure in the latest flowering of Muslim philosophy in Iran, on whom he had written a book before the revolution.[21] Although he participated in Khomeini's Cultural Revolution in 1980–1981 and carried out the Imam's order that "a fundamental revolution must take place in all universities across the country, so that professors with links to the East or to the West may be purged,"[22] Sorush did not approach Islam as an ideology. His perspective was a civilizational rather than an ideological one from the beginning.

In his celebrated article, "The Expansion and Contraction of the Sacred Law (shari'at),"[23] Sorush relied on the philosophy of science to establish the dependence of the normative validity of Islamic legal norms on the changing scientific world views of different epochs. As our world view expands with the development of natural sciences, he argued, there should be a parallel evolution of the norms of Islamic law. His argument was, however, flawed because the rules of Shi'ite jurisprudence have developed independently of science and have, in fact, not been responsive to changes in the natural sciences.

Sorush saw objective knowledge as the basis of modernism and as a universal ethos that shatters "the wall of civilization," allowing all contemporary cultures to put their "politics, government, the economy and morality...into a new order." Though it may be the "child of modernity and Western civilization...[it] is a child who leaves its mother immediately after birth and casts the shadow of its thesis over all peoples, local and foreign."[24] The West has nurtured "development and modernization" as its child in the course of a tumultuous history, he argued in another article in Kiān in 1995, and the most fundamental change in values that set modernism loose was its worldly turn of ethics. This worldly turn made happiness in this world rather than the other world the subject of ethics, and amounted to the transvaluation of values in trade, agriculture, and industry that "removed the shackles of mankind and prepared it for entry into the realm of development and modernism." The result was unprecedented economic prosperity and development that in turn fostered spiritual growth. The most important of the higher values that emerge in developed societies are the love of liberty and science. Whereas "ideology is the instrument of enslavement of the mind,...the democratization of dissemination of knowledge and its popular [as opposed to governmental] control...are among the most important causes and signs of democracy."[25]

Sorush's break with the twentieth-century apologetic Islamic modernism was more fundamental than his break with the political Islam of the 1970s and 1980s through his refutation of the Islamic ideology of Shariʻati. This break came with Sorush's advocacy of religious pluralism at the close of the century. Sorush had already spoken of cultural pluralism in the early 1990s, maintaining that contemporary Iranian culture was a composite of the (pre-Islamic) Persian, Islamic, and Western cultures.[26] A few years later, he proceeded from the affirmation of cultural pluralism to the more perilous advocacy of religious pluralism. In a 1997 article entitled "Straight Paths" (*Serāthā-ye mostaqim*), which significantly pluralizes the key Qurʼanic phrase, Sorush totally disregarded legalistic Islam and drew heavily on the tradition of gnostic mysticism (*'irfān*), especially in the poetry of his favorite Rumi, to establish the principle of religious pluralism. In the years after approaching Islamic jurisprudence from the perspective of the philosophy of science, Sorush had gradually come under the influence of the reformist cleric Mojtahed-Shabestari, who approached the norms of Islamic law from a hermeneutic perspective. Whereas Sorush had sought to reassess the norms of Islamic law in light of the advances in science, Mojtahed-Shabestari argued that the meaning of these norms depended on the historical context in which they were formulated. A new historical context therefore required a new reading of the Islamic norms. Sorush was quick to see the advantage of a hermeneutic perspective, focusing on meaning and its historic context, over the philosophy of science concerned with the truth value of propositions.[27] From this new hermeneutic perspective he could shift the focus of discussion from the religious sciences to religion itself, and write in 1999 of the *Expansion of Prophetic Experience:* "The prophet is a human being and his experience is human, so are his disciples."[28] Upon this premise, not only the entire corpus of the Sacred Law, but also the very expression of the Islamic revelation in the Arabic language and the culture that grew around it, could be consistently established as historically "contingent" rather than "essential" features of religion.[29]

Sorush has not been shy in making the political implication of his religious hermeneutics explicit. He began the essay on "Straight Paths" by noting that accepting religious and cultural pluralism necessitates the acceptance of "social pluralism," and ended it by affirming that "a pluralistic society is a non-ideological society" that is "[a society] without an official interpretation and [official] interpreters—and founded on pluralist reason."[30] More directly, Sorush advocated "religious democracy" but without deducing it from Islam. As democracy is majoritarian and the majority of Iranians are religious, he argued, democracy in Iran would naturally assume the form of a religious democracy. Sorush juxtaposed this underspecified idea of religious democracy with the view of the ruling clerical elite as "the fascist reading of religion," and spoke of them as the "bearers of religious despotism," affirming that "the new generation that has now arisen in Iran does not see the jewel of religion in jurisprudence and ideology."[31]

The man who made the decisive epistemic break with the apologetic modernism of the earlier generation, and offered a more rigorous critique of the foundations of theocratic government in legalistic Islam, was Mohammad Mojtahed-Shabestari. With the publication of *Hermeneutics, the Book and Tradition* in 1996,[32] Mojtahed-Shabestari drew on the mastery of modern hermeneutics he had acquired during his years in Germany to delineate a critical theory for rethinking Islam in the contemporary world. Noting that many observers insist that "the concept of tradition (*sonnat*) and its derivatives have primarily a religious-doctrinal sense for the Muslims," Mojtahed-Shabestari considered this idea the cause of "many difficulties and errors in the study of the problems of tradition, modernity and development in Islamic countries." He argued, by contrast, that the confrontation between tradition and modernity is easier in Islam than in Christianity, where "tradition" is tied up with the idea of the church as the vehicle of sacred history.[33] This may well be wishful thinking, but Mojtahed-Shabestari specified the conditions for speaking of faith in the contemporary world and within the limits of modern rationality as set by natural and historical sciences.[34]

Rather than beginning with the usual discussion of the eternal principles of Islam, Mojtahed-Shabestari's starting point in *A Critique of the Official Reading of Religion* (2000)[35] was the process of modernization. Islam is then defined hermeneutically and approached from the historical perspective of modernization. The key to the hermeneutic conception of Islam is that it is capable of different readings. The official reading (*qerā'at*) of Islam is historically contingent and only one of its many possible readings. This reading is severely criticized from the perspective of modernity. Modernization began about 150 years ago with the resolution of the Muslims to overcome backwardness by adopting a new style of life, and was at first called "the adoption of modern civilization" and "progress," and is now referred to as "development" (*tawse'a*). Mojtahed-Shabestari approached the Islamic revolution in Iran from this historical perspective: "When Iran's Islamic revolution attained victory in 1357 (1979), over a century had passed since the entry of our country into modern life, development and progress."[36] The process of modernization radically changed the character of Muslim societies and consequently the social functions of Islamic jurisprudence.[37] Not wanting to dissociate himself and the reform movement from the Islamic revolution, he argued, somewhat tenuously, that because the Constitution of 1979 was the product of rational law-making rather than traditional jurisprudence, and because it included values that were the "fruits of modernity (*modernité*)," the Islamic revolution was accompanied by a "rational humanistic" reading of Islam.[38] The "official reading of religion," however, originated in a phenomenon called "jurisprudential Islam" (*eslām-e feqāhati*), which justified totalitarian control of culture by theocratic government, and gradually gained the upper hand after the revolution.

The official reading of Islam had legitimacy during Khomeini's lifetime because the majority of the Iranian people accepted his charismatic leadership as a form of "political following" (*taqlid-e siyāsi*) of the religious jurist. Now that the majority has dwindled to a small minority, a crisis of legitimacy arises as modern political regimes derive theirs solely "from political rationality and popular vote."[39] The official reading of Islam was now undermined by a crisis of legitimacy for three reasons. It advocated non-participation, theorized violence, and lacked scientific validity. The loss of plausibility and scientific validity of the official reading of religion is in part due to the challenge by the reformists,[40] which has shaken the belief that there is only one correct interpretation of "the Book and tradition," and consequently the "absolute theoretical authority" of the religious jurists that prevailed before the revolution and under Khomeini.[41] Mojtahed-Shabestari's insistence on separating the form of government from Islam makes him deduce tolerance not from the principles of Islam but from the norms of the modern democratic state, which "acts as the protector of its citizens' liberties, not the guardian of the multiplicities of truth."[42]

The political implications of Mojtahed-Shabestari's religious hermeneutics were spelled out further. According to him, "a major element in modernization is the rationalization of the political order." In fact, "the most important source of tension between modernity and religion in Iran today is the political order."[43] Mojtahed-Shabestari used the hermeneutic principle that the meaning of religious norms is determined by their historical context to refute the fundamental claim that it is possible to base the state, or for that matter any social institution, on Islamic jurisprudence. Only "a small minority" of Muslim thinkers consider "the political instructions of the Book and the Prophetic Traditions to include even the form of government."[44] According to Mojtahed-Shabestari, this opinion is completely wrong. No political regime was founded on the basis of the science of Islamic jurisprudence in the past, nor could one be so founded in the future. This is because the science of jurisprudence can offer answers only to certain questions that arise in a specific historical context and within the institutional framework of existing political regimes.[45] Mojtahed-Shabestari thus explicitly refuted the two cardinal tenets of the official clericalist reading of Islam, namely that "Islam as a religion has political, economic and legal regimes based on the science of Islamic jurisprudence" suitable for all ages, and that "the function of government among the Muslims is the execution of the commandments of Islam."[46]

The advocates of Islamic modernism throughout the twentieth century and the Muslim world have generally maintained that Islam is the most perfect religion and therefore has the best answers to all problems of modern social and political organization, purporting apologetically to deduce democracy, equality of women, and principles of social justice and human rights from its sources. To them, Islam was the "Straight Path" and could, as such, generate the perfect, modern social and political system if only its fundamentals were reexamined correctly. The distinctive mark of the Shi'ite reformation of the 1990s, as formulated by Sorush and Mojtahed-Shabestari, is by contrast a critique, explicitly of political Islam but implicitly also of the apologetic Islamic modernism. The movement for the reformation of Islamic thought in Iran thus marked the birth of critical theory in modern Shi'ism. It offered a radical critique of contemporary Islamic thought for mistaking the historically contingent forms of Islamic religion for its revealed essence, and for disregarding religious pluralism as the inevitable result of different readings of the scriptural texts in specific human languages and socio-historical contexts. As more than one reading of revealed texts is inevitable, so there must be more than one straight path to salvation. Mohammad Khatami, elected President of the IRI in May 1997, subscribed to the view that there was more than one valid reading of Islam, and popularized it in his speeches.

The serious undermining of the legitimacy of theocratic government by this new hermeneutic pluralism cannot be doubted. It predictably touched a raw nerve and provoked the shrill reaction of the conservative Ayatollahs. One Ayatollah told his congregation: "Whoever says I have a new reading of Islam should be slapped in the mouth," and another blamed Khatami and his reform program: "This gentleman [President Khatami] says there are different readings of the foundations of Islam and religious beliefs. . . . The source of this danger is the slogan of civil society on whose side different readings of the foundations of religion take place."[47] In the fall of 1999, the hardliner

JRM (Society of the Militant Clergy) declared: "We must not permit the sacred principles of Islam to become subject of diverse interpretations of this and that individual," and Ayatollah Khaz'ali of the Guardian Council in unison warned President Khatami: "Nothing is dirtier than a pluralist reading of religion."[48] The consummate condemnation was predictably that of Ayatollah Mesbah-Yazdi: "Different readings of religion are the worst Satanic temptation!"[49]

The Ayatollahs defended their monopoly on authoritative interpretation of Islam against the new democratic hermeneutics not only with words but with the judiciary might of the IRI. In August 1999, 'Emad al-Din Baqi, a revolutionary turned reformist journalist, echoed the basic ideas of the new religious hermeneutics, using the neologism for ' "discourse," one of its key concepts. The ineffectiveness of "the discourse of jurisprudential Islam" (*goftemān eslām-e feqāhati*) in the first decades of the revolution had given rise to the new discourse focused on Islam and democracy, in contradiction to the discourse of jurisprudence and "especially the traditional reading of it." He proceeded to exercise his new freedom of interpretation to challenge the scriptural bases of capital punishment for apostasy and adultery in order to prove that it was not required by Islam. Baqi was tried in April 2000 and sentenced to four years in prison for "insulting sacred Islamic beliefs" and an additional three and one half years on other charges such as "spreading lies."[50] Two other journalists were also jailed for publishing his articles in the reformist newspaper, *Neshāt*.[51]

Akbar Ganji, another child of the Islamic revolution and former Revolutionary Guard, began a new career in Sorush's publishing house by transcribing his lectures for publication and became a leading figure in the new breed of reformist journalists. In a lecture at the University of Shiraz in June 1997 shortly after Khatami was elected President, Ganji branded the conservative proponents of totalitarian Islam fascists, supporting his categorization with an analysis of interwar European fascism as "the revolt against modernity and modernism."[52] The lecture was published shortly thereafter and resulted in Ganji's detention before the end of the year. In his defense, which was not delivered during the closed trial but was published in early 1998, Ganji documented "different readings of religion" even among the jurists themselves, and reaffirmed his definition of fascism as "opposition to modernity under the banner of pre-modern values."[53] In a series of articles in 1998 and 1999, Ganji maintained that Imam Khomeini himself had offered two different readings of religious government, the last (Absolute Mandate of the Jurist) being "a completely new reading of religion." This reading, in Ganji's opinion, put "the ideology of violence and the legitimacy crisis" in the context of the greatest rift in contemporary Iranian society caused by the "contradiction between tradition and modernity."[54] These and some earlier articles were published in January 2000 as a book that was reprinted several times during Ganji's second imprisonment and two subsequent trials.[55] While in prison, Ganji made a fundamental political break with the reformist thought of the religious intellectuals. In 2002, before his celebrated hunger strike in prison, he smuggled the *Republican Manifesto* into cyberspace, asserting boldly that Iran's Islamic regime would not be reformed. Its constitution had to be rejected before republicanism and democracy could be realized.[56]

The Dialectic of Tradition and Modernity and the Making of Post-Islamism

Sorush and his followers have been variously called Islamic reformists and religious intellectuals. Those in Western academic circles who considered the idea of modernization and the tradition-modernity dichotomy passé have been surprised by the hot debate on this subject in Iran since the mid-1990s.[57] However, in traveling from nineteenth-century European thought and, more immediately, the structural-functionalist sociology of post–World-War II to post-revolutionary Iran, the first term of the dichotomy—tradition—has lost the rigid fixedness attributed to it by classic eighteenth-century Enlightenment thought, and is seen in a fully dialectical relationship with modernity. Religious intellectuals were the architects of a critical theoretical framework for understanding the dialectic of tradition and modernity. The focus of this critical perspective is the tension between modernity and religion.[58]

Modernization had earlier been contrasted to "backwardness" and to "decline." In a series of books beginning in the late 1980s, Javad Tabataba'i had written on the irreversible decline of political thought in premodern Iran.[59] In the mid-1990s, the reformist periodical, *Kiān,* carried a series of articles on tradition and modernity, including a few by Sorush. In *How We Became What We Are: Search for the Causes of Backwardness in Iran,* first published in 1995, Sadeq Ziba-Kalam ridiculed the attribution, in Islamic revolutionary ideology, of all Iran's ills to Western imperialism. Iran's "backwardness, or to use a more polite euphemism, underdevelopment," is instead traced to a historical trajectory of social formation that sharply diverges from that of the West.[60] Ziba-Kalam's book was followed in short order by three neo-westernizing bestsellers in 1999–2000. These reversed Al-e Ahmad's diagnosis, replacing Westoxification with backwardness as Iran's disease, and proposing modernization, conceived as westernization, as its cure.[61]

During Khatami's election campaign in May 1997, Ganji published a series of dialogues with Iranian intellectuals. It was entitled *Tradition (sonnat), Modernity (modernité), Postmodern*. The "postmodern" did not do too well in Iran, and tends to be identified with a group of so-called Heideggerian (some would say fascist) intellectuals led by Reza Davari.[62] The postmodern trend originating in this group was created by Al-e Ahmad's mentor, Sayyed Ahmad Fardid, who elaborated the jargon of Islamic authenticity as a remedy for Westoxification.[63] It is more properly referred to as anti-modern.[64] The dialectic of tradition and modernity, on the other hand, continued to excite the imagination of the Iranian intellectuals. In the opening (*glasnost*) that immediately followed Khatami's 1997 victory in the presidential elections, Ganji led the new breed of post-revolutionary journalists in spreading the hermeneutically centered Islamic reformism. The debate was not confined to the reformist press and publications in Tehran. The periodical *Naqd o Nazar*, launched in the holy city of Qom in 1995, also published a series of articles on the "Sociology of Modernization" by Hossein Bashiriyyeh, a professor of sociology at the University of Tehran, and devoted a special double issue to *Tradition and Modernity* in 1999.[65]

The discussion of "modernity, pre-modernity and post-modernity," according to one observer, was "the most important discourse (*gofteman*) in our intellectual space and among all groups." The tradition/modernity dichotomy superseded the anti-Western, anti-imperialist, and center/periphery discourse. "The future of Iran," according to the same observer, "primarily depends on this movement of religious enlightenment (*rawshanfekri*) which is capable of bringing about a synthesis between tradition and traditional thought and the heritage of the modern world."[66] President Khatami echoed the same sentiment about the "new religious thinking" in a campaign speech in 2001.[67]

More rigorously, another reformist, Sa'id Hajjarian, proposed the deconstruction of tradition as the first step toward its reconstruction. For Hajjarian, the new religious intellectual "has to prepare a four-phase journey: the first from tradition to modernity; the second is a journey within modernity, the third is the journey from modernity to tradition; and the final phase is the journey within modernity while staying faithful to one's tradition."[68] In short, the search for an alternative modernity in Iran could be achieved only through the dialectic of tradition and modernity. As the dissident cleric

Hasan Yousofi Eshkevari put it in 2000, a critical assessment of both tradition and modernity was necessary to combine "the relevant and valid elements of both tradition and modernity" in "designing a kind of indigenous (Iranian-Islamic) modernity."[69]

Sorush, too, touched upon the debate on tradition and modernity. On the path to development, he observed, it is necessary to take advantage of traditions (*sonan*). Traditions are, however, both shackles and supports. It is necessary to take refuge in them and to seek liberation from them. The ethics of science and the ethics of wealth are two sets of constructive traditions that we now need more than ever.[70] Khatami, for his part, sees the revivalists and reformists lost in the mayhem of "the struggle between tradition and modernity," and acknowledges the tension between rationalism and legalism or "Shari'a-orientation" (*shari'at-garā'i*) with a view to helping them.[71]

In this debate, tradition and modernity were contrasted dichotomously, and even Javad Tabataba'i, the non-religious modernist who insisted on the irrelevance of the postmodern to the predicament of contemporary Iran, admitted the crucial importance of coming to terms with tradition.[72] President Khatami himself published a book on political philosophy in 1999. The ground he covered was the same as Tabataba'i's—the Platonizing adaptation of Greek political philosophy by al-Farabi (d. 950), its synthesis with the "eternal wisdom" of Persian statecraft by Abo'l-Hasan 'Ameri (d. 991) and Moshkuya (Miskawayh) Razi (d. 1030), and the juristic theories of al-Mawardi, Ghazali, and Nezam al-Molk; he ended with a discussion of the revival of political philosophy in Safavid Isfahan in the second half of the seventeenth century. Furthermore, Khatami shared with Tabataba'i the curious idea of the "decline" of Muslim political thought beginning at the very outset, after Farabi.[73] This investigation of neglected, nonjuristic elements in Muslim historical heritage was intended to guide the transition to modernity, and thus is fully in line with the reformist search for modernity in dialectical relation to tradition.

Although his tripartite division of practical philosophy into ethics, economics, and political science was adopted by medieval Muslim philosophers, Aristotle's *Politics* was his only major work not translated into Arabic.[74] The book became available in Persian to Khatami's generation only in the 1970s in a translation by Hamid Enayat. Thus, like Tabataba'i, Khatami brought in the sharply contrasting Aristotelian view of politics to highlight the shortcomings of Muslim political thought.[75] Khatami's explanations of the decline in Muslim political thought in terms of "the transition from political philosophy to royal policy (*siyāsat-e shāhī*)" and its imputation to the prevalence of "forceful domination" (*taghallob*) in Islamic history, however, carry little conviction.[76]

The gap between using Aristotle to criticize traditional political thought and the advocacy of democracy by the reformists remains largely unbridged. Sorush's idea of religious democracy was shared by Khatami, but neither of them elaborated it. Sorush held a purely instrumental, "managerial" view of democracy as "a successful and scientific method of management (*tadbir*) in the social arena."[77] He also sought to grant the management of political affairs normative autonomy from religion, and argued that religious jurisprudence is irrelevant to the justification of democracy, which should rest on purely rational grounds.[78] In a 1997 lecture, Sorush returned to medieval Muslim political philosophy as the art of civic government with a novel question: can politics, or the political sphere, have its own distinct ethics? To answer the question in the affirmative, he divided political ideas into theories of legitimacy, such as the *velāyat-e faqih,* and theories of political management, which were badly neglected by contemporary Muslims. His central argument, however, was that management is a rational and experimental affair. "Therefore, the managerial branch of government was essentially independent of religion."[79] This managerial conception of democracy was shared by Mojtahed-Shabestari who saw democracy as required by "the scientific management and long-term planning" typical of modern life, and derived it from the view of medieval Muslim philosophers as "management of the polity."[80] Sorush, however, later changed his mind and opted for a normative definition of democracy as resting on three pillars: rationality, pluralism, and human rights.[81] This, too, fell short of a justification of democracy within the normative framework of Islamic reformism.

The sociologist S. N. Eisenstadt has written about the modern totalitarian impulse as "the Jacobin dimension of modernity." Through Shari'ati's sojourn in Paris of the 1960s and of Beheshti's in Hamburg of the 1970s, this Jacobin political modernity entered the process of Iranian modernization in the form of political Islam.[82] The force of dominant political Islam seemed largely spent in Iran by the 1990s, however, while it continued to thrive under repression in countries such as Algeria and Egypt. In the decade preceding the Iranian revolution, in London and Hamburg, the influences fostering the liberal, non-Jacobin dimensions of modernity—in the form of Karl Popper's philosophy and Karl Rahner's theological hermeneutics—had also left their imprint on the intellects of Sorush and Mojtahed-Sabestari. What is interesting about the coming to fruition of these influences in the 1990s is that they were neither antireligious nor anti-moral, but on the contrary, represented an emphatic attempt to make moral sense of modernization and its normative governance. This search for an alternative modernity could be achieved only through the dialectic of tradition and modernity. Asef Bayat calls the outcome post-Islamism.

Bayat presents post-Islamism as an internally driven process that grows out of Islamism, or what I have called political Islam. "Islamism becomes compelled, both by its internal contradictions and by societal pressures, to reinvent itself, but it does so at the cost of qualitative shift. The tremendous transformation in religious and political discourse in Iran during the 1990s exemplifies this tendency."[83] Post-Islamism thus results from the fact that the process of Islamization in Iran reached a dead end: "Scores of old Islamist revolutionaries renounced their earlier ideas and warned of the dangers of a religious state to both religion and the state." They called for the secularization of the state "but stressed maintaining religious ethics in society."[84] Ghamari-Tabrizi comes to a somewhat similar conclusion: "the democratization of the entire edifice of Islamic knowledge production [is] one of the most enduring, albeit unintended consequences of the Iranian revolution." This is because the revolution has brought religion to the public sphere and thereby transformed it, producing an official and a dissident variant of Islam that are mutually contested and "competing to become hegemonic."[85]

The official version of Islam in the IRI was built on Khomeini's extension of the traditional authority of religious jurists over the insane, minors, and girls without legal guardians into the mandate to rule. While the reformist President Khatami was playing the somewhat ineffectual role of the leader of the loyal opposition in the IRI, Mojtahed-Shabestari seriously undermined the *political* authority of the jurists, and thereby Khomeini's painstakingly crafted constitutional structure. This paved the way for the naughtiest of the children of the revolution, Sorush, to dynamite the father's whole edifice by undermining the *religious* authority of the jurists that had not been disputed even by the Shah.

The specifically political idea in what Bayat calls post-Islamism is "religious democracy," defined very vaguely by Sorush in 1996 as a regime that "emanates from a religious society and serves the interests of the people."[86] Other reformists highlighted the "republican" dimension in their new reading of the Constitution of the IRI.[87] Khatami's Interior Minister, 'Abdollah Nuri, argued that "religious government" (*hokumat-e dini,* evidently his equivalent for *holumat-e eslāmi,* the slogan of the Islamic revolution) "derives its legitimacy from the popular vote, and has no legitimacy to rule independently of the vote of the people."[88] What he condemned, by contrast, was "state religion, not religious government.... The effect of 'state religion' was not and is not anything but the reduction of religion to an instrument for justifying power and the actions of the powerful."[89] In Nuri's post-Islamist reading, the "people," or for that matter the community of believers (*umma*), is a pluralistic unity in which different views and opinions among the citizens (*shahrvandān*) are recognized.[90] Religious democracy thus meant a blend of "Islam and republicanism, religion and democracy, the Revolution and reform, unity and diversity... ethics and politics, this world and the afterworld, God and the people."[91]

Bayat goes so far as to speak of "the coming of a post-Islamist society."[92] Unfortunately, social life and especially political life do not change that simply. The reformists were just as much children of the revolution and trapped in their past as the pragmatists and the hardliners. They could not free themselves from the old revolutionary rhetoric because they did not want to be traitors. Patterns of socio-political action are even more difficult to change than discourse. The children of the Islamic revolution could tread along different paths, but only those paved by Khomeini. Perhaps unbeknownst to them, the dead Imam determined the range on which they could roam on the highly uneven field chosen by him as the arena of post-revolutionary power struggle.

The Rise and Fall of President Khatami and the Reform Movement

"We the protesting Deputies have had a share and role in the Revolution and have struggled for its victory and consolidation in various arenas, have learned the lessons of honor, truth-telling, piety and freedom in the school of Imam Khomeini (God's mercy be upon him), and consider his way and Tradition (*sonnat*) the path to the salvation and high standing of the Islamic Republic of Iran."

So began, after a perfunctory quotation from the First Imam, 'Ali, in Arabic, the last letter of protest of February 17, 2004, from the 131 deputies of the Sixth Majles who had gone on strike in January, after the Guardian Council had disqualified 80 of them from running for the Seventh Majles. The reformists presented themselves as spokespersons for "the forces loyal to the Revolution and democracy (*mardom-sālāri*)," and complained that "the forces faithful (*mo'men*) to the Revolution and the regime" had no option but to retreat from political involvement. There was a reference to the rumor of the Supreme Leader's complicity in their disqualification, and oblique questioning of his authority to issue this particular "governmental order" (*hokm hokumati*). But the "clarity" (*shaffāfiyyat*) advocated by President Khatami and his reformist followers seven years earlier was totally absent.[1] There was strong evidence that Khatami himself believed the same rhetoric and was trapped in it.[2] The reformists ended their letter with an admonition in the manner of the councilors to old kings: "We are very worried about the future when our regime, with the nostalgia of its immense lost popular support, would be forced to submit to the open and hidden onslaught of foreigners." This letter was the sad epitaph for the reform movement that had began with electrifying effect in 1997 and caused a tremendous burst of enthusiasm in Iran and throughout the world.

The Rule of Law and the *Glasnost*

Khatami belonged to the revolutionary elite, as did many of his followers in the Majles. It is therefore important to view their reform movement as an attempt at reform from within the regime and from above. As such, it may be instructive to compare it to the reform movement in the Soviet Union under Gorbachev that began with an opening (*glasnost*) and a restructuring (*perestroika*).[3] These attempts to reform the regimes from within by Gorbachev and Khatami were less than a decade apart. Khatami was relatively successful in his *glasnost,* but failed, with one notable exception, in his *perestroika.* The Iranian opening of the public sphere in the reform movement was as impressive as the Russian, but the impetus to restructuring was extremely weak. The reform movement consequently failed to restructure the regime as it intended or, as in the Soviet Union, to unintentionally produce regime change.

An important issue in the constitutional politics of the Islamic Republic—namely the clash between the traditional hierocratic authority of the so-called sources of imitation and new system of theocratic government based on the Mandate of the Jurist—had been solved during President Hashemi-Rafsanjani's second term, before Khatami came to power. The institutionalization of clerical rule also involved a contradiction with the constitutional authority of the legislature as a rival principle of legitimacy, which was resolved by giving the six clerical jurists in the Guardian Council the authority to veto any item of legislation passed by the Majles. These contradictions notwithstanding, the clerical elite ruled Iran for over two decades through a number of key councils, and by controlling the Judiciary and the Ministry of Intelligence and using a subservient bureaucratic/technocratic second stratum without any significant power sharing with it.

Although the characteristic shared with other post-revolutionary regimes was a collective government emerging during the period of succession to the charismatic leader of a revolution, the regime of the Islamic Republic of Iran (IRI) was distinguished by its unique clericalism. The Islamic revolution established a hybrid political regime, with an elected parliament and President, but one subordinated to clerical authority—a theocratic republic, which can be characterized as a system of collective rule by clerical assemblies or councils under a clerical ruler styled the Supreme Jurist or Leader. The clash of clerical conciliarism with the democratization espoused by the reform movement also occurs alongside a non-institutional process of accumulation of power in the hands of the Leader, resulting in increasingly personal rule by him called clerical monarchy (*saltanat*) by its critics.

The Association of Militant Clerics (MRM) proposed Khatami as its presidential candidate after the former radical Prime Minister, Mir-Hossein Musavi, and reportedly five other clerics and ministers had declined to run.[4] He won nearly 70 percent of popular vote in an election with very heavy turnout in May 1997. At the time of his unexpected landslide victory, the institutionalization of clerical conciliarism was proceeding with full momentum. Early in 1997, following the advice of the influential Investigation Committee of the Assembly of Leadership Experts, the Leader, Ayatollah Khamenei, reconstituted the Maslahat Council with the mandate to assume its function of offering advice on major policies of the regime according to Article 110 of the Constitution. Following the advice of the same Committee, he broke with the precedence of having the President of the Republic as the chairman of the Council, and appointed the outgoing President, Hashemi-Rafsanjani, instead. The clear intention was to demote the elected President by appropriating the function of the determination of state policy to the Council. Here, we can see the two trends following the demise of the charismatic leader of the revolution clash. The trend toward centralization of power in the state, reinforced by Hashemi-Rafsanjani as President holding the chair of the Maslahat Council, was now reversed, curiously for his benefit, in favor of the trend toward clerical conciliarism by depriving the incoming President Khatami of the main institutional means for the determination of state policy. The election of Khatami to President suddenly pulled this quiet trend in clerical institutionalization into the arena of contested constitutional politics. The President as the head of the executive was pitted against the Leader at the apex of the system of clerical councils and courts.

The Iranian *glasnost* came as a radical break with the totalitarian ideology of the Islamic revolution. Back in 1992, Sayyed Mohammad Khatami had been forced to resign as Hashemi-Rafsanjani's Minister of Islamic Culture and Guidance for his liberalism and relaxation of press censorship by a newly elected Fourth Majles that was dominated by hardliners who feared "cultural invasion" by the West. If cultural invasion entailed liberalization and freedom of the press, the hardliners' fear was not paranoia. After his landslide 1997 victory, Khatami appointed Ata'ollah Mohajerani, one of Rafsanjani's deputy-presidents and a founder of the Servants for Reconstruction, his Minister of Culture and Islamic Guidance, and through him removed many of the restrictions on the press. Khatami's landslide victory was an unexpected and historically unprecedented event, and was instantly referred to as the historic "national event of 2 Khordad (23 May)," which date was later chosen by the coalition of his supporters as their designation. It reopened the question of the fundamental principles of order in the Islamic Republic for the first time since 1979. Khatami's platform of civil society and "the rule of law (*hokumat-e qānun*)" evoked an implicit contrast with "*hokumat-e eslāmi* (Islamic government)," the slogan of the revolution.[5]

Although "the rule of law" was accompanied by "civil society" in Khatami's program, it was more a matter of creating than mobilizing civil society, and of turning a shapeless mass into a public. The number of political associations rose from 35 in 1997 to 130 by 2001. The number of professional and advocacy NGOs, including women's (230 by 2000, 330 two years later), youth, and environmental, exceeded 2500 after 2001.[6] The Student's Office of Consolidation and Unity, whose leaders had earlier acted like officials of the revolutionary government, began an impressive news agency, ISNA, to publish a national student newspaper, *Āzar,* and some 700 local ones, and sponsor some 1,437 cultural, scientific, and social associations. A student leader could credibly claim: "The fundamental role of the student movement is to critique power. The student movement is not a political party, an institution, or a political actor; on the contrary, it is the antithesis of such powers. Its objective is to mobilize for democracy and human rights, and to reform power."[7]

A popular pro-Khatami press immediately flourished. Before long, a number of these newspapers were closed down by the clerical judges, while their editorial staffs were given licenses by the Ministry of Culture to start new ones. Between 1997 and 2002, 108 newspapers and periodicals were banned. The massive closure, however, came in April 2000 after the Leader declared the reformist journalism "a grave threat to all of us."[8] This press spread Khatami's new political discourse and neologisms such as "civil society" (*jāme'a-ye madani*), "legality" (*qānun-mandi*), and "citizens" (*shahrvandān*) used in his inaugural speech.[9] To these were soon added others: "pluralism" (*plurālizm, takkathur-garā'i*) as opposed to "monopolism," "law-orientedness" (*qānun-garā'i*), and finally, "reading" (*qerā'at*) [of Islam].

Khatami showed firm determination in promoting the most basic aspect of the rule of law. Political murders committed by the secret services of the Islamic Republic constituted a blatant breach of the rule of law. In January 1999, Khatami insisted on the arrest of a number of officials in the Ministry of Information (read Intelligence), including a deputy minister, Sa'id Emami (*alias* Eslami), for the chain of murders of a number of writers and liberal politicians carried out in November 1998 in defiance of the President and in order to discredit his reformist program.[10] Some of the conservative Ayatollahs were reliably said to have issued *fatwā*s (injunctions) justifying the killings. The reformist Ayatollah Musavi-Arbadili declared any such *fatwā*s invalid. Hojjat al-Eslam Mohsen Kadivar, a younger but prominent reformist cleric who had written a direct and detailed refutation of Khomeini's theory of theocratic government, delivered a speech in Isfahan in which he declared terrorism forbidden by the Sacred Law. Kadivar was arrested at the end of February 1999, and his trial by the Special Court for Clerics became a cause célèbre. The national press and student associations protested that the Court was unconstitutional, and that it was in contravention of the International Human Rights Instruments signed by the government of Iran that disallows special courts for special classes of persons. The Head of the Judiciary defended the legitimacy of the Special Court for Clerics on grounds that it had been approved by the late Imam Khomeini as the Supreme Jurist and by the Constitution. Disregarding the widespread public protest and Kadivar's elaborate defense, the Special Court for Clerics sentenced him to 18 months in prison in April 1999.

More institutionalized struggles were taking place between the Majles and the Guardian Council, on the one hand, and between the Judiciary and the press and the Majles, on the other. The paradox of Khatami's rule of law became evident when he and his supporters were seen to be powerless in either making laws or enforcing them. Their law-making power was blocked by the Guardian Council, and law enforcement by the clerically controlled Judiciary was unabashedly politicized by Khamenei's hardliners and turned viciously against the reformers.

Mellowing of the Power Struggle among the Children of the Revolution

The rift between the hardliners or "establishment clerics" and the "reformists" during the Khatami presidency (1997–2005) can be seen as a delayed but typical pattern of revolutionary power struggle.[11] The division of the loyal opposition to the pragmatists in power under Hashemi-Rafsanjani (1989–1997) into the radicals turned reformist, on the one hand, and the hardliners, who disowned them and defined their own contrasting outlook, on the other, has been traced. This transformation of identities greatly complicated the power struggle. The delay of two decades caused a great ideological turn in the position of the radicals, with a shift of focus from revolution and Islam to reform, democracy, and civil society. The ideological (*maktabi*) outlook of many of the radicals underwent a complete change, and the term *maktabi* (belonging to the School [of the Imam]) coined at the beginning of the revolution, died even faster than the loan word "ideology." The result was the mellowing of the revolutionary power struggle when it resumed in earnest in 1999.

Compared to other revolutions and the first round of the revolutionary power struggle in the Islamic revolution, the second round was mild. Some observers wondered why Saturn did not show an enormous appetite for devouring his own children in the case of the Iranian revolution, apart from the Mojahedin-e Khalq, who were decimated in the early 1980s. The resumed power struggle can be attributed to Saturn's unsatisfied appetite. The remarkable lowering of violence in the power struggle, however, was due in no small measure to the weakening of the power of revolutionary ideology. Saturn was not devouring his children as much as punishing them less severely.

The summer of 1999 was less glorious than its first half for the reformists. On July 5, shortly after Emami or Eslami was said to have committed suicide in prison, the reformist newspaper, *Salām,* published a secret letter written by him with an outline of the restrictive press law with provisions for clerical censorship which was under discussion in the Majles. The Special Court for Clerics immediately banned *Salām,* presumably giving itself jurisdiction to do so because the newspaper's editor was a cleric. Students in the University of Tehran protested against the closure of *Salām* on July 8 and their protest spread to other Iranian universities. The Revolutionary Guards intervened, alongside the regular police and the hooligans of the Helpers of the Party of God, causing a few deaths, many casualties, and hundreds of arrests.

The student riots of July 1999 marked a high point in questioning the principle of Leadership or theocratic government. The protesters' slogans, for the first time, included "Khamenei must go!" They were also the first signs of disconnect between the reformist President and the younger generation who had voted for him. A similar disconnect between the President and his female supporters had become evident by Khatami's failure to appoint a female minister. Emboldened by the suppression of the student riots, the hardliners proceeded with the closure of the reformist newspaper, *Khordād,* and trial of its editor, the former Interior Minister under both Hashemi-Rafsanjani and Khatami, 'Abdollah Nuri. The trial of Nuri in November 1999 by the notorious Special Court for Clerics was remarkable in many ways. There was hardly any legal argument in the charges, which were blatantly political. The main charge against Nuri was his criticism of Khomeini's assertion that Israel should be obliterated.[12] The trial also provided the occasion for the widespread questioning of the legality of the Special Court for Clerics as well as the legitimacy of theocratic rule and Leadership. The all-clerical jury turned in its verdict before receiving Nuri's final written defense, and he was sentenced to 5 years in prison.

Khatami's supporters in the reform movement were organized by Sa'id Hajjarian, the Vice-President of Tehran's newly elected Municipal Council, and by the President's younger brother, Mohammad-Reza Khatami, into the Islamic Participation (*moshārekat*) Front for the parliamentary elections of February 2000. They won by a landslide, with 69 percent of the electorate turning out, and dealt the clericalist groups a crushing defeat. They won a solid majority in the first round against the 17 other political groups that had competed for Majles seats. But the reaction of the Supreme Jurist and the clerical establishment was swift and determined. Hajjarian, the chief architect of the stunning reformist victory, was almost fatally shot in the head in front of the municipal council building in March 2000 just before Nawruz, the Persian new year (figure 5.1). When the doors of the new Majles opened, its reformist members were in for a rude awakening.

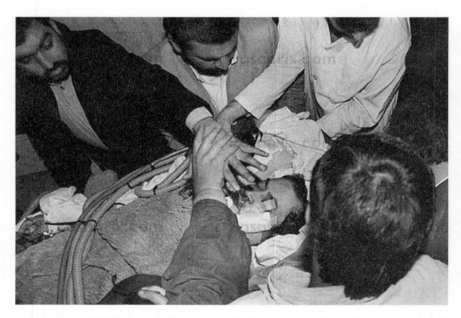

FIGURE 5.1 Sa'id Hajjarian, shot almost fatally in front of the Tehran Municipal Council building on March 12, 2000, shortly after the landslide victory of the reformists. (Supplied by SAA)

The crushing electoral defeat of clericalism in the 2000 Majles elections had some important but less obvious consequences. Hashemi-Rafsanjani, who had been sympathetic to Khatami and reformism until he was attacked by the journalists, notably Akbar Ganji, was badly humiliated in the Tehran election. He refused to take the seat he was given after the suspension of recounting, and threw in his lot completely with the Leader and the conciliar system. Many of the radical clerics, like Karrubi, had lost their seats in the Majles in 1992 and 1996, and became reformists as a result of their soul-searching outside the power loop. Although a few of them regained seats in the Majles in 2000, these clerics did not do nearly as well as Khatami's secular supporters. The top three winners of the Tehran seats were not clerics themselves but the brothers and sister of the reformist President and two jailed reformist clerics, Nuri and Kadivar. The reformist clerics who won in their own right had less influence in the new Majles. Karrubi had difficulty being elected as Speaker, Majid Ansari failed to keep his temporary position as Deputy-Speaker, and other clerics faced confirmation difficulties. This made these clerics feel threatened by their secular colleagues in the reform movement, and tended to push them to clericalism within the Majles.

In fact, signs of trouble multiplied before the new Majles was convened. In April 2000, the Guardian Council postponed the second round of Majles elections, annulled a number of elections won by reformists, and asserted its superiority over the Majles by virtue of its appointment by the Leader. The Maslahat Council, with its chairman Hashemi-Rafsanjani pushed into the clericalist camp, successfully preempted any Majles investigations into the breaches of the law by depriving it of the right to investigate not only the Special Court for Clerics but also any other organization under the control of Leadership, including the armed forces and the national radio and television. The reformist Majles, when it eventually convened, was too docile to challenge this arrogation by the Maslahat Council. By May 2000, all but one or two of the reformist newspapers were closed down, and many leading journalists were arrested and imprisoned. On August 6, 2000, the Leader told the Majles to stop its deliberations on the new press law, and clerical judges were emboldened to close down the last important reformist paper, *Bahār,* and to arrest more journalists.

The reformist Majles lost the chance it had at confronting the Leader, who had clearly stepped beyond his ample constitutional jurisdiction by telling Parliament to stop its debate, and to stand up as the Legislative Power against the Judiciary. It was too timid to react and challenge the authority of the

Leader when thus slapped in the mouth. The grave mistake of electing a cleric, Mehdi Karrubi, as the Majles Speaker became evident when he confirmed the authority of the Leader, as the Supreme Jurist (*vali-ye faqih*), to issue a "governmental order" (*hokm-e hokumati*) to the Majles, and defended it as the constitutional exercise of the Absolute Mandate of the Jurist. Two days later, Karrubi reaffirmed the value of this prerogative by pointing out that another "governmental order" had "solved" the problem of recounting the votes in the second round of elections in Tehran.[13] In retrospect, this was the last chance the Majles had to challenge the surreptitiously expanding system of conciliar clerical rule under Leadership by provoking a major constitutional crisis. It did not rise up to the admittedly daunting challenge and was doomed to suffer further humiliation.

The Supreme Jurist led the continuous assault with the use of the clerically controlled Judiciary through a group of former Ministry of Intelligence investigators who had been appointed judges toward the end of Yazdi's long tenure as the Head of the Judiciary. These judges began harassing the Majles deputies, as they had done with journalists, by summoning them to courts for expressing their critical opinions in parliament. The closure of the press continued beyond the dailies, and on the eve of the Nawruz 1380/2001, the most important of the remaining reformist magazines and monthlies were closed down. The political abuse of the courts to harass and sentence a number of reformist Majles deputies continued unabated.

The reformists were very much the children of the revolution, as were the "moderates" of 1979—the so-called religious-nationalist followers of Bazargan, Khomeini's revolutionary partner and the first Prime Minister of the IRI. It is no accident that in addition to the "reformist" children of the revolution, those chastised by the Leader and the politicized Judiciary under his command in the second, delayed round of revolutionary power struggle included these 1979 moderates. Bazargan's Islamic liberal nationalist movement, the Freedom Movement of Iran (*nahzat-e āzādi-ye irān*), had been junior partners in the initial Islamic revolutionary coalition in 1979. It was suppressed after some 90 of its members wrote a letter of protest to Hashemi-Rafsanjani in May 1990, and was banned from taking part in the 1992 elections.[14] This was another group of his children Saturn did not spare. The intelligence agents waged their war against the old moderates with the brutal murder of Bazargan's Health Minister, Kazem Sami, on 23 November 1988,[15] and the equally brutal murder of his Labor Minister, Dariush Foruhar, with his wife on 22 November 1998. Amir Entezam, Deputy Prime Minister under

Bazargan, having spent 17 years in prison, was arrested again in December 1999 for criticizing his notorious warden at the Evin prison and returned to prison after refusing to sign a "confession."[16]

Nevertheless, encouraged by Khatami's promise of the rule of law and his reining in of the intelligence agents, some members of the Freedom Movement of Iran and their sympathizers formed the Nationalist-Religious Coalition (*e'telāf-e melli-madhhabi*) in 2000, applying to the Ministry of the Interior for recognition and fielding some 30 candidates for the Majles elections. Their application was promptly rejected, however, as were their candidates.[17] In March 2001, the Tehran Revolutionary Court closed down the Freedom Movement of Iran. The Nationalist-Religious Coalition was also banned. Both groups were declared "illegal and outcast by the late Imam," and some 21 of their members, most notably 'Ezzatollah Sahabi, were detained.[18] A further 30 members, including Bazargan's Interior and Justice Ministers, were arrested a few weeks later in April 2001.[19] Those who were eventually brought to trial received rather harsh sentences in May 2003. All this was done by order of the Leader's men in the politicized Judiciary, while the President looked the other way.

Constitutional Politics of the *Perestroika*

The election of the rural, municipal, and provincial councils in February 1999 marked the height of Khatami's success in implementing his program of rule of law and democratization. The Organization of the Mojahedin of the Islamic Revolution, one of Khatami's key reformist allies, had also emphasized political participation through the councils as early as 1995: "The formation of the councils from the village and district to the highest national levels...is the most important factor for encouraging the people to exercise their rights and institutionalize the culture of popular participation."[20] The law concerning the organization and elections of the councils had eventually been passed in 1996, and Khatami promised to have them elected during his 1997 campaign. Participation was a major component of Khatami's favorite idea of political development. As he put it in a major speech, "the first step in political development is participation," and the election of the councils was "the most evident channel for participation."[21] The reformist Deputy Minister of the Interior responsible for carrying out the 1999 councils elections, Mostafa Tajzadeh, was a member of the Organization of the Mojahedin and considered the elections as the fulfillment of the major requirements of political development by extending participation to the most remote villages. Other reformists such as Ebrahim Asgharzadeh and Saʻid Hajjarian, who were running for the Tehran Municipal Council, recognized the councils as a new space for self-government, independent of the state and therefore more real than the much talked about civil society.[22] Hajjarian alternately included the councils among the institutions of civil society and considered them "the foundation stone of republicanism."[23] The elections took place as Khatami had promised. Over half a million candidates competed for seats in 35,000 villages and over 900 municipal councils. Some 80 percent of the popular vote (65% turnout) was reportedly cast for supporters of Khatami's reform movement who won the majority of the seats. On the second anniversary of his presidential victory, Khatami addressed the gathering of some 107,000 elected members of the village and town councils in Tehran, again emphasizing the importance of political development and the need to struggle for "the consolidation of Islamic democracy and popular government (*mardom-salari*)." He noted that sacred terms such as "revolution," "freedom," "Islam," and "*Leadership*" are not the monopoly of any group." The Leader was pointedly absent, and his message was read by the director of his office.[24]

In February 1998, President Khatami appointed a Commission for the Implementation and Supervision of the Constitution, citing Article 113 of the Constitution, one of the few remaining Articles unchanged from the original draft that made the implementation of the Constitution one of the main duties of the President. The Commission displayed little energy. Despite losing repeated rounds to the Leader and the resourceful Ayatollahs, Khatami made his presidential duty of safeguarding the Constitution a means for driving a wedge into the hitherto seamless edifice of monolithic Islamic-ideological interpretation of the law by clerical jurists. This episode and its background demonstrate yet again how constitutional politics are moved by vested interests independently of the personal inclinations of historical actors. In 1983, when the radicals were in power and pushing for centralization under Prime Minister Mir-Hossein Musavi with Khomeini's support, and the Guardian Council was on the defensive, it had sought the alliance of President Khamenei, and urged him to carry out the presidential responsibility according to Article 113. The latter, as a president seeking to increase his power against the Prime Minister and probably with little expectation that he would one day be the Leader, had already tried to set up a mechanism for implementing Article 113, but had been blocked by the Council.[25] Now with the blessing of the Guardian Council, he prepared the 1986/1365 Law of

Delimitation of the Functions, Powers, and Responsibilities of the President of the IRI. This law was enacted pursuant to Article 113 of the Constitution to define the President's authority "for the purpose of guarding (*pāsdāri*) the Constitution of the IRI."[26] Article 15 of the 1986 Law further gave the President the right to issue "warnings" to the three Powers in cases of constitutional violation.[27] In 1998, Khatami set up the new Commission to advise him on how to exercise this authority. The Commission advised him on one occasion to issue "warnings of constitutional violation" against the Head of the Judiciary at the height of the constitutional struggle, and he did so.

Meanwhile, the power of the clerical jurists of the Guardian Council to determine the qualification of candidates for all elected office, which was first effectively challenged by the disqualified clerical or clerically endorsed candidates, now became more widely contested. "Conformity with the standards of Islam" therefore became more fluid and contested with the widely accepted reformist position that different "readings" of Islam were possible.[28] This was particularly the case with regard to human rights and freedom of the press. Khatami and the chairman of his Constitutional Commission, Hossein Mehrpur, nevertheless avoided confronting the Guardian Council and the Judiciary, which under a more assertive Head, Ayatollah Mahmud Hashemi-Shahrudi, was putting forward its own claim to constitutional judicial review and considered the President's Commission a nuisance.[29] In January 2002, the Judiciary even denied Mehrpur's request to visit dissident political prisoners.[30] Finally, Khatami did not dare augment the power of the Commission in his last assertive endeavor to be considered shortly.

Meanwhile, the temporarily interrupted process of consolidation of the conciliar system had resumed in 2001, with the Guardian Council and the Maslahat Council turning their heavy guns on the Majles. Early in February 2001, the Guardian Council rejected the budget passed by the Majles, a matter that patently had nothing to do with the conformity of laws with Islam, and the Maslahat Council supported it without reservation. At the same time, the jurists of the Guardian Council went out of their way to assert that they had been too lax in disqualifying the Majles candidates and would be much firmer in rejecting any candidate they disliked in the forthcoming presidential elections (including President Khatami).

With Ayatollah Khamenei's decision to suppress the reform movement and block any further restructuring (*perestroika*) of the regime, the Guardian Council and the Maslahat Council assumed the functions of political control necessary for maintaining the system of clerical conciliarism, while the political abuse of the Judiciary to suppress the freedom of expression reached a new high. The state-favored *maraje'-e taqlid* spoke out in favor of theocratic government and against the Majles. Dissident clerics, however, could not be silenced. In fact, to Ayatollah Montazeri goes the credit of demanding in February 2001 that the Constitution of the Islamic Republic be revised, something President Khatami and his Majles supporters lacked the courage to do.[31]

Not until October 2001 did President Khatami join the fray of constitutional politics as the protector of the Constitution. He warned the Head of the Judiciary against the constitutional violation of the parliamentary immunity of several Majles deputies convicted by the politicized courts.[32] But this warning was ignored and the political abuse of clerically controlled judiciary power against legislators continued. Some 60 reformist legislators were summoned to court in the ensuing months, and four were sentenced. Deputy Loqmannia began serving his sentence in January 2002, but was pardoned by the Leader after a few days when his reformist colleagues walked out of the Majles in protest.[33]

Khatami took the next few months to prepare for one final confrontation. In an important speech, given on 28 August 2002, he renewed his vow with the nation and affirmed that he was not only the Head of the Executive Power but also the authority responsible for the upholding of the Constitution. He reaffirmed that "religious democracy" (*mardom-sālāri-ye dini*) and "rights of the people" were not empty slogans and that he was determined to realize the model of religious democracy proposed to the world by the Islamic revolution.[34] This speech was followed by the introduction in September 2002 of two pieces of legislation that provoked the constitutional crisis prefigured in the combination of the heterogeneous principles of theocracy and democracy in the Constitution of the IRI.

On September 1, 2002, the President introduced a bill to curb the Guardian Council's power of approbatory supervision based on its own constitutional interpretation of 1991. Predictably, it was vetoed by the Council. Khatami's second bill aimed at increasing the powers of the President as the guardian of the Constitution according to its Article 113. It was presented as an amendment to Khamenei's 1986 Law and was passed by the Majles in April 2003. It too was promptly rejected by the Guardian Council. The Commission was cautious and conservative, wishing to remain strictly within the confines of the Constitution, and its bill was consequently too timid to make a significant difference. It missed the opportunity to make the bold first step toward introducing a form of judicial review under the aegis of the President, which seemed technically possible,[35] by couching the bill in administrative rather than judicial terms. The proposed presidential commission was to be given the power of "inspection" to determine violations of the Constitution and was not explicitly given jurisdiction to hear cases of human rights violations. Only obliquely and at the end was the President given the power to provide a budget for compensating victims of human rights violations. Despite all the talk of reform, the global wave of the human rights revolution had evidently passed the Iranian shores without a ripple. But even this feeble attempt to provide administrative redress for human rights violations was too much for the Guardian Council. In April 2004, a despondent Khatami wrote about his dashed hopes to the relentless Guardian Council, and withdrew his bill.[36]

As resignation of the President and a national referendum were being discussed by the reformists as ways to overcome the recalcitrance of the Guardian Council and the Maslahat Council, Rahim Safavi, commander of the Revolutionary Guards, announced his readiness at the beginning of November 2002 to unleash revolutionary violence against the reform movement.[37] Meanwhile, the political abuse of the clerically controlled Judiciary Power had become more blatant. A number of reformists outside the Majles were arrested in the fall of 2002, and on November 6, a university lecturer and former Islamic student leader, Hashem Aghajari, was sentenced to death for his anticlerical remarks, which the judge considered insults to the Prophet. Students joined the constitutional struggle with protests against judicial abuse.[38] Unrest continued into December, resulting in numerous arrests, and even a hard-line judiciary spokesman resigned in protest against the gross miscarriage of justice in the Aghajari case.[39] At this point, Aghajari introduced a radically novel oppositional tactic into the constitutional politics of the Islamic Republic. Sensing the feebleness of the President as the leader of the uncoordinated opposition within and outside parliament, Aghajari refused to ask for the pardon hinted at by the Supreme Jurist and demanded instead that the unjust death sentence be carried out.[40] His example was followed by the one surviving "moderate" leader, the religious-nationalist dissident 'Ezzatollah Sahabi, who wrote an open letter to the Heads of the three Powers asking that he be executed rather than subjected to continued harassment after his release from jail.[41]

The legislative power of the Maslahat Council also came under reformist attack after their victory in the parliamentary elections of 2000. In May 2002, the Maslahat Council issued a statement in response to an article in the reformist newspaper, *Nawruz,* which had cited a number of instances of its legislation being unconstitutional. The Maslahat Council reaffirmed the constitutionality, with the Leader's permission, of its legislation in matters other than disputes between the Guardian Council and the Majles. This legislative power was implied in Clause 8 of the amended Article 110 of the Constitution, which gave the Maslahat Council responsibility for "solving the difficulties of the regime that cannot be solved through ordinary chan-nels."[42] The argument seemed logical, but it could only reinforce the growing conviction among some of the leading reformists by that time that their goal of democracy was not achievable within the framework of the existing Constitution. Writing in the same reformist newspaper, 'Abbas 'Abdi argued that reform was impossible within the existing constitutional framework and convoluted power structure and called upon Khatami to resign rather than give legitimacy to a lawless regime.[43] Many reformists realized by then that the discursive terrain was badly sloped against them and they had no chance to beat the hardliners at the appropriation of Islamic terms. Reformist jour-nalists 'Alavitabar and Jala'ipur called for deleting the qualification "religious" from "religious democracy," and Ganji did so when issuing his *Republican Manifesto* from Evin prison. Ganji stated that reformists were paralyzed by political deadlock, bluntly acknowledged that "there is no hope for democ-racy within the framework of existing laws," and advocated civil disobedience and boycotting elections as "the only way to open the door to reason and justice."[44] By December 2002, University of Tehran students were shouting "Death to Dictatorship" and "Khatami, Resign!"[45] Behzad Nabavi may have been one of the last to give up hope, but in May 2004 even he admitted that "young people no longer take us seriously when we speak of religious democracy."[46]

The loss of the only serious constitutional struggle Khatami and the reformists had mounted against the Leader led to widespread disaffection that manifested itself in the elections of the municipal councils in Tehran and some other major cities in February 2003. The same general disaffection with Khatami was evident in the widespread and continuous student protests and youth unrest in a large number of cities through the summer of 2003. The Majles reformists, to their great discredit, disowned the students.

As these events demonstrate, the major problem of the political wing of the reform movement as the true children of the Islamic revolution of 1979 and its undoing was a double disconnect: a disconnect between the President and the reformist members of the Majles at the organizational level, and a disconnect of both Khatami and the reform movement from the people in general and the new generation in particular, especially the university students. There was little coordination between the President and his cabinet and the reformist MPs, and even less between the reformists in the Majles and the newspapers and the press. Nor did the reformists reach out to the sympathetic groups in society. As a prominent reformist Mohsen Mirdamadi admitted, they did not have any committee for coordinating their activities with like-minded social groups.[47]

Meanwhile, the reformist children of the revolution were trapped as insiders (*khodi*) in their revolutionary discourse. The empty slogans they clung to for salvation in their last moment of desperation were in fact the heavy weights around their necks that drowned them. Building a coalition with outsiders—students, women, the urban poor, and citizens without impeccable revolutionary credentials—may have saved the reformists, but they were incapable of building the bridges. They chose perdition over treason to the revolution as its insiders.

Clerical Councils versus the Majles

The Constitution gave the Majles very little to use against the Guardian Council and absolutely nothing against the Maslahat Council. In 2001, the Majles had tried to use its power of confirmation of the lay members of the Guardian Council proposed by the Head of the Judiciary. On August 8, 2001, however, with the backing of the Leader, the Maslahat Council ruled that if the nominees of the Judiciary failed to obtain confirmation in the Majles in the first round, those nominees with the highest plurality of votes in the second round would be appointed to the Guardian Council. The rejected candidates were confirmed retroactively on a plurality of votes, with many of the reformist deputies turning in blank votes in protest. One candidate was even considered confirmed with less than a handful of votes out of 290. Two years later, in November 2003, the Head of the Judiciary proposed two other candidates, including a notorious mobster of the Helpers of the Party of God, who were rejected by the Majles for failing to obtain a majority. Majles Speaker Karrubi explained that the Leader had changed his mind on the subject. The Guardian Council did not insist on its newly acquired constitutional prerogative.

Yet the Guardian Council did not show the slightest interest in avoiding confrontation; it had simply chosen a different battlefield. The Council's function as the protector of the ideological foundations of the regime by now required not only filtering legislation but also controlling the elections politically. The September 2002 bill to restrict the supervisory power of the Guardian Council was predictably rejected by the Council. In March 2003, the Majles passed amendments to the electoral law with the same effect.[48] Khatami threatened to resign or put the bills to referendum. At this point, the Maslahat Council let its position be known by quadrupling the budget of the Guardian Council at a meeting on March 15. President Khatami and Majles Speaker Karrubi walked out of the meeting in protest.[49] That the Guardian Council would reject these attempts to restrict its power was a foregone conclusion. What the reformists had not expected, however, was that the Guardian Council would be fully supported by its sister Maslahat Council and given the budgetary means to punish them by depriving them of their parliamentary seats in the forthcoming elections of February 2004. The enlarged budget was used, among other things, to increase the number of Guardian Council inspectors and agents, reportedly to as many as 200,000 (Ehsani 2004). The Council made clear that "approbatory supervision" would henceforth mean practicing "continuous supervision" or vetting a candidate's competency at any time. President Khatami prepared to capitulate, telling the members of election supervisory boards on December 1, 2003, "Even if some renowned candidates are not nominated or qualified, the people should not withdraw. In this case we should look for a candidate whose thoughts are closest to our ideas and vote for him."[50] A month later, 3,600 of the 8,200 candidates were disqualified, including 80 incumbent members of the Majles.

The final and most resounding popular defeat of the reformist movement came in the presidential elections of June 2005. The reformist candidate, Khatami's lackluster Education Minister Mostafa Mo'in, was rejected by an unduly apprehensive Guardian Council but shrewdly reinstated by the Leader, who had a much better sense of popular opinion. He came in fifth in the first round and was eliminated.[51] The hardliner, Mahmud Ahmadinejad, who became the mayor of Tehran after the hardliners had won the municipal elections of 2003 in the first massive expression of disillusionment against the reformists, won the final round against Hashemi-Rafsanjani by a wide margin. The reformist Mo'in was just as much a child of the Islamic revolution as the hardliner Ahmadinejad. Both began as radical Islamic revolutionaries, committed to violence and wedded to ideology,[52] and their career paths diverged only in the mid-1990s. Quite a few students, presumably disillusioned with the reformists, had joined Ahmadinejad's campaign.

The ineffectiveness of the student organizations' anti-regime boycott of the presidential elections was demonstrated by the larger than expected turnout, even though the official 60 percent figure should be discounted. Finally, the Ahmadinejad vote also highlighted the reformists' alienation of the students and its failure to attract the urban poor. Trapped in their insider rhetoric and narrow vision and refusing to draw on the huge reservoir of secular professionals, the younger generation and the urban poor, Khatami and his reform movement came to naught also because of their failure to build bridges to these growing social forces that were easy potential constituencies.

Trapped in Their Own Rhetoric and Abandoned

The revolutionary rhetoric of the reformists and their profession of faith as followers of the line of the late Imam fell on deaf ears, except for those hardliners who resented this futile attempt to appropriate the revolutionary heritage they considered their own, and hastily closed two reformist newspapers. In truth, this was an overreaction on their part. Anyone who still cared for the revolutionary rhetoric would infinitely prefer to hear it from the mouth of Khomeini's true heir and successor. And the word was to come without delay. When casting his vote on February 20, the Supreme Jurist and Leader Ayatollah Sayyed 'Ali Khamenei said that he considered these elections particularly important "since you can see how those who fight the Islamic revolution and Iran, are trying to prevent the people from going to the polling booths."[53] After the withdrawal in protest of a further 1,179 candidates and the foregone victory of his hardliner followers in the elections that left at least eight persons dead in two reported clashes, he obliquely retorted to the reformists' admonitions by saying that the losers were "the United States, Zionism, and the enemies of the Iranian nation."[54] The reformists were thus hoisted on their own petard. After 4 years of insults and humiliation, witnessing the assassinations, near-assassinations, and imprisonment of their colleagues, they were still pathetically trapped in the net of their bombastic revolutionary discourse.

The reformist strike had begun in January by the members of the Majles who had been surprised by the rejection of their candidacy by the Guardian Council despite their impeccable revolutionary credentials. In the last week of January the Majles passed a bill "to solve the election crisis,"[55] which was promptly rejected by the Guardian Council. Interior Minister Musavi-Lari announced that he was not willing to hold the elections on schedule under the circumstances. The high point of the protest came in the first days of February after the Guardian Council, while restoring just under a third of some 3,600 (out of a total of 8,200) candidates it had originally rejected, not only refused to reinstate the 80 striking reformists but instead barred seven more of them. In response, 123 or 125 reformist Majles deputies handed in their resignations. Some 12 ministers and some 28 governors and deputy-ministers, representing the lay, "technocratic" second stratum in the administration, were also said to have submitted their resignations in sympathy. The main student organization, the Office for Consolidation of Unity (*daftar-e tahkim-e vahdat*), by contrast, kept its distance because the students had been badly let down by the President and the reformists during their prolonged sporadic protests through the summer of 2003, and only one group of students decided to support the striking Majles reformists at the last minute on February 3. On February 11, in the speech marking the twenty-fifth anniversary of the Islamic revolution, President Khatami let down his Interior Ministry and cabinet, and capitulated to the Leader, confirming that the elections would take place on schedule. This was yet another instance of the President's caving in rather than standing firm and provoking a constitutional crisis that might have been resolved by some concessions to the reformists, or by the dismissal and jailing of the President and the Interior Minister; Musavi-Lari went along with the elections, and nothing further was heard of the resignation of the cabinet ministers and provincial governors. The only deputy whose resignation was accepted happened to be a woman, Ms. Fatema Haqiqatju; the rest were said to require a case-by-case hearing and a vote by the Majles. These reformists thus continued to receive their paychecks until the expiration of their terms.

With their shoes piled up in the corner of the carpet for an extra cozy sit-in, the uncouth reformists, whose tieless white shirts and inelegant suits evoke Marx and Weber's contemptuous term "petty bourgeois" (*Spießburger*), gathered to protest their treatment by the clerical elite. President Khatami stayed away from the gathering in his elegant clerical attire, cutting a truly tragic figure. Mohsen Kadivar, the reformist cleric who had been jailed for over a year for writing an erudite refutation of Khomeini's theory of the Mandate of the Jurist, called on him to resign rather than accept an unfair election. More poignantly, in a letter urging the striking parliamentarians to push for a new constitution, the jailed reformist, Hashem Aghajari, aptly referred to the "Tragedy of Khatami"[56] (figure 5.2).

FIGURE 5.2 Pro-reform lawmakers listen to an address during a sit-in to protest the disqualifications from seeking election of over 3,000 of the 8,200 people, including more than 80 sitting lawmakers, by the hard-line Guardian Council in Tehran, Monday, January 19, 2004. (AP Photo/Vahid Salemi)

He was referring to the destruction of the "smiling Sayyed" (*sayyed-e khandān*), elected President in 1997 and 2001, by the ruthless Ayatollah, selected by his clerical colleagues as the Leader and Khomeini's successor. This destruction was already complete in 2000. It came in the spring and summer of 2000, at the very time of the astonishing defeat of the pro-clerical candidates in the national elections of the Sixth Majles, with the Leader's several deadly strikes: the almost successful assassination of the President's most important reformist aide, the clampdown on the pro-President reformist press, and, above all, his "governmental order" to the newly elected reformist Majles to stop its debate on the press law in August 2000. Khamenei embraced the President after each strike, and with each embrace came his affirmation that Khatami is one of us. Khatami did not have the courage to push him away and say he was *not* one of them. From then on, Khamenei knew he could do anything he wanted with the smiling Sayyed. Khatami's maudlin speech for Nawruz 1380/March 2001, which was read by many as his intention to quit, was that of a defeated man and reflected his sense that he did not have the strength to stand up to the Supreme Jurist and the price of his clinging to presidential power would be capitulation and further humiliation. The defeat of President Khatami and his reform movement and a hardliner takeover were foregone conclusions. Khatami's second landslide victory in the presidential elections of June 2001, when he won 77 percent of the popular vote, running against nine other candidates, only delayed the realization of true defeat.[57] The electorate still had faith in him, but massive disillusionment soon followed. The reformists were soundly defeated in the local elections of 2003, which delivered Tehran to Ahmadinejad, the national elections of 2004, in which the hardliners won the majority of seats in the Majles, and the presidential elections of 2005, in which Ahmadinejad was elected.

The analysis of the constitutional politics of the Islamic Republic from 1997 to 2005 demonstrates that the contradictions between two heterogeneous principles of the Constitution of 1979—namely, theocratic government and participatory representative government—can explain the confrontation between the Leader, or clerical monarch, and the President. The Leader stood for the first principle and aligned behind him were the conservative clerics who came to power as a result of the Islamic revolution and are in control of the revolution-generated system of collective rule by clerical councils, foundations (*bonyāds*), and foundation-supported unofficial groups, including the thuggish Helpers of the Party of God, the Judiciary, and the commanders of the Revolutionary Guards and its Mobilization Corps. The President stood for the second principle, which was fused in his new political discourse with the rule of law, democratic participation and civil society. This principle was increasingly referred to as the "republicanism" of the IRI in contrast to its "Islamicness." Behind him stood the technocrats for reconstruction, the reformist and excluded clerics, and the disenfranchised middle classes. The playing field was steeply sloped against the President and his supporters, given the Constitution and the rhetoric of the Islamic revolution. The reformists either made the tactical mistake of thinking they could appropriate the rhetoric of the Islamic revolution, or much more likely, did not have the courage to dissociate themselves from it because they were afraid of being called traitors. Either way, these good children of Khomeini's revolution lost the power struggle for reform.

6

Social and Political Consequences of the Integrative Revolution

THE INTEGRATIVE REVOLUTION IS AN EXPLOSION of political mobilization and participation. When the revolutionary power struggle comes to an end, participation is typically rolled back, but the social base of the political regime is (considerably) enlarged. This happened with the French and Russian revolutions as well as those of Mexico and China. Revolutions result in the displacement of one ruling class by another. One of the most important consequences of revolutions is the generation of a new political class consisting of a narrower ruling stratum and a much broader second stratum in charge of administration and political mobilization.[1] The process of the formation of the second stratum of the new political class takes at least a generation to unfold. The integrative impact of the revolution goes far beyond the circulation of elites, and changes the structure of society. This involves the integration of small towns on the periphery of Iranian society, and of the upwardly mobile section of the population, such as women and men who acquire higher education for the first time in their families. Social integration, however, does not automatically mean political participation. In fact, the formation of a new political class is conditional upon the exclusion of significant sectors of society.

Iran's New Political Class

Revolution changes the political order and the structure of the political community. The unsettled nature of the post-revolutionary political order expands competition for positions of power and entry into the second stratum. The 1979 moderates were ousted by the radicals by the end of that year, and the pragmatists replaced the radicals in Hashemi-Rafsanjani's administration, and the exclusion of the radicals was completed by the emergent hardliner faction in the early 1990s. The same instability is reflected in the high turnover of new deputies in the seven post-revolution parliaments, which parallels the high turnover of Jacobin deputies in the revolutionary assemblies after the French revolution.[2] The competition for entry into the new political class through the Majles provides a useful starting point for studying its gradual formation. Table 6.1 shows the turnover of Majles deputies in the Islamic Republic of Iran (IRI), both during the revolutionary decade and in the post-revolutionary Iran of Khomeini's successors.

In the past three decades, there has been a continual high turnover of Majles deputies. Consistently over 50 percent of the deputies are elected to parliament for the first time. This means that some 150 persons are recruited into the top

TABLE 6.1   Distribution of the Members of the Islamic Consultative Assembly (Majles)

Session of the Majles	1	2	3	4	5	6	7	8
Year of election	1980	1984	1988	1992	1996	2000	2004	2008[a]
Actual number of MPs	327[1]	277[1]	278[1]	268	265	297[1]	285[1]	285
First-time MPs	327	171	153	162	142	190	159	152
As (%) of total[2]	(100%)	(62%)	(55%)	(60%)	(54%)	(64%)	(56%)	(53%)
Gender								
Male	323	273	274	259	252	284	272	277
Female	4	4	4	9	13	13	13	8
Status								
Clerical	161	149	80	63	53	37	43	44
As (%) of total[2]	(49%)	(54%)	(29%)	(25%)	(20%)	(12%)	(15%)	(15%)
Lay	156	124	194	205	212	260	242	241
With some formal religious education	49	26	32	23	32	16	26	11

(continued)

TABLE 6.1   (continued)

Session of the Majles	1	2	3	4	5	6	7	8
Year of election	1980	1984	1988	1992	1996	2000	2004	2008[a]
Place of Birth[3]								
Cities	123	90	78	93	83	103	117	107
Small towns	147	150	161	122	113	176	137	155
As (%) of total[2]	(45%)	(54%)	(58%)	(46%)	(43%)	(59%)	(48%)	(54%)
Villages	50	35	45	45	67	18	18	21
Holy cities of Iraq	7	2	4	4	2	0	0	2
Education[4]								
High School or less	23	20	31	17	4	11	4	0
Bachelor degrees and diplomas	109	103	146	109	91	101	76	74
Graduate degrees	195	154	101	68	99	166	157	169

Sources: Āshenā'i bā Majles-e shurā-ye eslāmi, Tehran: Majles Public Relations Office, 1982/1361; *Mo'arefi-ye nemāyandegan-e Majles-e shurā-ye eslami,* Tehran: Majles Public Relations Office, 2000/1378 for the first five sessions and subsequent ones for sessions 6, 7, and 8. Compiled by Majid Mohammadi, except for session 7, which was added subsequently.

[1]Article 64 of the 1979 Constitution set the number of MPs at 270, providing for an increase of up to 20 every 10 years. The number was increased to 290 for the Sixth Majles. The actual numbers may be higher as they include the replacements for MPs who die or resign. The number for the first Majles is quite high because of the replacements for the MPs killed in the June 27, 1980 (Tir 7, 1359) bombing in the Islamic Republic Party headquarters in Tehran and the Iran–Iraq war. The deputies elected in the interim by-elections are included. One MP died in 2008 without assuming his seat and is excluded from the statistics.

[2]The significant trends are highlighted by the selective addition of percentages in these three rows.

[3]Population centers with less than 5000 people are considered villages; population centers with more than 100,000 people before the 1990s and more than 200,000 people after 2000 as well as provincial capitals are considered cities.

[4]Clerical degrees are also included for the first three sessions. The system of equivalence between clerical and secular degrees used by the Iranian Ministry of Sciences and Higher Education is also adopted here. A small number of MPs don't appear to have supplied information on their level of education.

political elite of the IRI via the Majles once every 4 years. The process is highly competitive, as the number of candidates is very large, but with the exception of a handful of deputies representing religious minorities and very few other representatives, this political elite is recruited from the ranks of those with revolutionary careers. The two other significant trends are highlighted by adding percentages to the actual numbers. There is a predictable decline in the number of clerics from 50 percent in the first two Majleses under Khomeini to about 15 percent in the 2000s. There is also a predictable opening of the political class beyond the numerically small group of clerics, who were the primary carriers of Khomeini's Islamic revolution, to the massive body of his lay supporters. But the most telling proof of the integrative dimension of the Islamic revolution is the overrepresentation of deputies born in small towns. The proportion of Majles deputies from small towns has fluctuated around 50 percent, a remarkable index of integration as less than 20 percent of Iran's population lives in small towns. The Islamic revolution has thus opened political careers to the children of the revolution from small towns on a significant scale.

Villages, where one-third of the population of Iran still lives, were better represented in the 1980s and 1990s (15% of deputies) but are the birth place of only 6 percent of the members of parliament (MPs) in the current decade. The representation of women, by contrast, shows a modest gain after the death of the patriarch of the Islamic revolution, tripling to just over 4 percent by 2000. With regard to the highest level of education attained by the MPs, there is a decline in the number of MPs who did not finish high school, roughly in line with the trend in the general population. The proportion of MPs with graduate degrees, on the other hand, dropped significantly in the late 1980s and 1990s to return to the level of the first two Majleses of the early 1980s. The decline represents the influx of the lay revolutionaries into the political class, for which the clerics shifting to other positions in 1988 made room. The restoration to the earlier level after 2000 in part reflects the rising level of education in the general population, but should mainly be attributed to the requirement of a higher degree for promotion in civil service extended to most revolutionary organizations in Hashemi-Rafsanjani's centralization endeavor. The elevation of the educational level of the new political class in the 2000s is thus the result of the intimidation of professors by diploma-seekers from the ranks of the revolutionaries, who were required to get grades for promotion in various organizations according to the government's bureaucratic scale, as much as genuine part-time study in the 1990s.

The composition of the new political class in the process of formation can be studied from the available occupational data on the Majles deputies. A

TABLE 6.2 Prior Occupations and Careers of the Majles Deputies after Khomeini

Session of the Majles	1	4	5	6	7	8
Year of Election	1980	1992	1996	2000	2004	2008
Education and teachers	127	47	33	52	74	79
As (%) of total [1]	(39%)	(18%)	(23%)	(18%)	(25%)	(28%)
Clerical professors and seminarians	101	29	15	9	14	12
As (%) of total [1]	(31%)	(11%)	(6%)	(3%)	(5%)	(4%)
Medical and other professionals	35	14	16	25	18	18
Nonmedical		24	0	1	1	2	2
Agriculture	13	1	0	0	0	0
The Bazaar	5	1	0	0	0	0
Workers	2	0	1	0	0	1
Private sector managers	1	4	3	4	3	3
Public and *bonyad* managers	1	3	6	9	6	8
Second stratum	31	156	193	195	171	161
As (%) of total [1]	(9%)	(61%)	(72%)	(66%)	(59%)	(56%)
Civil state employees	11	78	102	98	101	77
Local administration	—	19	19	29	16	27
Military and security	7	37	53	45	24	35
As (%) of total [1]	(2%)	(14%)	(20%)	(15%)	(8%)	(12%)
Judiciary	11	15	11	16	15	16
Leadership personnel	2	7	8	7	8	6
Other (including the press)	11	1	2	3	6	3
Total	327	256[1]	269	297	292	285

Sources: Āshenā'i bā Majles-e shurā-ye eslāmi, Tehran: Majles Public Relations Office, 1982/1361; *Mo'arefi-ye nemāyandegan-e Majles-e shurā-ye eslami,* Tehran: Majles Public Relations Office, 2000/1378 for the first five sessions and subsequent ones for sessions 6, 7, and 8.

[1]The significant trends are highlighted by the selective addition of percentages in these four rows.

[2]Occupational data on the 12 interim MPs in the fourth Majles are not available. The slight discrepancy in the total number of MPs for the fifth and seventh Majles in this Table and Table 6.1 is due to the addition of occupational data for the MPs elected in by-elections. The total for the first Majles in explained in Note 1 to Table 6.1.

remarkable profile of the new political class since the revolution emerges and is summarized in table 6.2.

Although the table depicts as much differentiation as possible among the children of the revolution, these differences are superficial and mask a fundamental unity of outlook. Teachers and university professors are in one category, but are separated from those in the national educational administration who are classified with the other "state civil employees." The latter category draws its members overwhelmingly from the bureaucracy of the revolutionary mobilizational structures such as the Jihad for Reconstruction. Those in local government have also typically been involved in these structures. Medical doctors and surgeons are also separated from the state employees, though the majority of them are in the public sector and universities.[3] It would also be misleading to assume that they represent the medical profession, many of whose prominent members have private practices and, at least in Tehran, often seek to emphasize their distinctness from the Islamic elite by wearing Western ties. Last but not least, the religious teachers and functionaries at the time of their election are separated from clerics who were either revolutionary or regular judges and are entered as "Judges," or representatives of the Leader in various organizations, or "political-ideological commissars" and commanders of the Revolutionary Guards who are accordingly classified in the "Military and Security" category. This seems justifiable as these clerics certainly do not represent the clerics who seek to preserve something of the traditional independence of the Shi'ite hierocracy, and its religious institutions of learning are subjected to the discipline of the Special Court for Clergy and other governmental agencies.

The startling evidence of the formation of a new political class is that over 60 percent of the MPs in the 1990s and 2000s were recruited directly from its second stratum, having served in the administrative cadre of the revolutionary and developmental administration, military, mobilizational and security services, and the Leader's clerical control agency. A further 25 percent or more consist of teachers and university professors employed in the national educational system, and medical doctors and surgeons in government hospitals and medical schools. This persistent representation of the intelligentsia is a significant feature of the new political class. The number of clerical Majles deputies had already dropped from 50 percent in the early 1980s to about 15 percent in the 2000s; however, there was also a change in the kind of cleric who sits in the Majles. The proportion of clerics in religious functions, including religious learning, drops from two-thirds (a third of the total MPs) in the first Majles to about a third (5% or less of the total MPs) in the 2000s. This means that the majority of the clerical deputies have had political careers as revolutionary judges, political-ideological commissars, and Islamic Revolutionary Guards Corps (IRGC) commanders or the Leader's agents, whereas only a minority of them remain religious teachers and prayer leaders.[4]

However, some categories had no representation in 2000, showing the strict limits to the integrative revolution in terms of actual political participation. Three very significant social groups, represented by occupations in agriculture, the bazaar, and organized workers, modestly represented in the First Majles of 1980, almost disappear in the 1990s and completely disappear in the 2000s. This shrieking silence means the complete exclusion of the bazaar association and guilds as well as workers' unions from the new political regime.

The circulation of the second stratum extends beyond the Majles into the administrative elite in post-Khomeini Iran, contrasting sharply with the remarkable stability of the top circle of the clerical ruling elite. The excluded radicals of the early 1990s turned reformists displaced the hardliners under Khatami in 1997, and a new group of hardliners displaced the reformists under Ahmadinejad in 2005. According to Mostafa Tajzadeh, Khatami's Deputy-Minister of the Interior for Political Affairs from 1997 to 2001, who presided over his distribution of the spoils of office, Khatami replaced almost all provincial governors (*ostāndār*s) and city administrators (*farmāndār*s) as well as a large number of district administrators (*bakhshdār*s). The sociopolitical background of the new administrators was completely different from those who replaced them in 2005. Tajzadeh later said: "We drew personnel mostly from the Ministry of Education; Ahmadinejad is bringing people with security and military backgrounds."[5] Ahmadinejad also brought in new men who were already feeding off the public trough, but this time in military (IRGC and Basij) and security services. He carried out the most drastic circulation of the administrative elite and low-level functionaries by systematically changing the heads of all sections of the central as well as local governmental bureaucracy. In provincial and local government, according to one account, he replaced almost all 30 provincial governors, some 290 of 340 city administrators, and about a third of the 800 district administrators.[6] Ahmadinejad also recalled more than 40 ambassadors and replaced the top management of the banks and, before long, forced the governor of the Central Bank to resign.[7] The one place he failed to deliver to his men was the Oil Ministry. He had slated 400 officials in the national oil industry for dismissal, but failed in this attempt, and his candidates for Oil Minister were repeatedly rejected by the Majles.

The circulation of elites and mobility into the second stratum are by no means confined to government bureaucracy. A very different indicator of the considerable enlargement of the political community is the change in the visibility of new names among the new elite and the second stratum. The system of registration of people with a first and a last name was introduced in the period of state-building and modernization of Reza Shah in the late 1920s and 1930s. The literate people in the cities chose last names for themselves, but among the lower classes in the cities and the peasants, the officials issuing them national identity cards often assigned them new names.[8] A systematic study of the shift in the pattern of names could demonstrate the extent of upward social mobility that resulted from the enlargement of the political society after the revolution, but a few examples can be offered impressionistically. Akbar Hashemi-Rafsanjani, the former President and current chairman of both the Maslahat Council and the Assembly of Leadership Experts, has written about how he was too poor to take the infrequent bus from his village of Bahraman, near the southeastern town of Rafsanjan, and rode on a donkey to the provincial capital and took a bus from there to Qom to study at a seminary. While a seminarian in Qom, he dropped the reference to his native village in his name, replacing Bahramani by Rafsanjani.[9] The former Prosecutor General (who took charge of the students who took over the American embassy in 1979) is from the small town of Kho'in, but the suffix of his name, Kho'ini-ha, making it a plural, is very bizarre. Another member of the clerical elite, Hasan Ruhani, former Deputy Majles Speaker who took charge of Iran's nuclear negotiations until August 2005, was born Hasan Fereydun, and changed his last name to the more respectable-sounding Ruhani (meaning man of religion; literally, spiritual). Former Minister of Intelligence and judge of the Special Court from Clerics was born Mohammad Darunparvar, and changed his last name to Mohammadi-nik. He was from the area around the shrine of Shah 'Abd al-'Azim in Ray (whose administrator he became after being pushed out of office) and became known as Sha[h'a]bdbol'azimi. Since that sounded low class, he decided to emphasize that he was a native of Ray and finally settled for Mohammad Mohammadi Rayshahri.[10] The same pattern of name changes fits many upwardly mobile members of the lay second stratum. The leading Islamic, later reformist, intellectual, 'Abdalkarim Sorush, chose a new first and last name for himself. The last name in his birth certificate is Hajj-Faraj-Dabbagh—which means Hajji Faraj, the tanner; the registering official must have written down the title Hajji and the first name, Faraj, as well as his father's or grandfather's profession, the tanner, all in the slot for the last name.[11] Mostafa Aqa-Mir-Salim, Minister of Culture and Islamic Guidance (1992–1997) and advisor to the Leader, greatly dignified his name by dropping the redundant *āqā* (Mr.), which might have been a similar scribal intrusion from an earlier generation. Mahmud Ahmadinejad's father, like another family of humble craftsmen in his native small dusty desert town of Aradan, which had changed its name from Kaffash (cobbler) to Pezesh-kpur (physician's son), had changed the family name from Sabbaghian (dyer) to Ahmadinejad (of the Ahmadi race); as President, Ahmadinejad declared a similar symbolic upgrading name change for at least one modest small town, changing the undignified name of Ghavbandan (cow-yoking) to Parsian (Persians).[12]

Social Stratification and Economic Inequality

The post-revolution enlargement of the political society went hand in hand with its decapitation, as most of the political elite of the Shah's regime and the rich industrialists and entrepreneurs went into exile. This initial leveling eroded before long. Post-revolutionary Iran can be taken as yet another example of the persistence of durable inequalities. This does not mean, however, an unchanging social structure. In the IRI, there is little long-term leveling but very considerable circulation of elites and social mobility, and a basic shift in the political basis of economic stratification.

Like most Islamic societies, Iran did not have a rigid system of social strati-fication based on status honor, but a relatively open one based primarily on access to political power. With the change of political regime after the revo-lution came a completely new power structure and a new pattern of social stratification based on the Shi'ite religious hierarchy. In the mainstream of Islam—Sunni Islam—the differentiation of the religious elite is rather weak and de facto. But in the Shi'ite branch of Islam, including the Iranians, cler-ical authority is well differentiated and strongly established as a hierocracy.

The Islamic revolution established a hybrid political regime, with an elected parliament and President, but one subordinated to clerical authority—a theocratic republic. Over time, clerical authority enhanced its control over the state, creating a new system of social stratification based on its control of political power. The country is divided into a small clerical elite of religious jurists (*mojtaheds*), which maintains its power through the system of conciliar, collective rule and is supported by a second stratum of lay civil servants in control of the bureaucratic administration, and a huge lay population, which has no share of political power but votes once a year for the President or the Majles or the local and municipal councils. Clerical families made up a component of the second stratum in the first two decades after the revolution. Access to political power through such family connections and nepotism is decisive and is a new basis for the new system of social stratification in Iran. The same is true of the military-intelligence second stratum whose economic empire is based on the IRGC.

Economic inequality in Iran before the beginning of industrialization in the 1960s was high, as it is in most predominantly agrarian, underdeveloped economies with large absentee landlords. According to one estimate by Iran's Central Bank for the urban areas in 1960, the Gini coefficient, the most common index of inequality in income distribution, was quite high. Inequality typically increased with rapid capitalist industrialization in the next decade and a half.[13] Massive confiscation of industries and banks after the Islamic revolution of 1979 reduced economic inequality but only back to the 1960 level. How can the quick erosion of the revolutionary leveling of 1979 be explained?

In addition to political connections, there is also an economic basis for social stratification. As in other Middle Eastern countries, government dominates the economy, and the beneficiaries of government contracts and concessions constitute a "state bourgeoisie," which owes its economic power and social rank to its ties with the state. In Iran, the *bonyāds*, which control over 40 percent of the economy, favored their own network of contractors and suppliers. These foundations, mostly run by clerics who are not responsible to government but answer only to the Leader of the Islamic Republic who appoints them on a personal basis, also create a secondary basis for rising post-revolutionary inequality and social stratification. Once again, clerical families and their relatives are prominent among the beneficiaries and contractors of these economic foundations and among government contractors. The term *āqā zādehgān* (sons of masters) was coined to refer to the new politicoeconomic elite consisting of the families of the clerical upper stratum. The IRGC military-industrial complex also has its own contractors and a host of satellite companies and partners that sustain a segment of the state bourgeoisie that has been getting rich fast. None of these economic bases, however, can be considered independent of political power but, on the contrary, need political ties to maintain their restrictive appropriation of economic opportunities. Iran's foreign policy makers wish to join the World Trade Organization to improve the country's international standing—a move that is shortsightedly opposed by the United States.[14] As Richard Haas, Middle East advisor to President George H.W. Bush and Colin Powell knew well, admitting Iran to the WTO would amount to a gift of a "Trojan horse," as it would erode an important economic base of the regime.[15]

The consolidation of the state-dependent network of military-industrial-commercial complex points to another remarkable and totally unexpected consequence of the Islamic revolution: the political disenfranchisement and economic marginalization of the bazaar. The sharp economic decline of the bazaar is remarkable considering the immense support it gave to Khomeini's revolutionary movement. It is also in stark contradiction to the Marxist theories of revolution, which see revolutions as the historic mission of social classes, either singly or in coalition with groups who share their interests.

Threatened by the Shah's modernization and economic development projects, the bazaar of Tehran played a very important role in the Islamic revolution of 1979 and was considered by some to be the eye of the storm, while others saw the revolution itself as the latest manifestation of the mosque-bazaar alliance that underlay the protest movements in Iran since the closing decade of the nineteenth century.[16] The Marxists would expect it to dominate a new petty-bourgeois post-revolution economic order and political regime. Yet the Islamic revolution has paradoxically led to the great weakening, if not destruction, of the bazaar as an autonomous economic community, making it hopelessly dependent on a variety of external state-controlled or state-regulated networks. Contrary to expectation, the revolutionary state infiltrated the bazaar and coopted its Islamic activists, who become incorporated into the political elite and set up a system of rent-seeking and distribution of concessions through government licensing. Revolutionary populism and the war economy intensified this infiltration, destroyed the old system of self-governance through communal trust and stable patterns of exchange, and shifted the nodes of the exchange networks outside the bazaar and into the military-industrial-commercial complex, which was externally controlled by the hydra-headed state and ultimately its Leader.

Growing regulations and the increasingly politically motivated "special licenses" for imports and distribution and the enormous growth of the politically controlled economic foundations (bonyāds) created from the confiscated enterprises reduced the economic importance of the bazaar and its autonomy. The bazaar's autonomy through cooperative hierarchy was replaced by a mode of governance through a state-manipulated coercive hierarchy linked to rent distribution and an overregulated market. As a result, the bazaar has lost its capacity for collective action and political mobilization, and currently remains largely passive despite its increasing alienation from the state.[17] Nevertheless, the bazaar has not given up its memory of heroic strikes despite its marginalization. In one rare instance in October 2008, the coordinated bazaar strikes in Isfahan, Tehran, and several other cities forced the government of Ahmadinejad to suspend the 3 percent value-added tax it had introduced for a year.[18]

Urbanization and Migration

Revolution and war produce social dislocation and mobilization. In the first years of the Islamic revolution, 1979–1982, there was an explosive geographic expansion of cities that followed the extensive land seizure by squatters and the so-called "revolutionary housing." Tehran doubled its size to 550 square kilometers, and Ahwaz tripled it to 75. The population of Karaj, Tehran's satellite city to the west where much land was seized by squatters, increased more than fourfold in a decade, from 138,000 in 1976 to 612,000 in 1986.[19] War was an even more powerful force for social dislocation and similarly created the urgent need for social and national reintegration. The population of the small town of Ramhormoz in Khuzestan near the Iraqi front typically doubled between 1980 and 1982, or nearly so, as a result of the influx of war refugees.[20] In 1990, two years after the end of the war with Iraq, there were still about one million displaced people in Khuzestan alone. The Soviet occupation and war added an even larger number of Afghan refugees to the mobile population. The population of Mashhad, partly because of the influx of Afghan refugees, more than doubled in a decade.[21] Revolution and war thus greatly accelerated the processes of internal migration and urbanization. According to the census data, by the end of 1996, about 25 percent of the entire population had migrated internally since the revolution. Migration slowed down considerably in the decade following the revolution and war (table 6.3).

Urbanization has been a powerful engine of social and political change throughout the Middle East since 1945, and can be considered a major precondition of the Islamic revolution of 1979 in Iran and, more generally, of the resurgence of Islam. The pace of urbanization was accelerated after the revolution, and its pattern was definitely affected by the integrative revolution (table 6.4).

Not only has the urban population grown from under a half to two-thirds of the total since the revolution, but most of that growth has taken place in

TABLE 6.3   Internal Migration in Two Decades after the Revolution

Year	Number of Migrants[1] (in thousands)	Total Population (in thousands)	Migrants as % of Population
1986	5,957	49,445	12
1996	8,719	60,055	14.5
2006	4,774	70,496	7

Source: Iran's National Census of Population and Housing 1375 and 1385 as reported in *Sālmāna-ye āmāri (Statistical Yearbook), 1365* [1986–7], 72; *1376* [1997–8], 69; and the website of the Statistical Office for the 2006 figure.

[1]Persons who migrated during the 10 years preceding the census.

cities with populations of between 5000 and 1,000,000, which now account for 69 percent of the urban population, as compared to 56 percent before the revolution. The integrative revolution has thus left its unmistakable mark on the pattern of distribution of the population in favor of smaller cities in this period of rapid urbanization. Small towns grow faster than larger ones as they become integrated into the national economy and polity. The preponderance of Tehran in the urban population is thus reduced considerably and that of other metropolitan cities slightly. This trend is atypical for developing countries and must be attributed to the impact of the integrative revolution in Iran.

Employment in the public sector provided the main pathway to upward social mobility in small towns. As the economy declined and the private sector shrank after the revolution, the public sector provided 43 percent of urban employment of 2.6 million jobs in 1986. The Basij militia also recruited heavily in urban areas among recent migrants. With the growth of the size of the state during Rafsanjani's postwar reconstruction, the number of public sector jobs in urban areas increased to 3.3 million, still providing 37 percent of the jobs in urban areas in 1996, despite the postwar growth of the private sector.[22] Together with the massive expansion of higher education and growth of university campuses in many cities, this expanding public employment created a new provincial middle class that immediately sought a voice in national politics.

The contrast between the social background of the clerical elite and the second stratum of the IRI and that of the political elite of Iran before the revolution is striking proof of the integrative revolution. Perhaps the best

TABLE 6.4   Urban Population during the Three Decades after the Revolution

Year	Urban/Total (in thousands)	Urban as % of Total	Distribution of the Urban Population in %		
			Tehran and Karaj	Other Metropolitan Areas[1]	Rest
1976	15,855/33,709	47%	29.5%	14.9%	55.6%
1986	26,845/49,495	54%	24.8%	16%[2]	59.2%
1996	36,818/60,055	61%	21%	14.6%	64.4%
2006	48,260/70,496	68%	17.6%	13.7%	68.7%

Source: Iran's National Census of Population and Housing data as reported in Sālmāna-ye āmāri (Statistical Yearbook), 1385 [2006–2007], 107–8.

[1]The four other cities with populations of over one million by 1996.

[2]With adjustment for the influx of the Afghan and Iraq war refugees into Mashhad and Shiraz, respectively, the downward trend would probably be continuous.

indicator of the integrative dimension of the Islamic revolution is the preponderance of those born in small towns among the Majles deputies since the revolution. They constituted the majority of the MPs in all but the two parliaments of the 1990s, with a further 15 percent of the MPs born in villages.

Social Mobility through Education and the Mobilization of Women

Another important prerevolutionary trend that was greatly accelerated during post-revolutionary reconstruction and acted as a powerful agent of social mobility was the expansion of higher education. After the Cultural Revolution and dismal shrinkage of their absolute and relative size in the 1980s, the universities expanded rapidly during Hashemi-Rafsanjani's presidency, quickly surpassing the prerevolution level both in absolute terms and relative to the size of Iran's population. The expansion continued under Khatami and beyond (table 6.5).

Women were conspicuous in the revolutionary mobilization against the Shah. After bringing them out in droves to demonstrate against the Shah and contribute to the success of the revolution, Khomeini thanked them and praised the model Islamic woman, which meant sending them back home

TABLE 6.5   Number of Students in Institutions of Higher Education in Iran
in thousands

Academic Year	Total	Per 1000 of Population	Regular[1]	Women	Open[2]	Women
[Prerevolution]						
1978–1979	234	7	234	—		
[Khomeini]						
1983–1984	151	4	151	45 (30%)	—	—
1986–1987	203	4	203	59 (29%)	[6][2]	[3(45%)][2]
[Hashemi-Rafsanjani]						
1991–1992	603	11	359	122 (34%)	244	n.a.
1996–1997	1,209	20	595	217 (36%)	631	251 (41%)
[Khatami]						
1999–2000	1,403	23	703	308 (44%)	726	337 (46%)
2004–2005	2,126	32	1,028	554 (54%)	1,098	530 (48%)
[Ahmadinejad]						
2005–2006	2,398	35	1,201	657 (55%)	1,198	575 (48%)

Source: Sālmāna-ye āmāri (Statistical Yearbook), 1362 [1983–84], 42, 91, 104, 111;
1372 [1993–94], 473; 1381 [2002–02], 48–49, 568, 575; 1984 [2004–05],
72–73, 573, 581–82.

[1]Including universities and teacher training colleges.
[2]The Islamic Open University *(Dāneshgāh-e Āzād-e Eslāmi)* began to admit a small number of students beginning in 1983. The figures for 1986–1987 are those admitted and not the total enrollment.

to the kitchen. The percentage of women in the active labor force dropped from the prerevolution 13 percent to about 8 percent in the first decade after the revolution, and did not return to the prerevolution level until the end of 1990s.[23] Meanwhile, the number of women with higher education increased enormously, and in the 2000s they comprised the majority of the students in the institutions of higher education in Iran. Social norms changed somewhat, too, with the average marriage age for women increasing by four and three years in the rural and urban areas, respectively, to over 23 years by the time of

the last census in 2006.[24] The immense discrepancy between female employment opportunities, on the one hand, and the new educational achievements
of women and the accompanying rising professional expectations, on the
other, generated immense frustration among women.

Women's leaders and their advocacy groups and associations enthusias-
tically embraced activism in the public sphere after the *glasnost* in the late
1990s. Thirteen women were elected to the Majles in 1996 and 11 in 2000.[25]
The second highest vote-getters in Tehran in both elections were women's
advocates, Faezeh Hashemi, the President's daughter who promoted women's
sports and launched the reformist newspaper *Zan* (Woman) in 1998,[26] and
Jamileh Kadivar, who had been elected to Tehran's first Municipal Council
in 1999.[27] Although Khatami disappointed women by not appointing one as
a minister, a large number of women's NGOs were allowed to register and
operate. By 2000, there were 230 women's NGOs and two years later their
number reached 330.[28] The presence of women in the electoral campaigns
of the reformist presidential candidates in May and June 2009 was spectacular. They formed the Women's Movement Convergence and held debates
with the representatives of the four candidates to put women's rights on the
agenda. Zahra Rahnavard became the first woman in the history of the IRI to
campaign alongside her husband, Mir-Hossein Musavi, who was the leading
candidate and claimed victory. Women were most prominent in the demonstrations that followed to protest President Ahmadinejad's stealing of the
election in June and July.[29]

Consequences of the Iranian *Perestroika:* Provincial Autonomy, Local Politics, and Presidential Populism

Local politics, completely stifled during the half-century of state-building and
centralization under the Pahlavis, reemerged in a new form: no longer as politics of the notables but as middle-class politics. This was a major impact of the
integrative revolution deepened by the war with Iraq. The citizens of Ardabil
had distinguished themselves in the war and formed their own brigade, the
Abu'l-Fazl al'Abbās Brigade, and the bazaar of Ardabil had supported it with
a so-called Salavāt [benediction (of the Prophet)] Café. The merger of the
veterans and merchants in demanding provincial autonomy was consolidated
by setting up a Commission for the Pursuit of Problems of the Urban Region
of Ardabil in the office of the city's Friday prayer leader in February 1991.[30]
This first manifestation of the politics of the new provincial middle class

used the post-revolutionary public space, such as the mosque of the Ardabili residents in Tehran, to lobby members of the ruling elite born in the area. The Commission organized a seminar on the "Growth and Development of the Eastern Region of Azerbaijan" on 19 July, 1992, which was attended by some 200 area notables. Meanwhile, the President had been greeted during his visit to Ardabil in October 1991 with the chant, "Hashemi, Hashemi, by the soul of the Imam [Khomeini] [let] Ardabil be a province."[31] The three Majles deputies from Ardabil were naturally drawn in and were instrumental in obtaining the final vote from a Majles apprehensive about possible rioting early in 1993, but the Majles was not the primary arena of lobbying for provincial independence. Ardabil was thus separated from Eastern Azerbaijan to become a new province, with public celebrations preceding the final reading and approval of the pertinent bill in April 1993.

Although a similar, popularly orchestrated attempt to make Qazvin a new province independent of Zanjan narrowly failed in the summer of 1994, the resulting spontaneous riots that followed persuaded the Rafsanaji government to separate Qazvin administratively and attach it to Tehran. It eventually became a province on its own. Given the special importance of the shrine city of Qom in the theocratic republic, there was no need to carry out lobbying in the public space to acquire the same status, and it was done behind closed doors. In 1995, it was made a province by a government decree with the personal endorsement of the Leader.[32] The new province of Golestan followed, with Gorgan as its capital. The trend toward increasing local autonomy led by the provincial middle class culminated in the division of the province of Khorasan into three provinces in this decade. The price of real estate in Bojnurd, which became the capital of the new province of Northern Khorasan in 2005, jumped twenty-fold within a year.[33]

In July 2006 President Mohammad Khatami offered the following justification of his administration's policy of "development of non-governmental formations." Political organizations set up by governments were "like artificial flowers put in a vase without roots; whereas political organizations should come out of the context of society, resulting in political parties and more extensive political organizations with roots among the people of the country."[34] His claim to strengthen civil society and "non-governmental formations" is born out by the sixfold increase in the number of women's NGOs from 67 to over 480 during his two terms in office (1997–2005).[35] The truth is that the undeniable importance of the social roots of political organizations is no substitute for decisive political action. Khatami and the reformists in full control of the Majles between March and August 2000 missed the opportunity to challenge the Leader constitutionally, and with their submission to his order to stop debating the press law,[36] the possibility of irreversible democratization was foreclosed, and the civic associations he had planted indeed remained vulnerable like cut flowers in a vase. The Ahmadinejad administration has had no difficulty rolling back the gains of the civil society NGOs, and certainly their political participation and agency. Those associations that are permitted to remain active can do so only on the condition that their activities have no political implication. Women's activities have notably been targeted for suppression. One of the last peaceful demonstration in Tehran was to protest laws discriminatory to women on the occasion of the Day of Women's Solidarity (*hambastegi*) on June 12, 2006. It was broken up by the police who detained 70 women. The trial of five of them was scheduled for March 4, 2007, and on that day, the police arrested 28 other prominent women activists who were holding a silent protest.[37] No demonstration was allowed on the subsequent Day of Women's Solidarity in 2007, and the police arrested eight women leaders on June 12, 2008, to prevent any gathering.[38] The lasting effect of the *perestroika* was thus not the creation of a civil society independent of the state. It was something else.

Before that early moment of decisive defeat, however, Khatami had had the chance to carry out his key measure for political development. In February 1999, he finally carried out the elections of the local and provincial councils envisioned in the 1979 Constitution (Articles 7, 100–106). Indeed, provisions for local and provincial councils had also been made in the 1907 Supplementary Constitutional Law but were never carried out. In retrospect, the creation of the councils must be considered his single, most remarkable achievement in democratization.

Khatami has to share this credit with Hashemi-Rafsanjani under whom the Law of the Organization, Functions, and Elections of the Islamic Councils of the Country and the Election of Mayors had passed in June 1996, pursuant to which his cabinet had approved the executive regulations for the election of the councils in December 1996. The most significant feature of the 1996 Law was that it gave the village and municipal councils the power to elect the headmen and mayors, respectively. In 2002, the councils were reorganized into a hierarchy of district (*bakh*), town (*shahr*), urban region (*sharestān*), and high provincial (*ostān*) councils. There were to be some 8000 councilors in 919 cities and 107,000 of them in 33,857 villages.[39] The huge turn-out in the 1999 elections undoubtedly reflected the general enthusiasm for the fulfillment of the century-old aspiration to local self-government. President Khatami and the reformists were, however, not adequately organized to take advantage of this achievement. In fact, the second councils elections in February 2003 demonstrated the spectacular failure of Khatami and the reformists to maintain their control and were the first unmistakable signal of complete popular disenchantment with them. Outside of the major cities, the turnout was not all that low (about 50% for all of Iran), partly because the Ministry of the Interior had stood its ground and the candidates were not vetted by the Guardian Council, and quite a few reformists seem to have been elected in smaller places. But the drop in participation in the big cities was sharp, and with less than a third of voters turning out (the official breakdown of the Tehran vote has apparently never been made public) the Municipal Council of Tehran went entirely to the pro-Khamanei hardliners. As several people told a researcher, "what can we expect from local councilors, when even the President of the country is stymied from pursuing his agenda?"[40]

Ahmadinejad began his presidential campaign as the mayor of the capital, having formerly been the first governor of the newly created province of Ardabil, and before that the city administrator of Maku and Khoy in Western Azerbaijan. His attempt to appeal to the urban poor neglected by the reformists did not stop in the shantytowns surrounding Tehran but extended to the most remote towns and their rural hinterland. He had an instinctive sense of the integrative dimension of the Islamic revolution missing in others and made it the cornerstone of his popularity as Iran's ninth President. In the first 2 years of his presidency, he is said to have traveled to and given speeches in some 2000 towns in all 30 provinces of Iran while being filmed to fill the airtime on the national television with ample footage. He held his cabinet meetings away from the capital in some of these towns, making them into something of a roadshow government. He received millions of requests and petitions, and would make a big display of largesse by promising roads, bridges, sports facilities, and other amenities.[41] The biggest victim of Ahmadinejad's populism was the Plan Organization, the chief organ of Iran's developmental state since 1947, which was restored during Hashemi-Rafsanjani's first presidency but closed down by Ahmadinejad in late 2006. He has reportedly read the planners' drafts and tailored his generous theatrical handouts roughly in line with the regional developmental recommendations, their gross inefficiency notwithstanding.

Nevertheless, local autonomy is poorly served and largely subverted by the centralized control of resources by the developmental state and its bias.

It cannot be said that Khatami thought out his idea of political development through participation. In fact, in their typical inattention and disarray, the reformist Majles not only failed to nourish the councils, but removed what little financial autonomy the councils had enjoyed by giving the central government the power to set the rates for and collect the local taxes with the Tax Amalgamation Law of January 2003.[42] The councils thus provide a space for local debates and a basis for lobbying, but have very little power, as municipal administration is actually carried out by a parallel structure under the central control of the Ministry of the Interior. They are expected to provide the mayor with broad guidelines and principles of urban management. But they have no formal role in planning structures and processes, and developmental planning is completely out of their hands. The main planning bodies at the national level, at least until Ahmadinejad closed down the Management and Plan Organization late in 2006 and took development into his own hands, were that Management and Plan Organization and the Provincial Office of Development of the Ministry of Interior. At the critical provincial level, there is the Provincial Planning and Development Council for each province. It is chaired by the centrally appointed Provincial Governor and its members are drawn from the centrally controlled administrative structure. It includes only one representative of the High Provincial Council and two MPs without voting rights.[43]

President Ahmadinejad's populist rhetoric and verbal acceptance of many local developmental projects during cabinet meetings in provincial towns notwithstanding, his government introduced a bill to the Majlis in the summer of 2006 that shifted the vetting of the council candidates to the Guardian Council and gave the Interior Minister the power to veto council decisions, including the elections of mayors and headmen. It is therefore not too surprising that his supporters won less than 5 percent of the seats in the councils. The popular turn-out increased to 60 percent in the December 2006 elections, but the reformists could win only 4 of the 15 seats in the Municipal Council of Tehran, and did not do well in other major cities. Just as the results of the February 2003 elections can rightly be interpreted as a negative vote against the Khatami government, those of December 2006 reflected disaffection with Ahmadinejad's government. The hardliners who had split from Ahmadinejad's factions and independent candidates won the majority of council seats in roughly equal proportions.[44] In Tehran, Mohammad Baqer Qalibaf, the chief hardliner rival Ahmadinejad had sought to unseat, was re-elected mayor of Tehran. In short, just like Khatami's participation through empowerment of civil society, Ahmadinejad's populism has been subverted by the centralizing bias of the model of the developmental state they share.

With the election of local and municipal councils by Khatami in 1999, a new institutional arena was opened for local politics. The Majles was being increasingly blocked in national legislation and policies, and local lobbyists were quick in making the MPs spokespersons for their local constituencies. Some of the municipal councils of the metropolitan cities have been more assertive and carved a significant role for themselves in the planning process. The Municipal Councils of Tehran and Isfahan have developed long-term plans for their own cities. The Municipal Council of Tehran, furthermore, soon became a training ground for national politicians. It was from the Tehran Municipal Council that Sa'id Hajjarian engineered the landslide victory of the reformists in the Sixth Majles in 2000, and where he was tragically and almost fatally shot on the eve of Nawruz, years ago. The Council served as the springboard for President Ahmadinejad in 2005, and will probably do so for the present mayor of Tehran, Qalibaf, in the 2009 presidential election.[45]

Despite the centralist bias of the developmental state, be it the republican-reformist variant under Khatami or the populist-revolutionary one under Ahmadinejad, local politics in Iran has begun a new life that cannot easily be subjugated to central control. The elections of the local and municipal councils are relatively free, as the central government has neither the interest nor the knowledge to vet the candidates, except in Khuzestan, in which Arab ethnic separatists gained control of the councils, and possibly other provinces in which ethnic separatists present a threat. The councils have injected great vitality into local politics, and have become centers of local lobbying with connections to the Ministry of the Interior and the Majles. The local councils have had a major impact on the Majles and have turned it into a platform for the promotion of local interests. This somewhat unexpected result was facilitated by the presence of a large number of MPs from small towns, the fractured nature of parliamentary representation in the absence of political parties, which would presumably have national rather than local platforms, and the severe weakening of the Majles as the national legislature by the Guardian Council and the Maslahat Council. The factors also reinforced the trend toward increasing provincial autonomy.

Iran's Foreign Policy

From the Export of Revolution to Pragmatism

FOREIGN POLICY OF REVOLUTIONARY REGIMES is closely linked to their domestic politics, or more precisely to the stage of the revolution. It is closely tied to the struggle of the pragmatic against the radical elements in the revolutionary elite in the early stage, and against the hardliners later in the post-revolutionary period. The first major foreign policy in revolutionary Iran was the typical one for all revolutions: the choice between the export of revolution—in this case the spread of the Islamic revolution beyond Iran—and accommodation with the rest of the world. The presidency of Hashemi-Rafsanjani meant a victory for the pragmatists in foreign policy, with the Gulf War (1990–1991) in its early years as the decisive point of transition.[1] Revolutionary rhetoric, which persisted for three decades, dies even harder in foreign policy, and that is why it is important to examine in close detail the key period of transition to pragmatism in order to reveal its limits.

The Gulf War as a Turning Point

The ideology of revolution supplies a powerful stimulus for its expansion, and mass revolutionary participation creates the precondition for the export of revolution through mass military mobilization.[2] As far as the wars that follow revolutions are concerned, this is only one side of the story, however. Equally important is the misperception of the robustness of revolutionary regimes by

neighbors who see revolutionary anarchy as weakness and perceive an opportunity to extinguish it by force.[3] Although Iraq invaded Iran in 1980 with such
a typical misperception, provocation in the form of the radical rhetoric of the
Islamic revolution was certainly not lacking from the Iranian side. Indeed,
the 1979 Constitution of the Islamic Republic of Iran (IRI) declared in its
Preamble that "in the development of international relations, the Constitution will strive with other Islamic and popular movements to prepare the way
for the formation of a single world community... and to assure the continuation of the struggle for the liberation of all deprived and oppressed people
in the world." To this end, the "ideologically-oriented" (*maktabi*) army and
the Revolutionary Guards would not only protect the integrity of Iran but
also assume "the burden of ideological mission, meaning the Jihad to spread
the rule of the divine law throughout the world."[4] As Mohammad Javad
Larijani, the Islamic revolution's first theorist of international relations, put
it: "After the victory of the Islamic revolution in Iran... Iran became 'the
Mother of the Cities (*omm al-qorā*')'of the Abode of Islam.... According to
the theory of Mother of the Cities, export of revolution and the defense of
the Islamic Umma as a unified community (*wāhida*) is essentially engrained
in the prestige of the Mother of Cities."[5]

The moderates, Prime Minister Bazargan and President Bani-Sadr, and
their Foreign Ministers, Karim Sanjabi, Ebrahim Yazdi, and Sadeq Qotbzadeh,
were committed to international law and diplomacy, but could not prevent or
terminate the occupation of the American embassy and hostage-taking by the
radicals on November 4, 1979. The occupation came a week after Bazargan
met President Carter's national security advisor, Zbigniew Brzezinski, in
Algeria, and was planned as a symbolic gesture to last 48 hours.[6] Those two
days were, however, sufficient only to bring about Bazargan's resignation. To
settle scores with the Great Satan and prove it impotent, Khomeini endorsed
the continuation of the occupation of the American embassy. The legacy of the
constantly televised 444-day hostage crisis left an indelible mark of national
humiliation on the American collective psyche, permanently imprinted an
image of Iranians as reactionary fanatics, and continues to haunt U.S.–Iran
relations. It has impeded improved relations between the two countries at
significant junctures.

Export of the Islamic revolution became Iran's official foreign policy after
the ouster of Bani-Sadr when, in October 1981, the radical Foreign Minister,
Mir-Hossein Musavi, set up a committee to "determine the basis of the
foreign policy from an ideological perspective" and drew up a "plan for an

Islamic front" worldwide. An Islamic Revolutionary Council was established as an umbrella organization covering the Supreme Council of the Islamic Revolution in Iraq (SCIRI), the Islamic Revolution Movement of the Arabian Peninsula, and the Islamic Front for the Liberation of Bahrain (already involved in the attempted coup in Bahrain in December 1981), all linked to the Islamic liberation movement unit of the Revolutionary Guards.[7] The Revolutionary Guards went to Lebanon in 1982, while the Iranian forces pushed the Iraqi army behind the border on July 13, 1982, declaring Jerusalem via Baghdad as their final destination.[8] Traffic signs showing the direction of Jerusalem were posted. General Shirazi, commander of the ground forces, declared that the "Islamic combatants of Iran" would soon be praying with the oppressed Iraqi nation in Karbala and attempt to eliminate the Zionist regime and liberate Jerusalem. Thus, "God willing, the ground would be prepared for the appearance of Imam Mahdi, the Hidden Imam."[9]

The suicide truck bombing against the American and French contingents in Lebanon claimed 361 lives, including 258 Americans,[10] in October 1983, and multiple bombings took place in Kuwait in December.[11] The "human waves" tactics organized by the clerical commissars, using poorly armed or unarmed young men over mined fields ahead of the army, proved an inefficient means for defeating Iraq and exporting the Islamic revolution, however, and the commissars claiming the presence and even sighting of the Hidden Imam on the Iraqi front was no more effective.[12]

The 1980s secret arms deal with Israel and implicitly the United States followed an earlier "October Surprise" secret arms-for-hostages deal in 1979 between William Casey and the Iranians through Israeli mediations.[13] Iran bought over $500 million worth of arms from Israel between 1980 and 1983, but despite the crash of an Argentine airplane carrying arms near the Soviet–Turkish border in July 1981, the deals were kept secret.[14] In another secret arms-for-hostages deal in 1985–1986, 2004 TOWs and over 200 spare parts of HAWK missile batteries were traded for three American hostages in Lebanon. It was misconceived and badly mismanaged, mixing long-term strategic considerations with the short-term and middlemen-driven arms sales. After national security advisor Robert McFarlane's unsuccessful trip to Iran in 1986 with a cake from President Reagan, the deal came to light as the Iran-Contra affair, or Irangate, because of the linkage of the arms-for-hostages deal with secret aid to the Contras in Nicaragua.[15] Majles Speaker Hashemi-Rafsanjani refused to meet McFarlane in Tehran. The repercussions of the revelation of the deal in Iran included the execution of the radical cleric, Mehdi Hashemi, in 1986. The time was not yet ripe for a pragmatic approach to foreign policy. It was evidently too risky for Hashemi-Rafsanjani to go beyond obtaining the badly needed arms for the war with Iraq toward a more general détente.

Nevertheless, like every other development in the IRI, the pragmatic approach was set in motion by a word from Ayatollah Khomeini. In October 1984, his contrary goals and contradictory assertion notwithstanding, he told a group of Iranian diplomats:

> We should act as it was done in early Islam when the Prophet...sent ambassadors to all parts of the world to establish proper relations....We should have relations with all governments with the exception of a few....

The radical Prime Minister, Mir-Hossein Musavi, immediately expanded on these instructions: "We do not want to export armed revolution to any country. That is a big lie."[16] Iran's revolutionary elite was thus slowly developing a pragmatic approach to foreign policy that required movement toward more open dealings and a general rapprochement with the United States. In October 1988, Hashemi-Rafsanjani, who was not yet the IRI President, declared that the export of the Islamic revolution could be achieved not by violence but only by setting up "a suitable model of development, progress, evolution, and correct Islamic morals for the world."[17] However, pragmatism was in practice often resisted by Khomeini, who found the acceptance of cease-fire with Iraq that ended the Iran-Iraq War on July 18, 1988, after eight years, like "drinking a cup of poison." It did not take long for pragmatism to be wrecked for the last time by Khomeini, who issued the infamous *fatwā* condemning novelist Salman Rushdie to death on February 14, 1989. The pragmatic trend could prevail only after Khomeini's death.

Hashemi-Rafsanjani became the IRI President in 1989 and sought to insulate foreign policy from domestic ideological politics by making it the responsibility of the Supreme National Security Council, which was newly set up by a 1989 constitutional amendment. As his foreign policy advisor, Sa'id Raja'i-Khurasani, put it, "no country conducts its foreign policy in the context of open domestic ideological discord."[18] He accordingly set up the Center for Strategic Studies in Tehran as a foreign policy think tank in July 1990. In the same month, Iranian Foreign Minister Velayati visited Kuwait to revamp Iran's relations with that country and the Gulf Cooperation Council (GCC) states.[19] In the crisis created by the Iraqi invasion of Kuwait in August 1990

FIGURE 7.1 United States–Iran relations have been haunted by the occupation of the American embassy in Tehran that began in November 1979. This 1983 commemorative stamp refers to the event as "the take-over of the U.S. spy den." (Supplied by SAA)

and the ensuing Gulf War, the pragmatic leadership of Hashemi-Rafsanjani succeeded in preempting the radical faction that sustained the original ideological attitude and advocacy of the export of Islamic revolution.

Iran's dual leadership during the transition following Khomeini's death allowed Hashemi-Rafsanjani to put pragmatism and economic reconstruction in place of ideology and mobilization. The foreign policy that accompanied this turn to pragmatism was characterized by the type of "hedgehog strategy" we may call "Islamic revolution in one country." The analogy from the comparative sociology of revolution can be helpful here. The initial impetus to export the Russian revolution at its outset gave way to a pragmatic, accommodating foreign policy in the attempt at economic reconstruction known as the New Economic Policy. The foreign policy of this new phase was most clearly manifest in the Rapallo agreement between Soviet and German governments, and in line with Lenin's position in his last years that a moderate foreign policy was required by the technical and capital needs of the New Economic

Policy. This developed after his death into the so-called hedgehog strategy of Stalin and Molotov during the era of "socialism in one country."[20]

Khomeini's death coincided with the collapse of communism. The latter event made Khomeini's motto, "Neither East nor West" (itself a modification of Mosaddeq's "negative balance" policy in the early 1950s) irrelevant. Iran's improved relations with the Soviet Union were both an effect of and a further stimulus to pragmatism in foreign policy. Early in 1989, Soviet Foreign Minister Shevarnadze visited Tehran, and Hashemi-Rafsanjani traveled to Moscow in June of the same year. The new Iranian policy, which Ramazani calls "Both North and South," opened the former Soviet Republics in particular up to Hashemi-Rafanjani's post-Cold War pragmatism, while the policy of the export of revolution to the southern shores of the Gulf was definitively abandoned.[21]

Diplomatic relations with Britain had been broken in 1980 and underwent a number of shifts in the following years. The British embassy was reopened briefly at the end of 1988, only to be closed again after the Rushdie *fatwā*. Following Iraq's invasion of Kuwait in 1990, diplomatic relations with Britain were resumed.[22] The decisive victory for the pragmatists in foreign policy, however, came in the Gulf War of 1990–1991.

Although this international juncture was highly favorable to Hashemi-Rafsanjani's pragmatic foreign policy, he had a very hard sell internally and needed the Leader's help to curb revolutionary radicalism. The abolition of the office of Prime Minister by the 1989 constitutional amendments had excluded the radicals from the administration, but they still remained in control of the Majles and resisted the onset of pragmatism in economic and foreign policy. It is true that the radicals were no more sympathetic to Saddam Hussein and his Ba'thist regime than were the pragmatists in power before the 1990 Gulf crisis erupted. Eight years of the devastating Iran-Iraq War had only deepened both groups' common hatred for a regime whose secular ideology they abhorred, and the radicals and the pragmatists alike supported the Shi'ite opposition to Saddam Hussein under the leadership of the Iraqi Shi'ite clerics. But the crisis of 1990–1991 forced each faction to weigh its natural hostility to Saddam Hussein against a countervailing tendency—namely, the anti-American and anti-Zionist sentiments that deepened as the war unfolded and Baghdad was devastated by allied bombing.

The initial reaction of both Iranian factions to the Iraqi invasion of Kuwait in August 1990 was one of serious concern. On August 14, however, Saddam Hussein made a desperate bid for Iranian support against the coalition forces by offering sweeping unilateral concessions to Iran ("everything you wanted!") regarding the disputes that had resulted from the Iran–Iraq War.[23] This found a responsive chord among some radicals who now reiterated the rhetoric of export of revolution: the former "Judge Blood" of revolutionary courts, Sadeq Khalkhali, denounced the Kuwaiti ruling family, while another radical Majles deputy cursed the House of Saud for inviting the infidels into the land of Revelation. Majlis Speaker Mehdi Karrubi promised that the Muslim nations would eject the American troops from Saudi Arabia ignominiously. The pragmatists in power, by contrast, were not greatly moved by the Iraqi overtures. Later disclosures indicated that they communicated the substance of the offers made by Iraq to the Kuwaiti Foreign Minister.[24] Iran also secretly communicated with the United States and allowed the U.S. Air Force to use Iranian airspace.[25]

At this point, the ruling diarchy, the Leader and the President, devised a division of labor that would allow the pursuit of pragmatism while keeping the radicals in check by preempting their revolutionary rhetoric. In September 1990, the Leader, Ayatollah Khamenei, sought to preempt the radicals' anti-American pressure by declaring combat against the United States to be a holy war or *jihad*. Meanwhile, President Hashemi-Rafsanjani and Foreign Minister Ali Akbar Velayati were vigorously engaged in diplomatic activities marked by particularly close contacts with Syria and Turkey. Since the Iraqi invasion of Iran in 1980, common enmity toward Saddam Hussein had brought the governments of Iran and Syria closer together, leading to cordial diplomatic relations and significant economic exchanges between the two nations. Late in September 1990, President Hafez al-Asad of Syria visited Iran for intensive discussions with President Hashemi-Rafsanjani.

Asad's visit, however, also marked the onset of a new round in the power struggle between the pragmatists in power and their radical opponents. Hashemi-Rafsanjani and his supporters seized the opportunity offered by the election of the Assembly of Leadership Experts to administer a serious defeat to the radicals.[26] With Ayatollah Khamenei's support, the clerical jurists of the Guardian Council rejected the candidacy of radical religious scholars by failing them at a humiliating examination in Shi'ite jurisprudence in their supervisory capacity. Those rejected included two leading radical clerics, Sadeq Khalkhali and the former Interior Minister and mastermind of the 1983 suicide bombing of the U.S. marines and founder of the Hezbollah in Lebanon, 'Ali-Akbar Mohtashamipur. Significantly, the leadership of the Association of Militant Clerics (*majma'-e ruhāniyun-e mobārez*) to which they belonged opted for pragmatism by excluding the radicals from the list of candidates it endorsed, supported by the Guardian Council in this move.

The pragmatists' domestic struggle against the radicals did not affect a primary goal of their foreign policy, namely championship of Islam and claim to leadership in the Muslim world. Reports of the October 1990 killings on Temple Mount in Jerusalem produced a wave of indignation and sympathy for the Palestinians in Iran as in other Muslim countries. Rather than allow Saddam Hussein to exploit this sense of outrage in the Arab world, Ayatollah Khamenei took the lead in a vigorous show of championing the Palestinian cause. Israel, Zionism, and American imperialism were strongly condemned in the press and in statements by Ayatollah Khamenei and the Iranian officials. Early in December 1990, an international conference was convened in Tehran to mark the third anniversary of the *intifada,* referred to as "the Islamic uprising of Palestine." The participants included the leaders of Islamist movements in the West Bank and Tunisia. This deft reaction on the part of Iran's dual leadership was similar to the earlier declaration of *jihad* by Ayatollah Khamenei and his sustained anti-American rhetoric throughout the crisis. The primary external objective of this policy was to preempt Saddam Hussein in his calculated bid to emerge as a champion of both Islam (through his declaration of holy war against the West) and of the Palestinian cause (through his espousal of "linkage" between the Gulf crisis and the Arab–Israeli conflict). It was part of a policy designed to prevent Saddam from wresting actual, or even nominal, Islamic revolutionary leadership from Iran. Internally, the policy preemptively disarmed the radicals.

Meanwhile, Ayatollah Khamenei had endorsed diplomatic efforts by the Iranian President and the Foreign Minister, who had concluded a round of negotiations with the President of Turkey, Iraq's northern neighbor, in November 1990. In December, Iran supported the United Nations Security Council resolutions against Iraq, and even as the Foreign Minister opened the conference on Palestine, the First Deputy President, Hasan Habibi, declared Iran's opposition to any concession to Iraq by the West.

A new round of confrontation between President Hashemi-Rafsanjani and his radical opponents began in January 1991, a few days before the outbreak of the Gulf war. The radical Majles deputies succeeded, by one vote, in dismissing the Minister of Health, who had the strong support of both the President and the Leader, and, on the eve of the air attacks on Iraq by the allied forces, Majles Speaker Karrubi once again denounced the United States. While the Iranian government declared its neutrality in the war, the radical clerics Mohtashamipur and Khalkhali strongly condemned the United States in the Majles, and argued that Iran should side with Iraq against the United States, the greater evil. A demonstration against the war on January 21, 1991, organized by the radical Association of Militant Clerics, proved an embarrassing failure, however, with fewer than 3000 participants. The radicals were also prepared to act within the Revolutionary Guards, and President Hashemi-Rafsanjani reportedly had to rush General Mohsen Reza'i, the IRGC commander, to Khorramshahr to stop a missile battery from firing at American forces.[27]

President Hashemi-Rafsanjani launched his official peace initiative, drawing in the Soviets and the European Union, while Foreign Minister Velayati conducted a busy round of shuttle diplomacy. Tehran became the major port of call for Middle Eastern, Soviet, and European diplomats; Pakistani volunteers, seeking to cross Iranian territory to fight on the side of Iraq, were denied permission. Immediately after the crushing defeat of the Iraqi army by the ground forces of the United States and its allies at the end of February 1991, the chairman of the Supreme Council for the Islamic Revolution in Iraq, Mohammad Baqer al-Hakim, began to urge a Shi'ite uprising against Saddam Hussein. This was done with the evident support of President Hashemi-Rafsanjani, who effectively put Iranian broadcasting facilities at the disposal of the rebellious Iraqi Shi'a. Nevertheless, the radicals failed completely to pressure Hashemi-Rafsanjani to give military support to the Shi'ite uprising in Iraq against Saddam militarily.[28]

In short, the pragmatic ruling diarchy was able to control Iranian foreign policy and the revolutionary rhetoric alike. Iran silently cooperated with the expulsion of Iraq from Kuwait despite Saddam's offer to give Iran everything it wanted and restore the 1975 border agreement, and confiscated the Iraqi planes that had been flown to Iran at the beginning of the war.[29]

Transition to Pragmatism in Foreign Policy: Both South and North

Pragmatism gathered force in Iran's foreign policy despite the lukewarm response from its Arab neighbors.[30] Hashemi-Rafsanjani resented this, but must also have concluded that Iran's strained relations with Egypt had to be improved. Iran had been carefully cultivating economic and political ties with the Gulf states, and Hashemi-Rafsanjani considered his diplomatic efforts hampered by not having diplomatic relations with Saudi Arabia. Negotiating to resume diplomatic relations soon began with Oman's mediation.

Meanwhile, the Syrians undertook to convey Iran's concerns to other Arab countries.

Saudi Arabia had been Khomeini's *bête noir,* and his agents had used the annual Hajj pilgrimage to spread the message of the Islamic revolution. At the end of July 1987, during the Hajj season, the Saudi police reacted violently and killed over 400 Iranian pilgrims. After this, all relations were broken. Hashemi-Rafsanjani reopened Iran's embassy in Riyadh on the last day of March 1991, and announced shortly thereafter that the Saudi government had agreed to increase the quota for Iranian pilgrims to Mecca from 45,000 to 100,000, and to permit them to hold rallies while on pilgrimage. The Saudi Foreign Minister, Prince Saud al-Faisal, visited Tehran in June 1991—the first visit by a senior Saudi official to Iran since the revolution.

Near the end of his presidency in March 1997, Hashemi-Rafsanjani met the Saudi Crown Prince 'Abdullah in Islamabad during an Islamic summit. Prince 'Abdullah visited Tehran a year later, when the new President, Khatami, hosted the next Islamic summit of the Organization of the Islamic Conference in Tehran in December 1997. In October 2002, Iran endorsed 'Abdullah's peace plans and said it would not stand in the way of an eventual two-state solution to the Israeli–Palestinian conflict.[31] Khatami's hardliner successor, President Ahmadinejad, seriously strained the relations between the two countries by using the meeting of the Organization of the Islamic Conference in Mecca during the second week of December 2005 to disseminate his idea of the Holocaust as a myth to capture the Arab street.[32] Nevertheless, even Ahmadinejad seems to have returned to his predecessors' rapprochement with Saudi Arabia when he visited King 'Abdullah in 2007.

Improved relations with the GCC states were marked by several high-level visits in 1992, including the visit to Tehran by the GCC Secretary-General.[33] In January 1993, Deputy-President Mohajerani proposed resumption of diplomatic relations with Egypt, and this time the Leader consented.[34] In 1994, first Iran's Foreign Minister, 'Ali-Akbar Velayati, and then Ayatollah 'Ali Taskhiri, from the Office of the Supreme Leader, visited Egypt. In December of that year Iran forgave half of Egypt's debt, and Egypt agreed to set up sugar factories in Khuzestan to repay the remainder.[35] Ayatollah Taskhiri visited Egypt again several times to firm up the agreement.

Pragmatism in foreign relations to the north was just as evident. The Soviet Union's disintegration suddenly opened Iran's northern neighbors to trade and cultural exchanges, and in 1991 Iran quickly established good relations not only with Tajikistan, Turkmenistan, and Azerbaijan, but also Armenia and even the Ukraine.[36] Rafsanjani's Minister of Economy and Finance, Mohsen Nurbakhsh, saw this newly opened area as a potential $8–10 billion market for Iranian exports, and Iran brokered the acceptance of the Central Asian republics as members of the Economic Cooperation Organization at its summit meeting in Tehran in February 1992, where the formation of the Caspian Sea Five—Russia, Azerbaijan, Kazakhstan, Turkmenistan, and Iran—was announced.[37] Khatami and Ahmadinejad have continued Hashemi-Rafsanjani's policy toward Central Asia. As a recent example, the first Kazakhstan–Iran forum was held in the Kazakh Caspian port of Aktau in October 2008, following oil and gas deals earlier in the summer and discussions about the construction of an oil pipeline through Turkmenistan.[38]

Last but not least, Hashemi-Rafsanjani made a serious attempt to improve relations with the United States. Systematic as Hashemi-Rafsanjani and his advisors were in both domestic and foreign policy, it is inconceivable that he would consider his post-revolutionary pragmatic reorientation of Iran's foreign policy complete without a rapprochement with the United States. There is incontrovertible evidence that he consistently sent signals to Washington for improving relations between 1990 and 1995, and that his signals were consistently ignored.[39]

The United States Rebuffs Hashemi-Rafsanjani and Woos Khatami Too Late

In response to the 1989 announcement by the first President Bush that "good will begets good will," Iran helped with the freeing of two American hostages in April–May 1990, for which Bush thanked Iran. In June 1990, some 3 years after the Irangate scandal, 'Ataollah Mohajerani, Hashemi-Rafsanjani's Deputy-President, proposed resumption of diplomatic relations with the United States in a newspaper article, but was sharply rebuked by the Leader. The Bush administration had a positive view toward improving relations with Iran, but national security advisor Brent Scowcroft judged that "the situation in Iran was delicate enough that nobody was prepared to stick his neck out and actually have a conversation with the Great Satan."[40] He was right because Hashemi-Rafsanjani could not yet face the radicals alone, and had to bring Khamanei on board, which he managed to do only during the decisive rhetorical shift to pragmatism during the Gulf War. Yet even after his silent cooperation with the United States in that war, Hashemi-Rafsanjani's expectation of finding a sympathetic interlocutor in the George W.H. Bush administration was disappointed. Secretary George Baker's assurance early in 1991 that Iran would be included in the "New World Order" was met with a scathing attack on the New World Order by the radical Behzad Nabavi,[41] not long after another radical, Hashem Aghajari, reaffirmed that "Our revolution is like all revolutions and must be exported."[42] The upshot was that Iran was excluded from the Bush–Baker New World Order. Hashemi-Rafsanjani had been party to the Israeli secret arm deals in the 1980s, and had departed significantly from Khomeini on Israel by indicating that Iran would agree to any solution acceptable to the Palestinians. He signaled his interest in taking part in the Madrid peace conference that convened at the end of October 1991, but Iran was not invited. Left out in the cold, the Leader, who had assumed the championship of the Palestinians in rivalry with Saddam Hussein a year earlier, gave the radical Mohtashamipur the green light to organize an anti-Madrid conference and build ties with the Hamas and other rejectionists.[43] President Hashemi-Rafsanjani also grumbled later that he was some $200 million or so out of pocket for arranging the release of the Western hostages from the Hezbollah in Lebanon in November 1991, and had not had a compensating response from the Americans. In that month President Bush lost the elections, furthermore, and his lame duck administration did not return Iran's good will gestures. Still, Hashemi-Rafsanjani had made a serious decision to try to open channels to the United States, and continued sending signals to Washington when President Clinton took office.

These signals too were ignored, and in May 1993 the United States left no incentive for President Hashemi-Rafsanjani to challenge the radicals by announcing its misguided policy of "dual containment" (of Iraq and Iran). When the chairman of the foreign policy committee of the Majles and Iran's former representative at the United Nations, Sa'id Raja'i-Khorasani, wrote a letter to the Leader suggesting reestablishing diplomatic relations with the United States in November 1993, he brought the ire of the radicals upon himself and was let down by the President.[44] Nevertheless, U.S. oil companies were resuming business and had surpassed the Japanese as Iran's biggest clients by 1994. Hashemi-Rafsanjani tried again with the offer of a billion dollar contract to the American oil company, Conoco, in March 1995. This episode of Hashemi-Rafsanjani's strong signals and unilateral economic offers has strangely been forgotten.[45]

The dual containment period demonstrated the power of the Israeli lobby in American foreign policy but also the deleterious long-term effects of the hostage crisis. Israel's assistance to Iran during its war with Saddam

Hussein was justified in terms of Ben Gurion's so-called periphery doctrine that the enmity of the surrounding Arab neighbors of Israel had to be countered by friendship with the non-Arab countries on the periphery, especially Iran and Turkey. When the Israeli Prime Minister, Yitzhak Rabin, and his Foreign Minister, Shimon Peres, began the long secret negotiations with the Palestinians that resulted in the Oslo "land for peace" agreement of August 1993, the periphery doctrine was reversed, and Israel aimed to improve somewhat strained relations with the United States by turning against Iran and presenting it as the new arch-enemy, forever the home of "Khomeinism" and of anti-American Islamic fundamentalism.[46] The powerful American Israel Public Affairs Committee (AIPAC) took its cue. The doctrine of "dual containment" was the brain child of President Clinton's Middle East national security advisor, Martin Indyk, and was first made public in May 1993 at the Washington Institute for Middle East Policy, a pro-Israel think-tank. It became official policy despite the vehement opposition of Edward Djerejian, Assistant Secretary of State under Warren Christopher. Christopher himself, however, having negotiated the final release of the embassy hostages, could not overcome his distaste for the Iranians and sided with Indyk. In 1994, revenge for the hostages was the unstated reason for the House of Representative's decision to allot an additional $18 million to be used by the CIA to overthrow the Iranian regime. In 1995, the ghost of the hostage crisis was effectively harnessed by AIPAC to push for an executive order banning U.S. investment in the Iranian oil industry in response to Hashemi-Rafsanjani's offer to Conoco in March 1995.

The American reaction was spiteful. President Clinton caved in to the pressure by AIPAC and Congress, and scrapped the deal with executive orders. But that was not enough. Iran had to be punished further by legislation. The House of Representatives passed the Iran–Libya Sanctions Law, with an astonishing 415 unanimous vote, to tighten sanctions and penalize, in violation of international law, non-American companies dealing with Iran.[47] Despite all this, Iran pushed the Lebanese Hezbollah to agree to a cease fire with Israel in Hashemi-Rafsanjani's last desperate signal to Washington, to which he got no response.[48] The demonized image of Iran persisted despite the election of Khatami as a reformist President. The ghost of the hostage crisis could not be laid to rest even in 2001, when the new Secretary of State Colin Powell favored improving relations with Iran. In July 2001, before the 9/11 terrorist attacks, AIPAC had flexed its muscle by blocking a U.S.–Iranian rapprochement, and lobbied to change the administration's proposal to extend economic sanctions against Iran from 2 to 5 years so as to send a clear message to the Iranians. AIPAC's great success was reflected in another nearly unanimous approval of the measure (490 to 6 in the House, 96to 2 in the Senate).[49]

President Khatami continued Hashemi-Rafsanjani's pragmatism in foreign policy, maintaining cordial relations with Saudi Arabia, the Gulf emirates, Egypt, and the European Union. He even signaled the cooling of the warm relations developed with the Palestinian Oslo rejectionists by reverting to Hashemi-Rafsanjani's earlier stand, and in his address to the Organization of the Islamic Conference summit in Tehran in December 1997, accepted the two-state solution to the Israeli–Palestinian conflict.[50] Ambassadors were exchanged with Britain in 1998 after the final diplomatic solution of the Rushdie problem with the declaration by the Iranian Foreign Minister, Kamal Kharrazi: "The government of the IRI has no intention, nor is it going to take any action what-soever, to threaten the life of the author of "The Satanic Verses.""[51] Khatami then paid the state visit to France planned by Hashemi-Rafsanjani but aborted by the intelligence agents.[52] He also visited Germany and Italy, and talked during the Pope's funeral with the President of Israel, who was a native of his own city of Yazd. Furthermore, he imaginatively generalized his predecessor's ad hoc pragmatism by making it into a policy for the "Dialogue of Civilizations" designed to end Iran's diplomatic isolation for good.

In an interview with Christiane Amanpour for CNN in January 1998, Khatami declared "an intellectual affinity with the essence of American civilization" as based on "religiosity, liberty and justice," and proposed an exchange of "professors, writers, scholars, artists, journalists and tourists" to chip at the "wall of mistrust between us and the U.S. administration."[53] During his visit to the General Assembly of the United Nations in September 2000, Khatami proposed to call 2001 the Year of the Dialogue of Civilizations, and his proposal was accepted. 2001, however, turned out to be the year of September 11. Khatami failed to reopen diplomatic relations with the United States and thus solve Iran's biggest international problem.

The real opportunity to do so was missed in the last years of the Clinton administration. During Khatami's first visit to the United States in 1998, the UN Secretary-General Kofi Anan had arranged a meeting between the American Secretary of State, Madeleine Albright, and the Iranian Foreign Minister, Kamal Kharrazi, but the latter did not show up,[54] and was said to be taking the day off for shopping. Much more significantly, the Clinton admin-istration finally agreed to make all the significant concessions demanded by Iran. In the spring of 2000, Secretary Albright's speech announcing America's readiness to acknowledge its responsibility for the problems in Iran–U.S. relations was welcomed by Khatami's key supporters in the Majles, but scathingly attacked by the Leader.[55] Foreign Minister Kharrazi, who was also close to the Leader, delayed any formal move until the November 2000 American elections. My interpretation of this last minute failure is that Ayatollah Khamenei did not give his permission to Kharrazi in September 1998 to meet Albright, nor to Khatami to make any grand gestures.[56] Khatami and Kharrazi did not dare disobey the Leader who wanted the United States to have to negotiate with his own men, such as the Larijani brothers. The strongest evidence for this view is that as soon as the Leader had installed 'Ali Larijani as the secretary of the Supreme National Security Council in the fall of 2005, the latter persistently proposed talks with the United States. In the spring of 2006, to Larijani's great embarrassment, and to the delight of his rival Ahmadinejad, his proposition was rejected by Secretary of State Condoleezza Rice, who had already sought $75 million to support democracy in Iran in February.[57]

In any event, President Khatami and Foreign Minister Kharrazi immediately regretted their mistake in not being responsive to Clinton's final offer, and did everything to cooperate with the United States after the invasion of Afghanistan in October 2001. In the words of the chief U.S. negotiator on Afghanistan, James Dobbins, Iran was "comprehensively helpful."[58] Iran's chief negotiator, Javad Zarif, even conveyed an offer to help rebuild the Afghan army under American leadership. By then, however, the atmosphere not only in Congress but also in the White House was passionately anti-Iranian. The Iranian proposals were ignored by an unsympathetic Bush administration dominated by Vice-President Cheney and Secretary of Defense Rumsfeld.[59] Nevertheless, the U.S.–Iran talks that began in connection with Afghanistan in November 2001 continued. In May 2003, Khatami and Kharrazi obtained the permission of Ayatollah Khamenei, who was alarmed by the initial success of the American invasion of Iraq, to engage in comprehensive talks with the United States, and felt that covered their back against the hardliners.[60] They sent Iran's proposal for comprehensive talks, including Hezbollah and Hamas, to Washington through the Swiss Ambassador on May 4, 2003.[61] Their offer was rejected, however.[62] Cheney and Rumsfeld's man, Undersecretary of Defense Douglas Feith, proceeded with his briefing for Washington officials on regime change. Feith's proposal has been described as "much more than just a contingency plan."[63]

The countering of Hashemi-Rafsanjani's attempt to improve relations with the United States by the dual containment policy of 1993 and the unanimous

Congressional slap in the face—in contravention to international law—with the Iran–Libya sanctions of 1995, renewed with another near-unanimous vote during the inordinately long chad-dangling disarray of the 2000 transition to the Bush administration, cannot simply be attributed to the influence of AIPAC and the Israeli lobby, great though it undoubtedly was.[64] Hashemi-Rafsanjani's failure in the 1990s was also due to the bitter memory of the hostage crisis of 1979 created by Khomeini to ensure the definitive routing of Bazargan and Bani-Sadr. Without the hatred of Iranians, irrevocably demonized for hurting the Americans' pride for 444 days, it would not have been so easy for the Israeli lobby to sow vengeance on such a fertile ground.

The tale of missed opportunities to improve Iran–U.S. relations in the post-Khomeini era of pragmatism and reconstruction shows democracy (in this case, the Americans') to be no less immune than revolution (in this case Iran's) to the hindrance of rational foreign policy by the animus of domestic politics. Clinton's first Secretary of State, Warren Christopher, who had conducted negotiations for the release of hostages in Algiers, developed a visceral distaste for dealing with Iranians, and it took his successor, Madeleine Albright, a professor of international relations, to restore a sense of the logic of geopolitics and long-term American national interest during the last months of the second Clinton administration. By that time, however, Leader Khamenei, who had just snatched an improbable victory out of the jaws of the resounding defeat of the hardliners by intimidating the reformists in the Majles, was not prepared to allow the reformists an easy victory in foreign policy and would not stop short of intimidating the docile President Khatami and Foreign Minister Kharrazi to forestall it. Given the impingement of revolutionary and democratic domestic politics on the foreign policies of Iran and the United States, it is reasonable to consider the failure of a rapprochement, when it seemed within reach, partly a long-term consequence of the Islamic revolution, attributable to the long-dead charismatic leader of the Islamic revolution. Khomeini thus continued to dominate Iran's foreign policy, no less than its constitutional politics, long after his death.

8

Iran's New Political Class and the Ahmadinejad Presidency (2005–2009)

AHMADINEJAD AS A LAY MEMBER OF THE SECOND STRATUM of the Islamic Republic of Iran (IRI) kisses the hand of the Supreme Jurist, something his two predecessors as the latter's clerical colleagues and Khomeini's disciples never did. This symbolic gesture of class subordination has left its mark on the psyche of Ahmadinejad and has been compensated for by an assertive and strong presidency and by disdain toward members of his own hardliner faction of the new political class, especially those who have formed the Majles majority. He has also found supernatural support from the Hidden Imam, of whose imminent reappearance Ahmadinejad is convinced. (According to the Shi'ite creed, the Twelfth Imam went into occultation in the ninth century and will return at the End of Time to save the world.) Ahmadinejad's election in 2005 was conditioned by the rise of the military-security second stratum of Iran's new political class and reflects its aspirations. It is as a representative of the hardliners from the second stratum that he has contested the pragmatist and the reformist definitions of Khomeini's heritage in seeking to articulate the consciousness of this new political class and its aspiration to rule Iran indefinitely. His alternative definition of Khomeini's heritage highlights what was left unclaimed by the previous two groups of the children of the Islamic revolution: populism, social justice, and unflinching loyalty to the martyrs of the revolution and war. He is thus a throwback to the early days of revolution.

Rise of the Revolutionary Guards and Ahmadinejad's Election

During the revolution in 1979, Ahmadinejad was an Islamic student activist at the Office of Consolidation of Unity and participated in the Cultural Revolution of 1980 by purging his own Science and Technology University in the Narmak district of Tehran. He joined the Basij during the Iran–Iraq War. In the winter of 1993, he was appointed the first governor of the newly created province of Ardabil by 'Ali-Mohamad Basharati, the hardliner Interior Minister imposed on Hashemi-Rafsanjani by the Leader and the Fourth Majels. Discovering small luxuries such as sauna in that cold province did not make Ahmadinejad a "conservative," as the media usually describe him, but an even more determined hardliner. As governor of Ardabil, he showed no qualms in following a factional political agenda, and in due course diverted about $1.2 million to the campaign of the hardliner Majles Speaker Nateq-Nuri against Khatami in 1997.[1] His rise to national prominence began with his election as the mayor of Tehran in May 2003, following the expression of deep disaffection in the municipal elections with Khatami's reformism.

By the time he aspired to Khatami's job, Ahmadinejad knew he was representing a force larger than himself that was not merely a reflection of the disaffection with reformism, but stemmed directly from Khomeini's revolutionary heritage. The hardliners who routed the reformists in the Tehran municipal elections of 2003 had said they elected Ahmadinejad mayor because of "his Basij militia mentality"; and as the mayor of Tehran, he put up a huge mural of a female Palestinian suicide bomber at a busy intersection of the city. Although he had to back off from his plans to make universities and city squares burial grounds for martyrs after a riot against the first burials by the students of the elite Sharif Technological University, Ahmadinejad nevertheless reburied the martyrs in some city parks and would affirm in February 2004 that what was needed to solve the problems of the country were "revolutionary forces who can come with the mentality of Basij members."[2] He had no more qualms than he had had as governor of Ardabil seven years earlier about putting the resources of the Tehran Municipality at the disposal of the hardliner candidates fitting that description in the Majles elections of 2004.[3]

In the 2005 presidential elections, he ran as the candidate for the Basij and to the memory of the martyrs of the revolution and war. The retrieval of the revolution slogan went hand in hand with the Basij candidacy: the blood of the martyrs of the revolution would not be in vain. "Some people keep saying that our revolution is aimed at establishing democracy. No. Neither in the

Imam's statements nor in the message of the martyrs ... has any such idea been considered." In another speech during his presidential campaign he described it as a push to capture the street, likened to a hill, in which the presidential palace was located, adding in martial terms: "Either we achieve our aim or we will become martyrs, injured or missing in action."[4] In this, he was assisted by the Basij militia, and enjoyed the decisive support of its leaders and the key elements in the Revolutionary Guards. His former superior and associate in the Hazma Headquarters in the early 1980s, Esma'il Ahmadi-Moqaddam, played a critical role in mobilizing the Basij and the Revolutionary Guards in 2005, and four years later as Iran's police chief, in suppressing popular protests against Ahmadinejad's electoral putsch in June and July 2009.[5]

For a dark horse to win the presidential elections on the blood of the martyrs in the revolution-weary Iran of 2005 was an astounding victory, and it cannot be explained by any sudden change in mood or volatility of the electorate. The explanation is fairly simple, however. A new machine for delivering the popular vote had come into existence in the IRI. In the presidential elections of June 2005, the Islamic Revolutionary Guards Corps (IRGC) and the Basijis perfected the new function of bringing voters to the ballot box, something they had begun experimentally in the municipal elections of 2003 and the Majles elections of 2004. The 2005 presidential elections could indeed be accurately described as their first electoral coup d'état.

There can be little doubt that the first decisive round of those elections that saved Ahmadinejad from elimination was highjacked by the bosses of the new machine, with the approval if not at the bidding of the Leader and Supreme Jurist. Two men from its military-security second stratum made a bid for the leadership of the new political class through the Presidency: Tehran's mayor, Ahmadinejad, and its police chief, Mohammad Baqer Qalibaf. Once the decisive choice between Qalibaf and Ahmadinejad was made by the Revolutionary Guard leaders in a meeting with the Leader, the plot was carried out and the first round of the elections was managed successfully. Assertions to this effect were immediately made by the reformist former Majles Speaker Karrubi, who was wrongfully eliminated to make room for Ahmadinejad, until he was intimidated by the Leader to keep quiet, and by Hashemi-Rafsanjani, the winner of the first round, especially after he badly lost to Ahmadinejad in the second round.[6] Ahmadinejad could count on the Basij, but the decisive factor was the last-minute backing of the Revolutionary Guards according to the instructions of the Leader's representative at the IRGC, Ayatollah Movahedi-Kermani. The IRGC deputy commander General Zolqadr later admitted that there was a "multilayered plan" to get Ahmadinejad elected, explaining that in "the complex situation where foreign powers…had been plotting,…one had to act in a complex manner!"[7]

Ahmadinejad's ascent had been too sudden and unpredictable to allow for any clear formulation of a broader political identity and ideological position. His supporters were at first mere copycats of Hashemi-Rafsanjani's Servants of Reconstruction, and during the 2003 municipal elections, the 2004 Majles elections, and the 2005 presidential elections called themselves Developers (*ābādgarān*), or in full, Developers' Coalition of Islamic Iran. Before long, Ahmadinejad seized upon social justice and clean government as the additional hallmark of his platform for Basij-driven revolutionary revivalism, and his supporters soon thereafter realized that the imitative "Developers" did not convey the desired throwback to Khomeini's pure revolutionism, and dug up the originalist designation, "the Principle-oriented" (*osulgarāyān*), from the hardliner editorials of the 1990s.

As its two other components had been appropriated by other factions, Ahmadinejad and his military-mobilizational team presented populism and social justice as the essential element of Khomeini's heritage or principles (*osul*) of the Islamic revolution, gradually labeling themselves as the Principle-oriented (*osulgarāyān*), meaning those who remain completely faithful to the original principles of the revolution. Distributive justice, "bringing the oil money to the people's dinner table,"[8] and fighting economic corruption were thus Ahmadinejad's chief slogans, and they were very effective in mobilizing the urban poor neglected by Khatami and the reformists. One of the reformist candidates, Majles-Speaker Karrubi, promised a lump sum payment to each Iranian citizen if elected, but he did not have the Basijis, with their 70,000 bases throughout the country, to get the urban poor to the voting box for him.

Ahmadinejad rewarded the Revolutionary Guards and the Basij handsomely for electing him. There was an immediate 74 percent increase in the development budget designed to help the Basij win government contracts. In November 2005, he declared a Basij week, and millions of Basijis on active duty and reserve made a symbolic human chain around Iran. Celebrating the Basij week three years later in November 2008, according to the Fars News Agency,[9] Ahmadinejad sought to define "the culture of the Basij" for the over 950,000 celebrant Basijis. All of Iran's successes were due to "the culture of Basij reigning in the nation and the country," and all the problems of the world are the result of turning away from "the human-producing culture of Basij." The world leaders should therefore think of "return to the Basij culture and thus taking a step for the salvation of human society!" Meanwhile, early in 2008, the Majles had seen to the material sustenance of the world-saving culture by recognizing the Basij Construction Organization, established in 2000, for securing no-bid government contracts. IRGC Commander General Ja'fari, who also assumed the command of the Basij, has overseen the closer integration of some 2,500 battalions of 300–350 each with units of the IRGC and regular army, thus blurring the line between their function as militia, morality police, and combatants against internal enemies and the Western cultural onslaught (figure 8.1).[10]

The IRGC has done even better. As the mayor of Tehran, Ahmadinejad had given many of the lucrative development projects for the capital to the Revolutionary Guards and waived the Tehran Municipality's financial claims against them.[11] In June 2006, the IRGC won a contract worth several billion dollars to build a gas pipeline, and later that year launched Oriental Kish, Iran's largest private oil company.[12] By 2006, according to its chief, IRGC's engineering branch, the Seal of the Prophets' Headquarters, had completed over 1200 projects, with another 247 in hand, including no-bid contracts for the Tehran Metro, Assaluyeh-Iranshar pipeline, and South Pars natural gas fields worth well over $1 billion each, and accounted for about 30 percent of the IRGC industrial and economic capacity.[13] The IRGC has significant

FIGURE **8.1** Iranian female paramilitary militias (Basij) hold their guns during a rally of paramilitary forces to support Iran's nuclear program in Tehran, Iran, Saturday, November 26, 2005. (AP Photo)

holdings in telecommunications and reportedly controls some 70 ports, charging its importing partners and satellite companies much lower import duties than the official rate.[14] The new IRGC commander, Mohammad-'Ali Ja'fari, emphasized the importance of the Revolutionary Guards construction projects and economic enterprises when he took over in September 2007. Nor is the IRGC left out of the informal economy: it reportedly controls extensive smuggling operations, through international airports and "invisible jetties" and sells Iraqi oil and Iran's heavily subsidized gasoline in the neighboring countries.

The industrial-military-commercial complex and its economic empire have not distracted the IRGC from politics, or more precisely their "Principle-oriented" attempt to take over the legislative and executive branches of government. Having gained control of the Executive with the Ahmadinejad presidency, the military-security second stratum announced its intention to take over the legislature too in the 2008 Majles elections. Brigadier General 'Ali-Reza Afshari moved to the Interior Ministry's elections office in preparation, while Major General Hasan Firuzabadi, chief of staff of the armed forces, warned that the reformists "must not be allowed to find their way into the Majles again to repeat their past performance."[15] IRGC General 'Ezzatollah Zargami, head of the national IRI Broadcasting, complied by refusing to air the latter's views, and the Leader's representative at the IRGC urged its officers to take an active part in parliamentary politics.[16] The most blatant statement came in a speech that was broadcast during the 2008 parliamentary election, in which the IRGC commander, General Ja'fari, told the Basij officers recently put under his command that the hardliners now controlled the Executive and Legislative, and "if the Basij members want to preserve this current and develop it, they must eliminate weak points." Furthermore, "to follow the path of the Islamic revolution, support for the Principle-oriented is the necessary, inevitable and divine duty of all revolutionary groups!"[17] The invasion of the legislature was successful, and the military-security stratum captured about a third of the seats in the Eighth Majles, strengthening their already substantial presence (figure 8.2).

The hardliners have not been entirely immune to the temptations and mellowing tendencies in the revolutionary process that produce pragmatism and moderation. This began with the Hashemi-Rafsanjani Thermidor of 1989–1997 and continued through the presidency of Khatami, 1997–2005. The military-mobilizational hardliners are the last and the rudest faction of the Islamic revolutionary elite to undergo moderation and corruption in power. In the past few years, the Revolutionary Guards have become the government's

FIGURE **8.2** President Mahmoud Ahmadinejad (right) with Yahya Rahim Safavi, Commander of Sepah-e Pasdaran (the Islamic Revolutionary Guards Corps [IRGC]) in front of the mausoleum of the late revolutionary founder Ayatollah Khomeini, just outside Tehran, Iran, Sunday, November 26, 2006. (AP Photo/Vahid Salemi)

biggest contractor by far, and expanded their economic enterprises. There are indications that petrodollars are finally sapping their hardliner revolutionary zeal. For example, the Revolutionary Guard General and Deputy Minister of Defense 'Ali-Reza Asghari, who disappeared or defected in Turkey in December 2006, was regularly in Syria for lucrative deals in olives and olive oil.[18] In April 2008, the Tehran police anti-vice chief, General Reza Zare'i, was found in a brothel, making six naked prostitutes pray to him.[19]

The Leader's Little Man Becomes His Own
with a Little Help from the Hidden Imam

In the early days of the revolution Ahmadinejad was involved with the Hojjatiyya,[20] a militant organization devoted to the Hidden Imam that was disbanded by Khomeini's order. He is reliably reported to have predicted his highly improbable election in the summer of 2005 as a favor from the Hidden Imam,[21] the Twelfth Imam believed to be in occultation until he returns as the Mahdi at the End of Time. According to a recent report, when being sworn in by the Leader as the IRI President, he remarked that the latter "thinks I am appointed president by him while I am the president appointed by the Lord of the Age [the Hidden Imam]."[22] In a national address shortly after this inauguration, he declared: "Our revolution's main mission is to pave the way for the reappearance of the Mahdi. Today, we should define our economic, cultural and political policies on the basis of the Mahdi's return." Ahmadinejad believed that the Hidden Imam had supernaturally intervened to make the eyes and ears of the delegates open to his message during the speech he delivered at the General Assembly of the United Nations in October 2005, and ended that speech with a prayer for his speedy return.[23] In an early cabinet decision, Ahmadinejad's administration allocated the equivalent of $17 million to the Jamkaran pilgrimage site near Qom and about a hundred kilometers south of Tehran, where the Hidden Imam is believed to have disappeared down a well, and to have ordered the building of a mosque revealed in a dream to a virtuous believer in the tenth century.[24] In November 2005, he even set a time for the return of the Mahdi in 2 years, by which time "we have to turn Iran into a modern and divine country to ... also serve as the basis for the return of the Twelfth Imam."[25] Furthermore, there are rumors that he superstitiously threw the names of the cabinet ministers before their presentation to the Majles in 2005 down the "well of the Lord of the Age" in Jamkaran, and had had plans as mayor of Tehran to build a good road connecting Jamkaran to the center of Tehran in expectation of the imminent appearance of the Mahdi.[26] Ahmadinejad's belief turned conspiratorial in May 2007 when he said foreign spies were asking about the whereabouts of the Hidden Imam in order to prevent his return.[27] A few months later, he said he felt the presence of the Hidden Imam in September 2007, when the President of Columbia University invited him to give a lecture but disgracefully insulted him during his introduction.

Ahmadinejad is thus using the Mahdi to strengthen his own purely secular authority vis-à-vis the Leader, Ayatollah Khamenei. Khamenei's office of the

Supreme Jurist (*faqih*) would evidently be made redundant by the return of the Hidden Imam. The clerical ruling elite, too, would be made redundant alongside the Leader. Several prominent members of the elite therefore dismissed Ahmadinejad's millennial expectations as misguided and superstitious in late 2007 and early 2008.[28] It is thus not surprising that they finally reacted to Ahmadinejad's evoking the Mahdi's direct backing. In April 2008 he told the Seminarians of the Mahdi in the city of Mashhad, "We see His hand directing all the affairs of the country. A movement has started for us to occupy ourselves with our global responsibilities. God willing, Iran will be the axis of the leadership of this movement."[29] His speech was not broadcast until May 6, 2008, at which point some leading members of the ruling elite and several clerics in the Majles and the press delivered their sharp rebuke.[30]

Ahmadinejad's adventures in foreign policy are related to his millennial expectation of the return of the Mahdi. When he made headlines throughout the world for saying that Israel (or, to use his exact words, "the Jerusalem-occupying regime" in this instance, "cancerous tumor" in others) "must disappear from the record of time" at the end of October 2005, he was simply signaling the return to Khomeini's intransigent revolutionism, and was in fact quoting the words of "our dear Imam."[31] But it did not take long for him to develop what had been said by many people in the Arab world and Iran beside Khomeini and Khamenei into his own original apocalyptic mix and basis of an unprecedented foreign policy. He combined it with the very accurate perception that the Holocaust had acquired a sacred quality in the West that trumped the value of free speech, but read it conspiratorially as a ploy for imperial hegemony. "Today," he declared in the remote town of Zahedan in Iranian Baluchestan on December 14, 2005, "they have created a myth in the name of Holocaust and consider it to be above God, religion and the prophets."[32] The source of this perception was his close foreign policy advisor, Moḥammad-'Ali Ramin, who had been educated in Germany but expelled because of his neo-Nazi connections. Iran could acquire new prominence in world politics by creating a historic alliance against Israel, the main beneficiary of the "Holocaust myth," with Germany, the Aryan nation that was its victim and had been reduced to considering its fathers criminals. Ahmadinejad launched this policy by writing a letter to German Chancellor Angela Merkle proposing such an alliance against "the victors of World War II." He then proceeded to convene an international conference of Holocaust deniers in Tehran and announced a Holocaust artistic competition to test the sincerity of the Western belief in the freedom of expression. The selected works were displayed in a Holocaust exhibition in Tehran in

December 2006, while the conference was opened, featuring David Duke of the KKK, Ramin's German and Austrian fellow "experts" on the "Holocaust myth," and some Iranians, including the 1980s radical cleric and founder of Hezbollah in Lebanon, 'Ali-Akbar Mohtashamipur.[33]

Ahmadinejad's millennial moves are fully in line with another bizarre act by him on the global scene. According to the Muslim apocalyptic tradition, the second coming of Jesus is the prelude to the reappearance of the Mahdi, and Ahmadinejad knew this full well: "Let me enlighten all Christians... that in the not-too-distant future the Prophet Jesus will rise again alongside the Mahdi to put an end to injustice in the world."[34] In May 2006, when Chancellor Merkl received her perplexing letter, Ahmadinejad wrote a similarly strange letter to President George W. Bush. The letter was sent through the Swiss ambassador in Tehran and was described by Ahmadinejad's spokesman and advisor, Gholam-Hossein Elham, as opening "new ways to solve current international tensions." The clue to the newness of the approach is supplied by the Leader and Supreme Jurist Khamenei, who evidently endorsed it by naming the Persian year 1385 (March 2006–March 2007) "The Year of the Prophet," referring to the year when Prophet Mohammad wrote letters to the world leaders of the time, the Iranian King of Kings and the Roman Caesar, to convert them to Islam. The Leader was not the only cleric to be persuaded to share Ahmadinejad's view of the world historical significance of his diplomatic letter-writing campaign. The Guardian Council Secretary, Ayatollah Ahmad Jannati, waxed ecstatic: President Ahmadinejad's letter to President Bush was the "result of divine inspiration" and should be made part of the syllabus at schools and universities.[35] Perhaps the best proof of the millennial context of these presidential ventures is the statement by the chief of Ahmadinejad's office that was to introduce the President's own prayer for the deliverance of the world by Mahdi in his Nawruz (Persian new year) address in March 2008: "Ahmadinejad's era is the period of [the Mahdi's] Lesser Advent (*zohur-e soghra*)!" In May 2008, less than two months into the new Persian year, Ahmadinejad reportedly told his cabinet to quickly wrap up unfinished Iranian internal business to be ready for the world revolution of the Mahdi.[36]

Populism and the Revival of Islamic Revolutionism

My sense is that Ahmadinejad psychologically needs the help of the Hidden Imam, readily available to all believing Shi'ites, to stand up to the Leader and to make bold decisions against his enemies as well as technical advisors. Millennial expectation is undoubtedly widespread in Iran,[37] and at least one other prominent member of Iran's second stratum, former Foreign Minister Velayati, shares it.[38] But it would be wrong to see Ahmadinejad's attitude as merely politically instrumental. In sharp contrast to Shari'ati's metaphorical use of the belief in the return of the Mahdi for revolutionary mobilization, Ahmadinejad's conviction is literal, and was expressed in the prayer that God may speed the reappearance of the Mahdi, with which he concluded his address to the UN General Assembly in 2005. Ahmadinejad does not use millennial expectation of the return of the Mahdi for mobilizational purposes. Instead, populism and loyalty to the martyrs of revolution and war serve him as an instrument of mobilization by reviving Khomeini's long neglected populist agenda of social justice. To prove his revolutionary toughness and opposition to America and Israel, Ahmadinejad stated that the Imam wanted Israel to be wiped off the map and denied the historical reality of the Holocaust, although his other motives were as important. His nuclear policy was also an astute tactic in domestic politics, and made him popular with the middle class.

The rejection of Hashemi-Rafsanjani's Thermidor was imperative for Ahmadinejad and the hardliners. In a throwback to Khomeini's original revolutionism, he mimicked the Imam's Cultural Revolution of the early 1980s in which he had played a part as a revolutionary student, announcing its resumption and appointing an extreme hardliner, Saffar Harandi, as his Minister of Culture and Islamic Guidance. Harandi has imposed a suffocating self-censorship on the press that is heavily dependent on the mercy of government to continue publication, and has repeatedly filtered thousands of websites and imprisoned the bloggers. In March 2009, a spokesman for the office of the Prosecutor General bragged that some five million websites had been closed because of their "onslaught on ethics and religious identity."[39]

Ahmadinejad also appointed the clerical hardliner 'Abbas-'Ali 'Amid Zanjani as Rector of the University of Tehran in the fall of 2005 to initiate a new round of purges, and set up a Cultural Revolution Council under his own chairmanship that banned "Western and vulgar" music from the national television in December of that year.[40] Protests during a speech by Ahmadinejad at the Amir Kabir Technological University in 2006 led to the harassment and expulsion of many students and the siege of the university by the Basij militia. The purges of liberal professors from all universities were completed before the academic year 2006–2007. Ahmadinejad's predecessors had done such a thorough job that he apparently needed to purge or forcibly retire only some 80 professors in the entire country.[41] As President, Ahmadinejad resumed the policy of the burial of "anonymous martyrs" in the universities. In February 2009, armed forces burying the presumably exhumed bodies of the martyrs of the revolution and war in the campus of the Amir Kabir Technological University violently attacked students carrying placards and shouting slogans such as "University is not a graveyard" and "Death to Dictatorship."[42]

The centerpiece of President Ahmadinejad's domestic policy is populism, however, and it is not confined to mere rhetoric but has political and economic consequences. As the mayor of Tehran, he had once donned the uniform of garbage men and said he would not trade his job of the people's street sweeper for anything. When casting his vote in a poor district of southern Tehran in the elections he won in June 2005, he repeated the refrain of his campaign: "I am proud of being the Iranian nation's humble servant and street sweeper."[43] As the people's President, he gives out his phone number and e-mail address, and travels to remote towns and provinces four days every three weeks to listen to residents and fix their problems. Ahmadinejad has held his cabinet meetings in small towns, mostly the poorer ones, addresses rallies in the provincial towns, and has reportedly diverted much of the government expenditure and investment away from Tehran. According to the Ministry of the Interior, during the first year of the new administration, the President and his cabinet visited 160 towns; and by the last year of his term, he had given speeches in more than 2,000 towns. During these trips, he makes on-the-spot grants for development projects and sports facilities and has given petitioners interest-free loans.[44] Other components of his economic populism include setting low interest rates, creating loan programs for newlyweds, increasing the minimum wage, and initiating a national school renovation project. A year after coming to power, Ahmadinejad circumvented a reluctant Majles and, using Iran's oil foreign exchange reserves, set up a substantial Imam Reza Love Fund to help young men and women to get married, find jobs, and set up homes.

A key economic component of Ahmadinejad's populism is the fight against corruption, squarely identified with Hashemi-Rafsanjani's reconstruction project, which he likes to refer to as the "Third Revolution." He has aligned his revolution against corruption and Western cultural invasion and for clean government. The roots of corruption are said to be the Iranian managerial class's lack of confidence in the Islamic culture, presumably the culture of the Basij. In the face of the cultural onslaught of the West, "these managers are weak in front of the enemies and look down on their own people."[45] Late in 2006, Ahmadinejad seized the opportunity to close down Hashemi-Rafsanjani's favored Manage-ment and Planning Organization after its head resigned in protest against his arbitrary and undue interference in the budgetary process, and took the devel-opmental planning entirely into his own hands. Ahmadinejad is said, however, to have kept the plan drafts and to tailor the generous handouts and promises during his provincial tours roughly in line with regional developmental plan recommendations.

Arguably the most important component of his populism is the distribution of the stocks of all nationalized industry as "shares of justice" (*sahām-e 'edālat*) on a per capita basis among the entire population of Iran. The program has boosted the President's popularity. Mimicking Mongolia's model of privatiza-tion, Ahmadinejad presented his plan for privatization through social justice to the Majles in October 2005, proposing to transfer 80 percent of the stocks of all state-owned enterprises estimated at $115–120 billion in three years. Of the assets, 40 percent was to be distributed as shares of justice, beginning with the lowest decile of the population. In addition, 35 percent was to be offered to the public through the Tehran Stock Exchange, 5 percent was to go to the workers, and 20 percent was to be retained by the state. The actual distribu-tion of shares, worth about $540, with the promise of an annual 11–15 percent dividend, began in four "deprived" provinces in February 2006. The plan has not been completed, but it is clear that it has resulted in partial denationaliza-tion rather than privatization, with a mammoth holding company possessing the shares of some 500 enterprises in 30 provinces and 337 town cooperatives as of 2007.[46]

Ahmadinejad's Relations with the Clerical Elite, the Majles, and His Own Stratum

Ahmadinejad's symbiotic relationship with the hardliner Ayatollah Mesbah-Yazdi, whom he considers his spiritual mentor, is in some ways indicative of the most positive rapport between the clerical and the military-security elements of Iran's new political class. Mesbah-Yazdi espoused Islam as an ideology in the early 1980s; he emerged as one of the chief opponents of Khatami's program of the rule of law in 1999 and was Hashemi-Rafsanjani's rival for the presidency of the Assembly of Leadership Experts in December 2006. Ahmadinejad followed the teachings of Ayatollah Mesbah-Yazdi in excluding democracy from Khomeini's alleged heritage, as did the clerical hardliners the latter had trained in the Haqqani School in Qom who became the Leader's hacks in the Judiciary and the Executive. Far from giving up the fight against Khatami and the reformers, Mesbah-Yazdi used a period-ical published by his organization to recruit for a shady Headquarters for the Devotees of Martyrdom commanded by an Ahmadinejad supporter, Mohammad Reza Ja'fari. A group of Basijis inspired by Mesbah-Yazdi had carried out a set of serial murders for alleged sexual sins in the city of Kerman in 2002, with copycat vigilantes replicating them in other cities. The trial of the six men began after Ahmadinejad was elected President in 2005, and their ringleader said he had met Ayatollah Mesbah-Yazdi and been told that violence in carrying out the religious duties of "commanding the good and forbidding the evil" was praiseworthy. He explained the motive for killing the victims he considered morally corrupt: "Why should we allow a revolution for which so many martyrs paid with their blood to go to waste at the hands of such individuals?" Mesbah-Yazdi publicly proclaimed his support for such violence early in 2006, declaring: "We must wipe away the shameful stain whereby some people imagine that violence has no place in Islam.... We have decided and are determined to argue and prove that violence is the heart of Islam."[47] The President and his mentor used their considerable influence at all levels of the judiciary hierarchy, including the Supreme Court, to secure the acquittal of all six Basiji murderers in the name of God in April 2007.[48] That summer Ayatollah Mesbah-Yazdi invited the President to give the commence-ment speech for the graduating class of clerics at his institute in Qom.[49]

Ahmadinejad's other strong supporter in Iran's ruling elite is Ayatollah Ahmad Jannati, the powerful Secretary of the Guardian Council and the chief gatekeeper in vetting candidates to all elected offices, who had put him on the Council's payroll as an election inspector and enabled him to become part of the hardliner elections network that evolved during Nateq-Nuri's 1997 campaign. The 1997 hardliner group included Ahmadinejad's future Interior Minister, 'Ali Kordan, who played a critical role in his own election eight years later.[50] Jannati took all twelve members of the Guardian Council to see Ahmadinejad upon his election to congratulate him and assure him that he had the Council's full support.[51] This was followed by the Ayatollah's support for Ahmadinejad's attempt to convert President Bush.

Ayatollah Jannati's unprecedented gesture of support was significant indeed. Having followed his repentance for lapsing and letting in reformers in 2000, he resoundingly defeated Khatami and the reformists and closed the gates to their candidacy and reelection in 2004, a task he would perform with even greater success in the 2008 Majles elections. Jannati did not have to worry about the Seventh and later the Eight Majles whose candidates he had vetted properly. As the Majles began to know its place and became more compliant, the tension in its relations with other organs of the regime somewhat surprisingly shifted from the Guardian Council to the presidency. Ahmadinejad showed the same imperiousness in dealing with the hardliner Majles as Jannati had toward the reformist one he had defeated.

When Ahmadinejad sent a bill to the Majles to use 8 billion dollars of Iran's oil foreign exchange for his Imam Reza Love Fund, the Majles found the figure alarming and rejected the bill. The President went ahead and set up the Fund anyway, though it is not clear how much foreign exchange he diverted to it.[52] In 2007, the Majles reacted against being ignored and countered some of the arbitrary acts of the President, who refused to consider himself accountable. It restored daylight savings time, which Ahmadinejad had abolished as un-Islamic by an executive order, and insisted on submission of a line-budget. The Majles also passed legislation to supply cheap gas to villages during the 2007–2008 winter. Ahmadinejad wrote to Majles Speaker Haddad-'Adel in January 2008 saying the Legislature was infringing upon the prerogatives of the Executive branch in requesting budgetary specification and interfering with daylight savings time, and he flatly refused to implement the last item of legislation. Rather than responding in kind and provoking a constitutional crisis, the Majles Speaker timidly begged the Leader and Supreme Jurist for help in a letter to which the latter tersely replied: "All lawful legislation that has gone through the proper procedures stipulated in the Constitution is binding for all branches of government."[53] This ruling had little or no effect on Ahmadinejad's behavior in 2008. He has refused to allow any budgetary scrutiny, pushing the Majles to seek the help of the Maslahat Council, which has instead seized the opportunity to insert itself into the budgetary process. He has also refused to increase the number of university students as legislated by the Majles despite the approval of the Guardian Council.

The Majles has had little success exercising its theoretical control over the government budget as the President refused to share necessary budgetary information. It can, however, still exercise its power of supervision over the Executive through confirmation and dismissal of ministers. In August 2008, Ahmadinejad's hardliner opponents in the new Majles dismissed 'Ali Kordan, the Interior Minister, shortly after his confirmation had been pushed through in an irregular fashion, for faking an Oxford University doctorate and attempting to bribe the Majles deputies. Ahmadinejad backed his old friend, counting on him as the Interior Minister for reelection in 2009, and said Kordan also had the backing of Ayatollah Khamenei. But the hard-liners retorted that the Leader was misrepresented and did not confirm his support.

Ahmadinejad's relations with the members of his own military-security stratum outside the Majles has not been smooth either. He cannot be said to have emerged as its undisputed leader, say, as Nasser did for its Egyptian counterpart after Egypt's July 1952 revolution. His "Well Serving Faction" did poorly in elections for municipal councils in December 2006, whereas his rival hardliner in the 2005 presidential elections, Mohammad Baqer Qalibaf, who became the mayor of Tehran, did very well and has secured the support of the economically conservative Coalition Groups alienated by the anti-corruption campaign, as well as that of Hashemi-Rafsanjani. Like Ahmadinejad, Qalibaf is a member of the military-security second stratum vying for the leadership of the new political class. He moved from the Revolutionary Guards into the Unified Forces of Order to become Tehran's Police Chief, and in that capacity set up the IRI's first female police force. Ahmadinejad eliminated the training program for this female force, and must have been miffed when his own initiative to court women's support by allowing them to watch men's soccer games in the summer of 2006 was overruled by the religious authorities.

Rather than targeting the poor like Ahmadinejad, Qalibaf courted the young in the Iranian electorate during the 2005 presidential elections, donning a white suit and flashy sunglasses. In response to a memo he wrote to President Ahmadinejad, the latter reportedly scribbled on the margin: "Go eat shit!"[54] Qalibaf was not intimidated and continued to challenge Ahmadinejad's leadership of the new political class for a while, but gave up the effort by 2009 and decided not to run for President against Ahmadinejad. Qalibaf was not alone in challenging Ahmadinejad, however.

Ahmadinejad does not seem to have succeeded in winning over the Revolutionary Guards, unlike some of the ruling clerics, to seeing the Holocaust initiative his way. The popular Baztab website associated with the IRGC described it as "adventurism at the expense of national interests" and rebuked Ahmadinejad for deviating from the position of Imam Khomeini, who had never doubted the Holocaust.[55] In January 2007, another faction of hard-liners, inclined to administrative pragmatism or rationality, split off from the Ahmadinejad faction, calling itself the Creatively Principal-oriented (*osulgarāyān-e khallāq*). Clear evidence of Ahmadinejad's arbitrariness and lack of leadership capability for dealing with hardliners in the Majles and his own cabinet came to light in the last months of his first term after the electoral putsch of June 2009. After going along with Ahmadinejad and the Leader in June and suggesting that the reformist presidential candidate Mir-Hossein Musavi be put on trial, prominent hardliner parliamentarians he offended broke ranks with Ahmadinejad. In the latter part of July, they linked together his arrogant refusal to obey the Leader's order (of July 18) to dismiss the relative he had appointed deputy-president with the inhumane treatment of the detainees from the protests after the Leader was forced to order the closure of the Kahrizak prison where many of them had died through neglect. Smelling blood, several hardliner ministers, notably the Minister of Culture and Islamic Guidance Saffar-Harandi and Minister of Intelligence Hojjat al-Eslam Mohesni-Ezhe'i, stormed out of the cabinet meeting in which Ahmadinejad confirmed his support for the relative, Esfandiar Rahim-Masha'i (who nevertheless felt compelled to resign later). Mohesni-Ezhe'i's parliamentary ally who chaired the Majles Intelligence Committee declared he had changed his mind about broadcasting confessions of the alleged velvet revolutionaries.[56] Ahmadinejad reacted by dismissing Mohesni-Ezhe'i and Saffar-Harandi, as well as the Ministers of Labor and Health. This prompted the Majles Deputy-Speaker to say that any further cabinet meeting before the end of Ahmadinejad's term would be illegal without a Majles vote of confidence. National Radio and Television chief and a former commander of the Revolutionary Guards, Ezzatollah Zarghami, had the Leader's order read out a week after it was issued, and another Revolutionary Guard commander said Ahmadinejad should have obeyed the Leader's order. Ahmadinejad's powerful clerical supporter, Guardian Council Secretary Ayatollah Jannati, similarly chided him for his disrespect for the Mandate of the Jurist.[57] Even the Basij militia would not tow Ahmadinejad's political line, and a spokesman for it said it set up a think-tank to "introduce our elite into government" and propose a "desired cabinet lineup" to him.[58]

The Revolutionary Guards' Electoral Coup to End the Republic and Inaugurate Clerical Monarchy

During the campaign for the presidential election of June 12, 2009, Ahmadinejad modified his approach to social justice, partly shifting his rhetoric to corruption among powerful members of the clerical elite and their sons and to the creation of aristocracy (*ashrāfiyyat*) by Hashemi-Rafsanjani, and partly replacing rhetoric with action by distributing potatoes, oranges, and especially government checks before the election.[59] To these were added

FIGURE **8.3** Former Iranian President Mohammad Khatami (right) and Mehdi Karrubi (left), Leader of Iran's reformist National Confidence party, attend a party congress in Tehran on October 16, 2008. Karrubi had already declared that he was running against President Ahmadinejad in June 2009. Khatami was to do the same early in 2009 but withdrew in March in favor of Mir-Hossein Musavi. (Getty Images/AFP)

a dose of nationalistic chauvinism fired by the projection of the IRGC in the geopolitics of the region. He performed well in the debates with other presidential candidate, and seemed to be doing well by the end of May.

The two candidates fielded by the reformists who survived the scrutiny of the Guardian Council, Mir-Hossein Musavi and Hojjat al-Eslam Mahdi Karrubi, organized highly efficient campaigns that brought out the marginalized and disaffected groups in the population, putting the turnout to over 80 percent of the electorate (figure 8.3). Karrubi was helped by Karbaschi and the Servants of Construction who put together a team for the revival and reconstruction of the economy. Musavi's campaign was critically helped by his wife, Zahra Rahnavard, a leader of the women's movement, and former university president who championed women's issues in the campaign and brought out women and students in massive numbers (figure 8.4). He had an early endorsement from Khatami, and enlisted the support of Hashemi-Rafsanjani as his campaign was gathering momentum. He had learned the lesson about the cost to the reformists of alienating Hashemi-Rafsanjani in 2000, and welcomed his support. Support for Musavi snowballed in the early days of June and must have caused some concern on the part of the Leader and Ahmadinejad, who considered him a safer rival than Khatami and Qalibaf who had been persuaded not to run.

The polling hours were extended on June 12 because of the massive turnout. Already at noon, Ahmadinejad's website had called the election the "Third Revolution," following the Revolutionary Guards' earlier warnings about the reformist plots for a "velvet revolution," which was to be foiled.[60] SMS services, used by the campaign organizers, were shut down, and mobile and internet networks and services went out. The plans for foiling the velvet revolution attempt and for initiating the "Third Revolution" were put into effect two hours after polling stations were closed and many of them were still counting the vote. While the security forces had blockaded the Interior Ministry and were surrounding the campaign headquarters of the reformist candidates and setting up positions at nodal points across the capital, the Ministry of Interior declared a landslide victory for the incumbent President Mahmud Ahmadinejad. The press had been told to expect the results late on

FIGURE 8.4 Mir-Hossein Musavi, the leading reformist candidate, and his wife, Zahra Rahnavard, attending a campaign rally in south Tehran on May 30, 2009. Musavi claimed victory late in the evening of June 12. (Getty Images/AFP)

Saturday or Sunday June 13 or 14 but the announcement was made a little after midnight from the so-called aggregation (*tajmī'*) room in the Ministry of the Interior, from which the representatives of the candidates were excluded, as was Hojjat al-Eslam Nateq-Nuri of the Leader's Inspectorate who was among the members of the clerical ruling elite accused of corruption by Ahmadinejad during the presidential debates. Ahmadinejad was declared the winner with 63 percent of the popular vote as against Musavi's 34 percent, and Karrubi, who had beaten Ahmadinejad in the first round of the 2005 election until the Guardian Council intervened, was said to have received fewer votes than the number of spoiled ballots. At the same time, the leaders of the main reformist organizations were rounded up, notably Mohsen Mirdamadi, Zahra Aghajari, 'Abdullah Ramazanzadeh, and Mohammad Reza Khatami (released the following day) of the Participation Front, and Behzad Nabavi and Mostafa Tajzadeh of the Organization of the Mojahedin of the Islamic Revolution. This move in particular can only be explained by premeditated theft of the election and by no other motive.[61]

The Basij militia had been used very efficiently in 2005 to engineer the election of the then obscure candidate Ahmadinejad. As President, instead of perfecting the techniques of ballot stuffing developed in 2005, he decided to save the Basij for dealing with the aftermaths, leaving the electoral engineering to his Interior Minister Sadeq Mahsuli, the underling who had taken over the Interior after the Majles dismissed Kordan, Ahmadinejad's top election engineer and first choice for the task, for faking a Ph.D. degree. It is reasonable to assume that the IRGC leaders had contingency plans that were carried out once they knew the elections were going very badly for Ahmadinejad.

The greatest puzzle is why the Leader Khamenei went along and endorsed the hastily announced results even before they were officially presented to him by the Guardian Council as required by law. He clearly could not think that Musavi would be a more serious threat to him than Khatami had been, especially now that his grip on the military-security apparatus was even more firm. Khamenei may not have anticipated the outburst of popular indignation and anger, but could surely not underestimate the cost of Hashemi-Rafsanjani's alienation. The puzzle remains, though the possibility of human error and poor judgment, greed for power and the rumors of intrigue by his son Mojtaba, the foremost *āgāzadeh* of the realm and staunch Ahmadinejad supporter, cannot be discounted. On the contrary, they appear to be confirmed by Mojtaba's leadership of the Basij in the suppression of subsequent protests.[62]

Electoral fraud was evident from the preposterous figures announced by the Ministry of Interior and instantly rekindled the power struggle between the hardliners and the reformists, which was immediately fueled by the massive public outrage at the theft of the popular vote.[63] The reformists' instinctive reaction was to bemoan the end of the republicanism of the IRI as instituted by Imam Khomeini. The editorial of Musavi's organ, *Kalemeh-ye Sabz* (Green word) was entitled "Political Coup, End of Republicanism," and asserted that its engineers "have with this attempt put their seal on the end of the republicanism of the regime."[64] It also published the announcement by the Association of Militant Clerics (MRM) apologizing for its failure "to protect the vote of the people" and demanding the annulment of the presidential election.[65]

Musavi called for a demonstration to protest fraud in the election on June 15 but cancelled it at the last minute. Nevertheless, crowds gathered spontaneously and began the march, and before long, their number exceeded a million. Demonstrators who had marched silently on June 15 knew how to apportion the blame according to the importance of the two principle actors in their slogans, softly chanted to avoid provocation: "Death to the Dictator" (=the Leader Khamenei) and the milder and more contemptuous "Liar!" and "Ahmadi[nejad], shame on you; go open a vegetable stand!"[66] The pressure was coming from below and spontaneously. As Musavi had cancelled the march, the vast majority of the demonstrators did not know that he and Zahra Rahnavard had in fact joined it, any more than they knew that Khatami and Karrubi had. As one of them put it, "we don't really have a leader."[67] In a different spot, the spontaneous pressure from below was articulated by the former President Khatami's brother, Mohammad-Reza Khatami, just released from detention, who told the crowd: "keep your protests going until the results are annulled and there is a new election."[68]

Propelled by this massive popular enthusiasm, Musavi proved equal to the task of leadership. He had been savvy in adopting the color green suggested to him during the campaign by his internationally inspired young supporters but presented it in Islamic terms and as the color of the Family of the Prophet (*ahl-e bayt*). Though stunned in the day of the putsch, his old revolutionary instinct told him he should contest the hardliners' appropriation of Islamic slogans instead of using any which may give the hardliners a pretext to identify the protest against electoral fraud as the movement for a velvet revolution promoted, as Khamanei was nevertheless to put it within a few days in his Friday sermon, by a "Zionist-American millionaire" (meaning George Soros).

Musavi reportedly told his supporters to use two slogans only: "God is Great!" and "There is no God but God."[69] The symbolism of protest, the march from the Revolution (*Enqelāb*) Square to the Freedom (*Āzādī*) Square, was carefully planned to reflect the teleology of the Islamic revolution according to the reformist camp. Even the generation born after the revolution filled the air of the city of Tehran with cries of "God is Great!" (*Allāhu akbar*) from their rooftops at night, as had been done in the nights of the Islamic revolution in 1978–1979.

On June 14, Basij militiamen attacked the dormitory of the University of Tehran, killing at least seven students. Violence also erupted at the end of the peaceful, silent march of June 15 in Tehran, claiming at least fifteen lives. Pro-Musavi protests were also held in other major cities on that day, resulting in a number of deaths that raised the total number to at least 32.[70] The clampdown on the opposition continued on the following day, with the arrest of many more reformist leaders and human right activists in Tehran, Tabriz, and elsewhere.[71] Beating and intimidation of demonstrators at their homes by the Basij continued late into the night. During the very large demonstration in Tehran to mourn the deaths on June 18, Musavi and the demonstrators, wearing black in addition to green ribbons, chanted "God is Great" and demanded "protection of their vote and the restitution of the republicanism of the Islamic revolution."[72]

In his Friday June 19 sermon, Ayatollah Khamenei sternly warned the opposition against further public demonstrations and told its leaders they would be responsible for any "chaos, violence and bloodshed."[73] Many thousands nevertheless defied him by demonstrating and were violently suppressed. Neither these tough words nor repeated warnings by the police and Revolutionary Guards deterred continued popular defiance in the form of sporadic demonstrations in Tehran and other major cities, notably Tabriz, Isfahan, and Shiraz, and cries of "God is Great!" from rooftops throughout July. These demonstrations of popular resistance were clearly spontaneous and without any direction from the reformist candidates, Musavi and Karrubi, who were encouraged to remain firm and refuse to compromise, however. Meanwhile, the number of deaths was approaching 200 by mid-July, and the number of detainees must have remained at least ten times as many, despite releases, including 140 ordered by the Leader in late July.[74]

The hardliners continued their power struggle against the reformist children of the revolution that now took the form of ruthless suppression. On August 1, 2009, two days before their President was sworn in by the Leader, the Revolutionary Guards put a hundred reformist detainees on a show trial for plotting a velvet revolution in collusion with foreign powers on the basis of coerced confessions in what appears as an attempt at their final liquidation. The move was clever because the Revolutionary Guards could count not just on the effectiveness of torture but also on finding enough rats among the hundred detainees who had turned around more than once from radical to pragmatist to reformist and would not find it impossible to go over to the hardliners under duress. The first two televised confessions in fact included one such rat, 'Atrianfar, a former member of the military-intelligence second stratum who had attained the rank of deputy minister, and showed no difficulty whatsoever in obliging his old military intelligence friends by turning in his newer reformist colleagues and glibly confirming their alleged ties with unnamed foreign puppeteers who were staging a velvet revolution.[75] 'Atrianfar was impressively adroit in handling the discourse he had shared with the hardliners as an erstwhile radical: that of foreign conspiracy to destroy the Islamic revolution. The common revolutionary discourse put the reformists at a grave disadvantage in the summer of 2009, after their star had fallen, just as in the spring of 2000, when it had been on the ascendance. Once more, the defeat of the reformists in the revolutionary power struggle was facilitated by the fact that the old political rhetoric of the revolutionary discourse, shared with hardliners in their radical days during the first decade of the Islamic revolution, unmistakably worked against them.[76]

To conclude this chapter as the crisis remains unabated and seems far from closure at the beginning of August 2009, Iran's new political class may or may not be ready to displace the remaining republican component of the IRI regime by unabashed class rule, but Ahmadinejad certainly proved himself incapable of leading it in the crisis caused by his electoral putsch.

9

Khomeini's Successor

Ayatollah Khamenei as the Leader
of the Islamic Republic of Iran

AS THE PRESIDENTS OF THE ISLAMIC REPUBLIC OF IRAN HAVE CHANGED, there has been remarkable stability at the apex of the Islamic order, with Ayatollah Sayyed 'Ali Khamenei having served as the Leader and Supreme Jurist since Khomeini's death. The gradual extension of Ayatollah Khamenei's control over the political, judiciary, and economic institutions was the counterpart to the progressive marginalization of Hashemi-Rafsanjani in the mid-1990s and to the decline and fall of Khatami in the early 2000s. It took the form of the penetration of the Judiciary by securing the appointment of the Ayatollah's own men, thereby "politicizing" it, and more surprisingly, by penetrating the state bureaucracy and lastly the legislature. Khamenei considered the military-security elite his men and let two of them run for President in 2005. The victory of his preferred candidate, Mahmud Ahmadinejad, in 2005 and the electoral putsch of June 2009 did not end the Leader's dominance, but modified it as the military-security elite represented by the President has become increasingly vocal in speaking for Iran's newly maturing political class.

Neopatrimonial Domination and Growing
into the Office of Leadership

The Supreme Jurist of Khomeini's novel theory of theocratic government prevailed over the "sources of imitation" of the traditional Shi'ite hierarchy.

But a revolution whose avowed goal had been to save Shi'ite Islam from the onslaught of secularism and westernization could not abolish the positions of its custodians or the independence of the traditional Shi'ite hierocracy based on religious learning through the seminaries. The attempt to organize the Shi'ite clerical body by the Islamic Republican Party in a one-party system failed, and Khomeini abolished it in 1987. In the same year, he set up the Special Court for Clerics to keep them in line, but the measure of political control and clerical disciplining it could achieve had limits. Nor was the Leader's appointment of the Head of the Judiciary sufficient to obliterate the Judiciary's institutional autonomy. Limited but effective institutional pluralism thus persisted in the Islamic Republic of Iran (IRI), and is perpetuated by clerical conciliarism, while the authoritarianism of the Leadership principle is combined with transmuted mobilizational features and attenuation of revolutionary ideology into loyalty to the Mandate of the Jurist. Furthermore, the hydra-headed consolidation of the revolutionary power structures alongside the state bureaucracy has created a political regime that has been typified as "fragmented authoritarianism."[1] What observers have

FIGURE 9.1 This mural in a busy Tehran thoroughfare depicts Imam Khomeini and Leader Khamenei. The caption reads: "We will continue on the Path of the Imam and the martyrs of the revolution." The Supreme Leader [Khamenei]. (Photograph by James Hill/Contact Press Images)

not sufficiently noted about the post-revolutionary regime is its neo-patri-monialism.[2] To concentrate power in his own hands, the Leader has had the enormous resources of his economic patrimony, the *bonyād*s and their nodes of connection with the industrial complex and import trade, and he has done the same with the vast sector of the economy under his control through the foundations. To this economic patrimony should be added the extensive Leadership Office with its various branches and huge discretionary budget. Leadership (*maqām-e rahbari*) was never asked to account for his patrimonial dispensations and expenditure of his Office, but the hardliner Majles, in an astounding feat of self-limitation, exempted all financial and political activi-ties under Leadership from parliamentary oversight in the last days of 2008. Their supreme guardian and guardian of their Guardian Council could no longer be expected to be accountable to the people even theoretically. All he was expected to do was to follow the path of Imam Khomeini as the supreme leader of the Islamic revolution (figure 9.1).

The Supreme Jurist and the Subjugation of the Shi'ite Hierarchy

Khomeini's Mandate of the Jurist and the traditional juristic authority of the Shi'ite Grand Ayatollahs or "sources of imitation" were categorically different, one relating to the state and the other to the hierocracy and their respective authority systems. Khomeini himself rejected the original 1979 compromise that had made the *marja'iyyat* (being a source of imitation) a condition for the Leadership of the Jurist or membership in the alternative Leadership Council, and both these provisos were eliminated with the 1989 constitu-tional amendments. Ayatollah Khamenei as Khomeini's successor tried his own hand at solving the contradiction between the two principles in favor of the state-centered Mandate of the Jurist, but failed. The attempt is neverthe-less worth considering in some detail. When Grand Ayatollah Abu'l-Qasem Kho'i died in August 1992, the Head of the Judiciary, Ayatollah Mohammad Yazdi, suggested that his followers and the Kho'i Foundation should recognize Ayatollah Khamenei as the source of imitation and pay their religious taxes and voluntary contributions to him. Ayatollah Yazdi made a more elaborate argument when Grand Ayatollah Golpaygani died in December 1993. The plurality of the sources of imitation, he argued, had been acceptable before the creation of the Islamic Republic, but was intolerable now that an Islamic state was securely in place. The existence of several sources of imitation was intoler-able when "guarding the sovereignty of Islam is an incumbent necessity."[3] As religion and politics were not separable, both the centralization and the unification of religious and political authority were needed for the preservation of the Islamic state. Yazdi, however, could not carry the day. As the second best interim solution, the ruling clerical elite promoted an aging Ayatollah who was rumored to be senile, Mohammad-'Ali Araki, into the position of *marja'-e taqlid*. Their endorsement was accompanied by the promise to bring out Araki's manual (*resāla-ye 'amaliyya*), which was eventually published in mid-August 1989. Meanwhile, they advised Khomeini's followers in law and ritual (*moqalledin*) to imitate Araki, and the latter permitted them to continue following Khomeini's rulings.[4]

When Grand Ayatollah Araki died at the age of 101 in December 1994, the ruling clerical elite was ready to push for the final realization of Ayatollah Yazdi's project of abolition of the institution of *marja'iyyat*. The project, however, foundered on the resistance of the Qom Seminary Professors (*modarresin-e hoza-ye 'elmiyya-ye Qom*) who assumed responsibility for the designation of religious authorities on the basis of the traditional principle of superiority in learning (*a'lamiyyat*). Despite all the imaginable arm-twisting to make them recognize the Leader of the Islamic Republic, Khamenei, as the sole source of imitation, the professors of the seminaries of Qom proposed seven religious authorities as possible sources of imitation. The fact that Ayatollah Yazdi had achieved the minimalist goal of having Khamenei, designated Grand Ayatollah, included among the seven was cold comfort and fell far short of the objective of declaring him the *sole marja'*. President Hashemi-Rafsanjani stepped in to help Khamenei save face by saying the latter had no intention of being a *marja'* inside the country and his *marja'iyyat* was only effective abroad. Khamenei himself reiterated this but could not disguise the embarrassment of the regime in the speeches he made after the event.[5] In the statement of Khamenei's promoters in the first days of December 1994, there were references to the Imamate of Khamenei, in an attempt to transfer the title of Imam from Khomeini to him.[6] The title was sporadically used in the next three years, but slowly disappeared after the challenge to the Mandate of the Jurist by dissident clerics in 1997.

The *marja'iyyat* crisis had repercussions beyond Iran and resulted in a split between the Lebanese Hizbollah's spiritual guide, Ayatollah Muhammad Fadlallah, who opted for Grand Ayatollah Sistani, and its political leader, Hojjat al-Eslam Hasan Nasrallah, who critically depended on Iranian government aid and chose Khamenei.[7] This in turn had an impact on Khamenei's very curious and otherwise inexplicable decision to decline the position of *marja'iyyat* in Iran, while accepting it for the Shi'a outside of Iran. Nasrallah was predictably appointed his representative in Lebanon.[8] By separating the two principles tenuously linked in the 1979 Constitution, the 1989 amendments had resulted in a new dualism of political and religious authority, representing a compromise between traditional and innovative principles, between *marja'iyyat* and *velāyat-e faqih*. This compromise proved stable and survived the failed attempt to establish Khamenei as the sole *marja'*.

Ayatollah Yazdi knew in the early 1990s that the great age and imminent death of the Grand Ayatollahs Kho'i, Golpaygani, and Araki meant a unique opportunity for solving the problem created by the incompatibility between the old and the new principles of Shi'ite authority. This attempt at its solution failed, however, and the regime's structural fault line was not repaired. With Grand Ayatollah Sistani's eminence in Iraq since 2003 and a new generation of jurists in their sixties and seventies forcing its way into the highest Shi'ite clerical rank, the issue could only be shelved, not solved.

This did not prevent Khamenei's far-reaching practical measures to tighten his bureaucratic and financial control over the religious institution and to establish a system of surveillance under Leadership that greatly undermined the autonomy of the Grand Ayatollahs and thus of the Shi'ite hierocracy generally. Khomeini had been content to continue acting through a consortium for distributing stipends from the Grand Ayatollahs to seminarians of the Qom Learning Center (*hawza*) and just set his own stipend as the highest. Khamenei reorganized the consortium for the distribution of stipends into a Hawza Management Center with a "Statistical Office" for collecting information on the seminarians and preachers that created a modern surveillance system as an instrument of political control through information. The vast financial resources at the disposal of Khamenei compared to other Grand Ayatollahs' meager resources through voluntary donations put him in a position to control and manipulate the impaired hierocratic authority structure, while a bureaucratic network extends over the seminaries to standardize the syllabi and find employment for its graduates.[9]

Since the declaration of his *marja'iyyat* abroad, Ayatollah Khamenei has supplemented the discretionary budget of the Leadership Office in Iran with the collection of religious dues from the rich Shi'ites in Kuwait and other Gulf countries.[10] After the invasion of Iraq in 2003, his representative 'Ali al-Tashkiri frequently returned to Iraq to distribute largess to the *madrasas* and other religious institutions in the Najaf Learning Center and through other Shi'ite clerical networks abroad, thus bringing them under Ayatollah

Khamenei's influence, making credible his claim to be the spiritual leader of all the Muslims of the world.

Protecting the Islamic Revolution against Cultural Invasion by the West

Khamenei had meanwhile been carving a special position for himself in contradistinction to Hashemi-Rafsanjani's pragmatism and economic reconstruction. The new mission may have been suggested to him by an open letter published in June 1991 by 35 professors. Taking their cue from Khomeini's famous pronouncement against East and West during the Cultural Revolution in 1980—"We are not afraid of military attacks, we are afraid of colonial universities"—these post-Cultural-Revolution-purge professors claimed that the undermining of tradition, the family, and social mores by the spread of such notions as "one-world culture," "the global village," and "the new world order" constituted a Western cultural invasion.[11] In a series of sermons that continued through the assassination of dissident intellectuals by the Devotees of Pure Mohammadan Islam in 1994–1995, the Leader championed the protection of the Islamic revolution against the Western cultural onslaught. The hardliners' alarm was heightened by the convergence of Sorush's reformism with the formation of the Servants for Reconstruction by Hashemi-Rafsanjani's top technocrats in January 1996. The technocrats announced in their founding statement that enough had been done for "strengthening the values of the revolution and the regime.... Now the time has come to utilize our skills and efficiency to face the challenges arising from the lack of development and to strengthen our economic policies...." The hardliners took this statement to be the declaration of the end of the revolution. As a journal of the Helpers of Hezbollah put it the following month: "it amounts to the death of the revolution as well as of Islamic values."[12]

In response, as satellites were being impounded and state-controlled public media incessantly sounded the alarm about the Western onslaught, the Leader's pronouncements on the subject were collected and published by the Ministry of Culture and Islamic Guidance later in 1996 under the title of *Culture and the Cultural Invasion* (*Farhang va tahājom-e farhangi*). Ayatollah Khamenei reassured the hardliners that the revolution would not end: "Do not think that the revolution has ended; it continues." It is "not a struggle of today, or one day, two days, one year or two years. It is the struggle of generations." The Islamic republic therefore needed to be defended: "Groups of the faithful, mobilized forces, the Hezbollah fighters should act in such a way throughout the country that America, the Zionists, and the rest of the enemies of the Islamic republic lose any hope [of winning]."[13]

Khamenei's apprehension of the Western cultural invasion shaped his consistent outlook that has found repeated expression in the current decade. Preparing to clamp down on reformism despite its resounding victory in the 2000 parliamentary elections, he stated: "I have now reached the conclusion that the United States has devised a comprehensive plan to subvert the Islamic system. This plan is an imitation of the collapse of the former Soviet Union." Three years later, he told the Iranian nation that "Iran's enemies, more than artillery, guns and so forth, need to spread cultural values that lead to moral corruption."[14] He proceeded to attribute the following remark to one such American enemy: "Instead of bombs, send them miniskirts."[15] In January 2005, he explained a new method of subversion: "In the present postmodern colonial era, the arrogant powers are trying to influence other nations with the help of their agents, by spending money and through propaganda tactics and colorful enticements."[16] He developed this interpretation of the velvet revolutions of the decade, offering an inimitably smooth Persian equivalent for it, "soft overthrow" (*barandāzi-ye narm*), which by 2007 became part of the official terminology of the Iranians for several arrests, including some American-Iranian scholars. Khamenei was convinced of a countervailing Islamic soft power that he sought to harness, using the extensive resources of the Iranian Leadership office and other means. He has consciously sought to ride the wave of Islamic resurgence in this decade, and his official website accordingly calls him the "Supreme Leader of Muslims."[17]

Growth of the Leader's Personal Power: His Pick from the Second Stratum

Khamenei had begun as the weaker partner of the post-Khomeini diarchy but clearly became the dominant one in the last years of Hashemi-Rafsanjani's second term. As the Leader, Khamenei reinforced the ties he had carefully cultivated with the Revolutionary Guards, whose commander, Mohsen Reza'i, he retained until 1998. He also quickly changed his modernist predisposition and saw the Leader's commonality of interest with the traditionalist clerics in charge of the theocratic conciliar system. The legitimacy of Leadership was inextricably bound with that of clerical conciliarism and undermining it was self-destructive. The modernist disposition he had displayed in the different office of the IRI President did not befit his new supreme office and was quickly discarded.

During the first decade or so as Khomeini's successor, Khamenei tended to rely on Iraqi exiled clerics of Iranian descent—the so-called returnees (*mo'āvedin*)—to strengthen his power as these clerics were aliens without deep social ties or influence. Foremost in this group was Ayatollah Mahmud al-Hashemi/Hashemi-Shahrudi, the first chairman of the Supreme Council for the Islamic Revolution in Iraq (SCIRI), who was appointed to the Guardian Council in 1995 and became the Head of the Judiciary in 1999. Another prominent returnee is 'Ali al-Taskhiri, who was appointed to the new Office of the Supreme Leader with Shahrudi in 1989 and was put in charge of international relations with the Muslim world.

The initially cordial relations between the Leader and President Hashemi-Rafsanjani became strained after the Majles elections of 1992, which brought the hardliners into the majority in the Fifth Majles. With Hojjat al-Eslam 'Ali-Akbar Nateq-Nuri as the new Majles Speaker, the hardliners immediately set out to obstruct Hashemi-Rafsanjani's economic reconstruction and privatization, and gravitated toward Khamenei, who found their support convenient in the bid to increase his power. The President, under pressure from both sides, bowed to the wishes of the new Majles and appointed hardliners close to the Supreme Jurist to key Ministries of Interior and Islamic Guidance. Meanwhile, the Leader would not miss any opportunity to replace other Hashemi-Rafsanjani men with his own. In 1992, for example, the Leader used his prerogative (added by the 1989 constitutional amendment) to oust the President's brother as the head of the national radio and television and replace him with 'Ali Larijani. Larijani had briefly held the Ministry of Culture and Islamic Guidance after Khatami was ousted by the Majles hardliners earlier in the year. That Ministry did not revert to a Rafsanjani man, but went to one of Khamenei's: Mostafa Mir-Salim. The final break between the two men came in the last year of Hashemi-Rafsanjani's second term, when Deputy-President Mohajerani's proposal to amend the Constitution to allow him to run for another term was vetoed by the Supreme Leader, who, after failing to secure a declaration as the sole "source of imitation," was less and less inclined to share power. Instead, he accepted the advice of the Assembly of Leadership Experts to revitalize the Maslahat Council in the spring of 1997 and leave it to Hashemi-Rafsanjani in order to ease him out of the presidency.

Having failed to amend the Constitution and remain President, Hashemi-Rafsanjani supported the candidacy of his former Minister of Culture and

Islamic Guidance, Sayyed Mohammad Khatami, in the 1997 presidential election. Like his predecessor, Khatami in turn felt compelled to accept Khamenei's men in some key positions in the Executive. The Leader's clerical commissar for universities, Hojjat al-Eslam Qorban-'Ali Dorri-Najafabadi, notably, became his Minister of Intelligence and Security.

During Khatami's presidency, Hashemi-Rafsanjani's men were gradually pushed out of the administration, and the former President lost much political clout. After the refusal by the clerical hardliners of the JRM to put them on their list, Rafsanjani's second stratum organized themselves into a party, the Technocrats for Construction (*kārgozārān-e sāzandehgi*), mounted a vigorous campaign during the 1996 Majles elections, and appeared as partners in Khatami's reform administration in 1997, with Mohajerani taking the key position of Ministry of Culture and Islamic Guidance. Other Rafsanjani lackluster technocrats, too, continued to serve under Khatami. The hardliners, however, went after Rafsanjani's men with the Leader's blessing. Their first victim was the Secretary-General of the Technocrats for Construction and the mayor of Tehran, Gholam-Hossein Karbaschi, who was put on trial for corruption in 1998. Hashemi-Rafsanjani's inability to protect his protégé was a foregone conclusion. It was damaging to his reputation within the ruling elite, and was seen as his final capitulation to Khamanei. Hashemi-Rafsanjani himself was forced out of the reformist camp. This was the reformists' costliest mistake. Akbar Ganji, heady with his utopian optimism transferred from the myth of revolution to that of inevitable democracy,[18] implicated Rafsanjani—as His Eminence dressed in red (modeled on Cardinal Richelieu)—in the murders ordered by the *eminences grises,* presumably 'Ali Fallahian, Gholam-Hossein Mohseni-Ezhehi, 'Ali Razini, and Mostafa Purmohammadi, the clerical hardliners in the Ministry of Intelligence trained by Ayatollah Mohammad-Taqi Mesbah-Yazdi at the Haqqani School.[19] This ill-conceived attack, and Hashemi-Rafsanjani's humiliating defeat in the Tehran 2000 Majles elections, alienated him from the reformists, and he threw in his lot entirely with the Leader. He could no longer be said to have much of an independent power base and become just an influential advisor to Khamenei. Before long, Khamanei also forced former Deputy-President Mohajerani, out in December 2000, while Khatami gave the latter a nonpolitical position as the Director of the Dialogue of Civilizations to pave his exit from politics into increasing obscurity. Rumors and complaints about Mohajerani's second and third wives resulted in his dismissal, while the first, Jamileh Kadivar (the sister of the dissident reformist cleric), was active as a Majles feminist reformer.

Another key *Kārgozār*, Mohsen Nurbakhsh, who had managed the Central Bank and Ministry of the Economy for Rafsanjani, was eased out of power and died in 2003.

Meanwhile, throughout the Khatami presidency, the Leader's men were being put in charge of the politicized courts and charged with the suppression of the press and harassment of the reformists. The constitutional theocracy was thus imperceptibly turning into a system of neo-patrimonial personal rule by the Leader, with increasing politicization of the Judiciary and ad hoc infiltration of a variety of governmental organs. The Islamic Revolutionary Guards Corps (IRGC) generals, Mohammad Baqer Zolqadr, Ahmadinejad's former commander at the Ramazan Headquarters of the Revolutionary Guards in the 1980s, and 'Ali-Reza Afshari were placed in the Interior Ministry and put in charge of internal security and conduct of the 2008 Majles elections. The Leader intensified his use of laymen—often nonentities—from the intelligence apparatus, inspectorates, and revolutionary and mobilization corps to concentrate power in his own hands. Beginning with the February 2004 Majles elections, he endorsed their intention to invade not only the Executive and the Judiciary but also the Legislature. In May 2004, he also appointed a former IRCG commander, 'Ezatollah Zarghami, as the head of national television and radio. Although invasion had been ongoing throughout the 1990s, it culminated in the preponderant presence of the military-security personnel in the Eighth Majles elected in 2008. The loud announcement of this invasion as an express goal by the hardliners in 2008 marked a new stage in the consolidation of Iran's new political class; and the Leader was determined to make the new class his own. The victory of the hardliners in the 2004 and even more in the 2008 Majles elections, many of whom were the former personnel of the Leadership Office or the Leader's men in the security apparatus and mobilization,[20] strengthened Ayatollah Khamanei's agglomeration of personal power in relation to the Majles. It was presumably the zeal of these men of the Leader that induced the Majles to deprive itself of the theoretical right to demand accountability from the Leadership Office and anything related to the Leader in December 2008.

At the end of February 2007, finding the Maslahat Council Chairman Rafsanjani heady with his recent election as President of the powerful Assembly of Leadership Experts, the Leader added Ahmadinejad's Minister of Intelligence and Security, his Deputy-President, two other military-intelligence men and one Mo'talefa hardliner to the Maslahat Council to balance the number of Rafsanjani pragmatists on the Council (8 to 8).[21] The

Leader's shift in favor of the military-intelligence men made the mainstay of the regime, the hardliners who subscribe to the Mandate of the Jurist and obey the Leader, a more heterogeneous group. Iran's new political class is a composite group, consisting of the clerical elite and the military-security second stratum, whose composition has been changing in favor of the latter. The traditionalist clerics and the military-mobilizational apparatchiks are two different political formations. It is true that they share power in the IRI structure and are further linked by the network of economic clientelism that has grown between the *bonyāds* and the IRCG economic empire around the military-industrial-commercial complex. However, the network of economic clientelism is not strong enough to ensure the smooth functioning of the system, hence the crucial neo-patrimonial role of the Leader in balancing the two political factions of the hardliners while managing a modicum of "negative integration" of the reformers as a loyal opposition. In the spring of 2008, the Judiciary, controlled by the Leader, ended the suspension of publication of three reformist papers, most notably *Sharq*. After completing his second term as President-cum-Leader of the Opposition, Khatami was allowed to create a foundation, *Bārān,* and transfer most of the members of his cabinet into its board of trustees. He continues to enjoy the privileges of a former President.

Seven important ministries went to men from the military-security segment of the second stratum in 2005. The one exception was the Ministry of Foreign Affairs, for which the Majles rejected Ahmadinejad's candidate and forced him to accept Manuchehr Mottaki, who belonged to a hardliner Majles faction whose offer of cooperation Ahmadinejad had turned down during his campaign.[22] In addition, he appointed two clerical hardliners who had been involved in the chain murders stopped by Khatami in 1999: Hojjat al-Islams Gholam-Hossein Ezhehi, Minister of Intelligence and Security, and Mostafa Purmohammadi, Minister of the Interior until 2008. The election of Ahmadinejad with the backing of the Leader-controlled security and mobilization apparatus in June 2005, the Majles law of December 2008, and especially the sham reelection in June 2009 can thus be seen as the culmination of the trend in accumulation of personal, extra-constitutional power by the Leader.

The men from the military-security second stratum promoted by the Leader seem to have gradually come into their own since 2003, making a bid for the representation of the new political class in the Majles and thus the future takeover of Iran. The control of a personal system of power is difficult, and the hardliners, formerly Khamanei's men, are not as easy to control as they appropriate the positions they attained through the Leader's favor. With the Majles and presidency as their additional power bases, the second stratum of Iran's new political class may decide to shake loose the tutelage of the Leader. The military-mobilizational hardliners turned politician have not remained united so far, however, and quite a few of them in the Majles and local government have distanced themselves from Ahmadinejad and formed their own factions. Many of them in the Majles did not endorse Ahmadinejad for a second term in 2009. Furthermore, the difficulty in controlling Ahmadinejad seemed to have motivated the Leader to begin tilting the balance of power back towards the clerical elite and Hashemi-Rafsanjani's faction in 2008, and even making a rare kind gesture toward the reformist loyal opposition.

The most assertive of Khamenei's new men is President Ahmadinejad, who has been claiming the direct blessing of the Hidden Imam and cultivating popularity with his program of economic populism and an assertive intrusion into foreign policy. The President's economic populism had been countered by the Leader's assumption of a greater role in economic policy. According to his instructions, the Maslahat Council has bypassed the Majles and determined the guidelines for the resumption and acceleration of privatization and strengthening of the market economy. In preparation for the ouster of Khatami and the reformists, Khamenei had recruited his own team of technocrats to take over the economy, or more precisely the sector of the economy which was not already under his loose control. With the expansion of the reach of the clerical conciliar system and the growth of the personal, extralegal power of the Leader, both of which are typical modes of post-revolutionary concentration of power, the trends toward centralization set by Hashemi-Rafsanjani and democratization initiated by Khatami have been reversed. The pro-clerical Developers, who won the Seventh Majles elections in 2004 with the help of the clericalist Guardian Council a year earlier, had a plan of their own for *perestroika*. The plan, as unveiled by their leader Haddad-'Adel, whose daughter is married to Ayatollah Khamenei's son, proposed to make Iran into a new China or Japan by performing the economic miracle of combining political and religiocultural conservatism with economic liberalization. This policy seems highly unrealistic because it requires the destruction of the economic base of the Islamic Republic. In any event, it was set aside by Ahmadinejad when he was elected President a year later. Leaving Ahmadinejad to implement his populist programs of social justice, diversion and personal dispensation of state funds into the provinces and small towns, international sable-rattling and nuclear bragging, Khamenei bypassed the hardliners in the Majles and charged his Maslahat Council with legislation to pave the way for Iran's projected Asian-modeled economic miracle under the Mandate of the Jurist.

The Maslahat Council submitted its guidelines for economic policy requested by the Leader late in 2004. He approved them in May 2005, and received supplementary guidelines fundamentally reinterpreting Article 44 of the Constitution in July 2006. These, too, were approved by the Leader. The completed guidelines were given by the Leader to the Executive for implementation in November 2006. These guidelines amounted to a radical reinterpretation of the letter and spirit of Article 44 of the Constitution, which divided the economy into three sectors: the private, the cooperative, and the public. The public sector dwarfed the other two, but public ownership was somewhat incidentally qualified by the proviso, "as long as it does not work against the interests of society." The new constitutional interpretation implied that public ownership was four times more likely to work against the public interest than not. Except for the extractive oil and gas industries, the state was ordered to gradually divest 80% of its ownership of economic enterprises in the public sector. The Maslahat Council guidelines for privatization, endorsed by the Leader, clearly trumped Ahmadinejad's privatization through shares of justice. In the early months of 2007, Khamanei praised the publication of the guidelines as an "economic revolution" and chastised the government for the slow pace of privatization.[23]

To counter Ahmadinejad's intrusion into foreign policy, the Leader set up a new advisory Strategic Council for Foreign Relations in June 2006, appointing former Foreign Ministers 'Ali-Akbar Velayati and Kamal Kharrazi to it.[24] It is interesting to note that Ahmadinejad's most significant act of defiance of the Leader to date has had a constitutional basis. The control of foreign policy through the Supreme National Security Council has been part of the growth of the Leader's personal, extra-constitutional power. He had chosen Hasan Ruhani as its chairman until 2005, and 'Ali Larijani after August 2005, even though Article 176 of the Constitution names the President as the Council's chairman. On October 20, 2007, President Ahmadinejad asserted his constitutional prerogative and replaced Larijani with one of his own men, Sa'id Jalili. The Leader was forced to fall back on his more modest constitutional power, and immediately appointed Larijani as one of his two representatives on the Supreme National Security Council to enable the latter to appear side by side with Jalili at the nuclear negotiations with the

European Union Foreign Minister, Javier Solano, on October 24 and show up the new man as an incompetent negotiator.[25] 'Ali Larijani was elected to the new Majles in March 2008, defeated the incumbent Majles Speaker, and took his place. In April 2008, Ahmadinejad dismissed two of the Leader's men from his cabinet, the Minister of the Economy, Davud Danesh Ja'fari, and the Minister of the Interior, Mostafa Purmohammadi.[26] This was apparently enough for the Leader, who seemed to have lost patience and cut the President out of the nuclear loop in June 2008. Ahmadinejad remained silent when Iran said it would agree to suspend uranium enrichment for six weeks at the beginning of July 2008, and Foreign Minister Mottaki, when accepting the proposal by the permanent members of the UN Security Council and Germany (5+1) to resume nuclear talks, went out of his way to contradict him concerning the Holocaust!

The Leader can be said to reserve the right to authorize any talk with the Americans now as much as he did when Khatami was in power. He reaffirmed, in January 2008, his view that "any relations would provide the possibility to the Americans to infiltrate Iran and . . . relations with America have no benefit for the Iranian nation now"; nevertheless he added that "Undoubtedly, the day the relations with America prove beneficial for the Iranian nation I will be the first one to approve that."[27]

At the beginning of the Gaza war, Ayatollah Khamenei took the initiative by issuing a *fatwā* on December 28, 2008, declaring anyone who would die defending the Palestinians a martyr in *jihad*. Over ten thousand volunteers quickly signed up and gathered in Tehran. The volunteers sacked the British embassy and threatened those of Jordan and Egypt, and finally occupied Tehran's Mehrabad airport, demanding transportation to take them to Gaza. They disbanded on January 4, 2009, when the Ayatollah told them Iran's hands were tied. Ahmadinejad was kept out of the picture from the beginning to the end, except for dispatching his brother to receive insults while persuading the volunteers that their work of consciousness-raising was complete and they should now go home.[28]

The reelection of Ahmadinejad may well be the beginning of the end for the Leader because it has changed the robust post-revolutionary regime he ruled into a more fragile one by creating a rift in its ruling clerical elite. Ahmadinejad appears to have succeeded in unifying the key elements in the military-security second stratum to assume the leadership of Iran's new political class, at least for going along with the electoral putsch of June 12, 2009. But quite apart from the cost to the regime in loss of legitimacy and popular support, the putsch created great tension between the military-security second stratum and the ruling clerical elite. Ahmadinejad's assault on Hashemi-Rafsanjani, Nateq-Nuri, and other important members of the ruling clerical elite during the June 2009 election and its aftermaths seriously strained the orchestrated unity of the two components of Iran's new political class. By identifying squarely with his men in the military-security apparatus headed by Ahmadinejad, the Leader and Supreme Jurist alienated an important segment of the ruling clerical elite and diminished his ability as the regime arbiter to engage in the balancing act he had learned from Khomeini.

The damage done to the relations between the clerical and the military-security components of Iran's new political class by the resumption of the power struggle among the children of the revolution with the June 12 putsch was even greater. Hashemi-Rafsanjani was now a powerless man, all his men in positions of power having long been ousted by the Leader except for the eight in the Maslahat Council who were equally matched by the Leader's men.[29] We will not know the extent of his support in the other clerical council he chaired, the Council of Leadership Experts, as, rumors notwithstanding, the Revolutionary Guards did not allow him to convene either council.[30] He remained silent for a month, then appeared to have come to terms with the Leader and was allowed to lead the Friday prayer on July 17. In his sermon to a raucous audience of sympathizers of the reformists, Hashemi-Rafsanjani picked up the major reformist theme in the power struggle and empha-sized the "republicanism" of the IRI. Having reminded the audience of his credentials as a revolutionary leader from the beginning, he reiterated the position he had staked out for himself as a candidate in the 2005 presidential elections that the IRI regime derived its legitimacy from the people and all its major offices were elective.[31] This time, however, he waxed more eloquent and skillfully invoked the authority of the father of the Islamic revolution to prove that the people's consent was essential for the legitimacy of all govern-ment. Imam Khomeini was said to have mentioned to him a little-known *hadith* attributed to the First Imam, 'Ali, which makes the consent of the people the exclusive basis for the legitimacy of political rule.[32] A few days later, Khatami, Hashemi-Rafsanjani's successor as IRI President, refused to accept the Guardian Council's certification of the election and proposed a national referendum on the matter.

Meanwhile, the reformists sought to draw the Grand Ayatollahs into the power struggle, but the majority of these "sources of imitation" did not respond, proving the Leader's successful domination over the Shi'ite learning center in Qom.[33] A delegation from the women's movement could secure an audience only with Grand Ayatollah Sane'i, and letters from the reformists candidates Musavi and Karrubi remained largely unanswered. Two Grand Ayatollahs ambiguously supported the reformists, while three others joined Sane'i in expressing their unequivocal support. The leading oppositional Grand Ayatollah, Montazeri, however, fiercely condemned electoral fraud and declared Ahmadinejad's government illegitimate in a number of proclamations and *fatwās*.[34] The most vehement personal attack on the Leader himself came from a leading radical cleric and the founder of the original Hezbollah in 1979, Hojjat al-Eslam Hadi Ghaffari.[35] In a gathering of Karrubi supporters in early July 2009, Ghaffari reminded Khamenei that Imam Khomeini had found his understanding of the Mandate of the Jurist defective,[36] and invited him to a debate as a fellow-cleric. Declaring that his body was accustomed to prison cells, he accused Khamenei of "turning religion into lying," and stated flatly that "the result of your leadership is the ruining of the reputation of the clergy," adding that his "clumsy defense of Mr. Ahmadinejad" was a grave mistake.[37]

Clerical Monarchy: Who Guards the Guardians?

The greatest challenge to the legitimacy of Leadership and the entire system of clerical conciliarism dependent on it came with the landslide victory of the reformists in the winter of 2000. Ayatollah Khamanei was not daunted and acted with singular determination to stem the incipient tide as early as August of that year by ordering the Majles what not to do. From that point on, he entrusted the neutralization of the Majles to the Guardian Council formally and to the purposefully politicized Judiciary informally. When the taming of the Majles as the only organ of popular will in the IRI was ruthlessly completed, the hardliners of the Seventh and currently the Eighth Majles turned to the Leadership for protection—this time not against the Guardian Council, which had no reason for further opposition, but against the Executive Power, now headed by one of their own who had turned out to be a most imperious President.[38] The Leader, as the supreme arbiter over the Three Powers of the Republic,[39] graciously obliged and took the humbled Legislative Power under his protection. As an expression of its deep gratitude and in an astounding feat of self-limitation in December 2008, the Majles exempted all activities under the auspices of Leadership from accountability to the people and its elected representatives.[40] By explicitly giving up this fundamental right of oversight as a derivative of national sovereignty the Majles has greatly weakened the "republican" aspect of the IRI and its elected organs vis-à-vis the appointive organs, including the Guardian Council, which for this and other reasons was unlikely to find this legislation unconstitutional.

Although several characterizations of the regime by outside observers have been offered, there is another coined by the former reformists. As the emphasis on the "republican" character of the regime by the early reformists in the 1990s appeared less and less convincing with the resurgence and victory of the hardliners in the 2000s, disillusioned reformists offered a new typological description of it: new Sultanism. The term *saltanat* was increasingly used by Mohsen Kadivar to refer to what he characterized as the "appointive Mandate of the Jurist system." The term means "monarchy" and is pejorative only within the ideological vocabulary of the Islamic revolution. Akbar Ganji, now in exile, has sought to highlight its pejorative aspect by coining the term "latter-day Sultanism" and supplying a Weberian sociological genealogy for it.[41] Clerical monarchy, however, seems more neutral and closer to Kadivar's Persian term. Clerical monarchy is a constitutional regime, its constitution defining rule by clerical councils under the Leadership of the Supreme Jurist. The Guardian Council guards the ideological foundation of the regime, while the Mandate of the Jurist makes the Leader the supreme guardian of the people living under that regime. The advisory function of the Maslahat Council is to assist the Leader with guarding the interest of the regime (*nezām*), only indirectly identifiable as the public interest or interest of the people. Clerical monarchy has a neo-patrimonial feature made all the more conspicuous by the growth of the personal, extra-constitutional power of the Leader and the recent exemption of his political and economic patrimony from parliamentary oversight. That this Constitution is not democratic and, in my opinion, not acceptable in the contemporary world is a matter of great political and moral concern, but is not a sociological issue. The sociological issue is the goodness or lack of fit between the constitutional structure of the regime and the power structure that sustains it.

The power structure that sustains clerical monarchy includes the Revolutionary Guards who are constitutionally designated not the guardians of the people or of the regime, but *of the Islamic revolution*. That their coming of age and their assumption of the leadership of Iran's new political class are throwbacks to Khomeini's revolution should not come as a surprise in view of their fundamental constitutional and ideological asset. They must have judged they got as much mileage from this asset as they could by June 2009 and embarked unabashedly on stealing the presidential election in their bid for the regime takeover with the blessing of the Leader.

Whatever his intention, the regime crafted by Khomeini installed the emergent political class and suited their interests admirably. But the composition of Iran's new political class was changing as it was beginning to take shape when he died, and has changed drastically since. Numerically and otherwise, the clerical elite has been replaced by the military-security second stratum, albeit below the level of the ruling clerical councils. It is not at all clear that the present Constitution can accommodate the political ambitions of this stratum and ensure its continued harmonious relation with the clerical elite. Can clerical monarchy survive the military-security stratum's bid for hegemony within the new political class after the reelection of its first President, Ahmadinejad, in 2009? The answer depends on the Leader's skill as a neo-patrimonial monarch in controlling his praetorian Revolutionary Guards and on the compliance of the weakened clerical elite. Whatever the answer may be, clerical monarchy entered a new phase after June 12, 2009.

'Attaollah Mohajerani, Hashemi-Rafsanjani's Deputy-President and Khatami's Minister of Culture and Islamic Guidance, was quick to see the change in the character of the IRI regime after June 12:

> The Supreme Leader decided to replace the Islamic Republic by Islamic Government...Mssrs Musavi, Karrubi and the JRM clerics who issue statements believe they can protect the republican regime and the vote of the people. But it is as clear as the day to me that on 22 Khordād 1388 (June 12, 2009), four months into the thirtieth years of the revolution, the era of the republic in our country came to an end.[42]

Readers in Iran would immediately recognize "Islamic government" as the battle cry of the hardliners such as Ahmadinejad's mentor, Ayatollah Mesbah-Yazdi, against democracy and thus see the acuity of this perception. Strictly speaking, however, Khamenei was not willing to tear aside the ample constitutional cover of the Absolute Mandate of the Jurist over his accumulated personal, patrimonial power. On the contrary, he was just discovering the appeal of the authoritarian travesty of the rule of law into rule by law. In his historic Friday sermon a week after the June 12 election, he found it easy to steal Khatami's slogan of the rule of law to whitewash his authoritarian and neopatrimonial rule through the law of the IRI. Having reassured the opposition that "the legal structures for elections in our country do not leave us room for vote-rigging," and that investigations should be carried out only through legal channels that remained open, he affirmed: "I do not submit to illegal precedents," and urged the audience to "Remember the last will and testament of the late Imam, law is the last word. We should consider law as the last word."

The sermon was the Leader's firm and uncompromising response to a week of unexpected and massive demonstrations that would have unnerved a weaker man. He knew that his determination in stemming the tide of reformism after another massive electoral victory in 2000 had paid off handsomely, and must have assumed the reformists would prove as feckless in 2009 as they had nine years earlier. If so, it seems at the time of this writing (July 2009) that he greatly underestimated the extent of the popular pressure from below and its effect on stiffening the reformists' backbone. Be that as it may, after invoking the support of the late Imam for his version of the rule of law, Khamenei ended his sermon with a prayer to the Hidden Imam that included the following pledge: "We will fulfill our duty. We said what had to be done and we would continue. All I have is my life. I am disabled also. I will sacrifice all I have for Islam and the revolution."[43]

I take this confession of disability and supplication for help to the Hidden Imam as a subconscious inkling that he may have made a grave mistake in his unqualified backing of Ahmadinejad against Hashemi-Rafsanjani, Karrubi, and Khatami who were not attending his sermon. And he must have remembered Hashemi-Rasfanjani's warning in the last days before the June election that his overdue dependence on the Revolutionary Guards put him in peril. Be that as it may, he was disabused of the assumption that Ahmadinejad, a month after endorsing his duplicitous reelection, was now his man when the latter ignored his order to dismiss the newly appointed Deputy-President Rahim-Masha'i.

Whatever his reasons, Ayatollah Khamenei's backing of the June 2009 putsch now appears as a costly mistake. One bad mistake, exactly thirty years or one generation after the Islamic revolution of 1979, the revolution that replaced the turban for the crown in Iran, and Khomeini's successor has changed the apparently robust post-revolutionary developmental course of the first and only theocracy in modern history into his fragile personal rule over an inharmonious amalgam of clerical conciliarism and brute post-revolutionary military-intelligence domination. The IRI regime is now critically dependent on decisions made by one man, the Leader, and is for that reason of a comparable degree of fragility to the neo-patrimonial regime of the Shah in the latter part of 1970s, obvious differences between the two notwithstanding.[44] The result may strike us as highly paradoxical, but we should remember the original astronomical meaning of "*revolutio*" as the movement of stars back to their original position.

10

The Hardliners, Foreign Policy
and Nuclear Development

THE NEGATIVE U.S. RESPONSE discussed in chapter 8 is not sufficient to explain
the failure of pragmatism in Iran's foreign policy from 1989 to 2005. There
were also significant internal obstacles. Two important features of the "great
revolutions" account for the shaping of post-revolutionary foreign policies and
for their distinctive direction for a long time after the revolution. The first is
ideological and the second is structural. First, the universalist ideology and
international orientation of the revolution create "fifth columns" in a number
of foreign countries with special claim to attention and resources that strongly
affect the revolutionary regime's subsequent "realistic" calculations of its geopolitical interests. Second, the typical revolutionary condition of dispersion of
power or "multiple sovereignty" that results from the collapse of the old state
is only gradually transformed by the post-revolutionary centralization of power
and state rebuilding, and leaves a permanent residue of semi-autonomous
military-intelligence and economic-industrial baronies.[1] The military-mobiliza-
tional-intelligence cartel develops special ties with the fifth columns and becomes
tangled with economic baronies as it creates its own economic empire.

Foreign Policy Cartels and the Failure of Pragmatism

In Iran, revolutionary committees, Basij militias, and other mobilizational
structures were not disbanded but developed into self-interested cartels under

the auspices of the Revolutionary Guards. The foundations (*bonyāds*) set up to harness the confiscated and nationalized economic enterprises to the goals of the Islamic revolution also developed foreign policy interests. The extensive holdings of the larger foundations have drawn them into economic ties with the defense industries and the Islamic Revolutionary Guards Corps' (IRGC) economic empire, and they have developed ties with members of the political elite influential in foreign policy. The board of directors of the Imam Reza Foundation, headed by the Friday prayer leader of Mashhad since 1979, 'Abbas Va'ez-Tabasi, for instance, brings together, among others, the former Foreign Minister Velayati, and Va'ez-Tabasi's son, Naser, one of the most important of the *āqāzādegān* with extensive interests in trade with Central Asia, and the brother-in-law of Ayatollah Khamenei's son.[2] The bazaar-*bonyād* rent-seekers, politically represented by 'Asgarawladi's Mo'talefa, also have extensive political ties and foreign policy interests.

The result of the development of special interest cartels is a hydra-headed political structure alongside the clerical conciliar oligarchy and the bureaucracy of the central government. This pattern of cartelization of economic-military interest has a direct impact on foreign policy and greatly reduces its effectiveness and independence from domestic politics. The dominant cartel in Iran since the Hashemi-Rafsanjani presidency has been that of the Revolutionary Guards. Here a key role is played by the Qods Force of the IRGC, which was set up as a carefully selected elite force of some 1,000 after the Iraq war with connections to the Shi'ite fifth columns abroad, and is used as a direct instrument of foreign policy. Some 400 Revolutionary Guards are deployed in Lebanon and are involved in training the Hezbollah. The IRCG has close ties with the foreign operations section of the Ministry of Intelligence and Security as well as its own intelligence and unconventional warfare units, while the Qods Forces have directorates for operations in several countries and their sections and officers are in many Iranian embassies.[3]

The military-intelligence cartel, and less frequently the interlocking economic cartel, is able to sabotage the official pragmatic foreign policy with impunity. Shortly before the scheduled state visit to France by President Hashemi-Rafsanjani in August 1991, for instance, the Shah's last prime minister, Shahpur Bakhtiar, was brutally murdered in Paris. The assassination of Bakhtiar also sabotaged the rapprochement with the United States,[4] and may well explain why the first President Bush and his national security advisor, Brent Scowcroft, did not reimburse Hashemi-Rafsanjani for his out-of-pocket expenses for securing the release of hostages in Lebanon.

Hashemi-Rafsanjani's attempts to improve relations with the European Union were irreparably sabotaged by Minister of Information Hojjat al-Eslam 'Ali Fallahiyan, who organized the assassination of a Kurdish opposition group in Germany in September 1992, the shooting of Rushdie's Norwegian translator in October 1993,[5] and the explosion at the Jewish center in Buenos Aires that killed 80 people in July 1994. Sabotage may or may not have been the primary motive behind these acts of terrorism, but the fact remains that in a fashion typical of regimes saddled with fifth columns and cartel baronies, Hashemi-Rafsanjani and Khamenei were unable to control them.

The Rushdie *fatwā* became an especially easy tool for sabotage. Ayatollah Hasan Sane'i, the head of one of the Khordad Fifteenth Foundations, announced in November 1992 that the $2 million bounty had been invested and that sum along with the profits would go to whoever carried out the order of execution.[6] By the February 1997 anniversary of the *fatwā,* the amount was announced to have reached $2.5 million.[7] In 1998, just as the Foreign Ministry claimed the Rushdie problem was solved and ambassadors would be exchanged with Britain, and as President Khatami declared that the *fatwā* was not in force, a huge mural was unveiled in Tehran with Khomeini's picture and the following caption: "The duty of all the Muslim people is to kill Salman Rushdie!" A new bounty of $2.8 million was put on Salman Rushdie's head in 1999, just as the Iranian Foreign Ministry had agreed to drop Khomeini's *fatwā* in its negotiations with Germany to attract German investment. On the anniversary of the *fatwā* on February 14, 2000, the bounty was confirmed, with the reaffirmation that it would be paid with interest!

Iran's policy of export of revolution in the early 1980s made the Shi'ite communities in Lebanon, Iraq, Bahrain, Saudi Arabia, Pakistan, and Afghanistan into bases for organizing pro-Iranian fifth columns. The greatest success came with the radical Hojjat al-Eslam Mohtashamipur's organization of the Hezbollah in Lebanon and its attack on the U.S. marines in 1983. In Afghanistan, the Taliban's decimation of the Shi'ite Hazara and their massacre of some 2,000 Afghani Shi'ites and eleven Iranian diplomats after the capture of Mazar-e Sharif in August 1998 brought the two countries to the brink of war, the need for which was obviated only by the American invasion of Afghanistan in October 2001. The U.S. invasion delivered Afghanistan to a Northern Alliance government coalition in which Iranian former clients predominated. When the invasion of Iraq followed in a little over a year, some 2,000 Revolutionary Guards and paramilitaries immediately moved to Basra behind American armored columns advancing toward Baghdad in March 2003,[8] and it became clear before long that the U.S. invasion of Iraq would have the same unintended consequence as that of Afghanistan, namely delivering the country's government to Iran's clients.

In Pakistan, however, initial success by Iranian agents and diplomats in the 1980s soon provoked a sharp Sunni reaction and plunged Pakistan into an escalating Shi'ite–Sunni sectarian conflict that continues unabated to this day. 'Allāma 'Arif Husyan al-Husayni, who had been studying in Najaf during Khomeini's exile there, spent some four years in Qom before returning to Pakistan in 1978. In 1980, he helped Mufti Ja'far Husayn, a prominent figure in the Shi'ite community, found the *Tahrik-i Nifaz-i Fiqh-i Ja'fariyya* (Movement for the Implementation of the Shi'ite Law) and organize its protest demonstrations until he was assassinated in August 1988. This set up a chain reaction over which Iran had no control. Sunni Mullahs responded by setting up some dozen militant sectarian organizations. The most notable of these is the *Sipah-i Sahabah Pakistan*, founded by a Deobandi cleric, Mawlana Haqnawaz Jhangvi (assassinated in 1989), to demand that the Shi'a (over 15% of the population) be declared non-Muslim.[9] Over 200 people were killed in sectarian violence in the Punjab Province of Pakistan between 1989 and 1994, another 200 died in a "five-day war" in the Northwest Frontier Province in 1996, with some 70 more deaths in the first ten days of August 1997 in anticipation of the fiftieth anniversary of the foundation of the country.[10] Iran cannot be said to have gained anything by this continued violence.

In Saudi Arabia, the likely involvement of Iran in the massive explosion at the Khobar Towers incident that killed 19 Americans and injured some 500 in June 1996 could plausibly be attributed to the Shi'ite fifth column in the Saudi oil region. All in all, the cost of the fifth columns was greatly outweighed by its benefits in term of the growth of Iran's regional power.

On the other hand, the serious cost of foreign policy cartels, most notably that of the Revolutionary Guards and its intelligence arm which act as a state within the state, became evident during the Khatami administration. The constructive dialogue with the United States after the invasion of Afghanistan was torpedoed by the Guards' giving refuge to a large number of al-Qaeda members fleeing Afghanistan, while the direction of the Hezbollah secret operations by 'Imad Mughniya from Tehran and the shipment of 50 tons of weapons and explosives to the Palestinian Authority on January 3, 2002, may have provoked President Bush's "axis of evil" State of the Union speech of January 29.[11] The U.S. invasion of Iraq in the spring of 2003 provided another opportunity for Iran to take advantage of its influence over the Badr

Brigade of the Supreme Council for the Islamic Revolution in Iraq, which it had helped organize in Iran, to obtain an American promise to disband the Mojahedin camp in Iraq. The deal was wrecked, however, apparently by the Revolutionary Guards' overestimation of the value of al-Qaeda members kept in Iran as a bargaining chip,[12] though this account has been recently disputed by Hillary Mann Leverett, who was involved in the negotiations in the 2001–2003 period.[13] Possibly the most successful act of sabotage by the military-intelligence cartel was the sending of arms to the Palestinian Authority, without the knowledge of the Iranian government, in a ship called *Karin A,* which was discovered by the Israelis on January 2, 2002, leading to the "axis of evil" speech at the end of that month.[14] Last but not least, the likely involvement of some al-Qaeda guests of the Revolutionary Guards in the Riyadh bombings of May 12, 2003 put a definite end to the U.S.–Iran constructive engagement after the invasion of Afghanistan.

Even though Ahmadinejad is one of them, his opponents from the Islamic Republic of Iran's military-mobilizational second stratum within the *Pasdārān* (Revolutinary Guards) cartel have not stopped acting as loose cannons during his presidency. In March 2007, the Revolutionary Guards arrested 15 British sailors on Iraqi waters to the great embarrassment of Ahmadinejad's government, and it took him about a month to secure their release as an Easter gift to the British people. More significantly, in early April 2008, the Qods commander, Qasem Soleimani, conveyed a proposal for comprehensive talks with the United States through the Iraqi President, Jalal Talebani,[15] preempting any initiative by Ahmadinejad in his state visit to Iraq later in May 2008.

President Ahmadinejad's Hardliner Populism and Nuclear Policy

Leader Khamenei's promotion of the hardliners and their takeover of the Majles in 2004 and of the presidency in 2005 made the military-intelligence cartel dominant in foreign policy, setting the stage for a return to an aggressive foreign policy. The United States' invasion of Afghanistan and Iraq, resulting in the destruction of Iran's strongest regional enemies, created unparalleled opportunities for Iran to expand its regional power. Exaggeration by revolutionary leaders of the foreign threat to strengthen their internal position is the typical pattern after revolutions. In the case of Ahmadinejad, he did not have to try very hard. The Bush policy of regime change gave Iran the incentive to push for nuclear development as a defense against the short-term regime change and the long-term U.S. nuclear threats.

In his first few months in office, Ahmadinejad launched an aggressive foreign policy in place of Khatami's Dialogue of Civilizations. He firmly rejected the two-state solution to the Israeli–Palestinian conflict accepted by his two predecessors. In October 2005, as we have seen, he affirmed: "As the Imam said, Israel must be wiped off the map," and in December he made his bid to capture the Arab street for the IRI by declaring the Holocaust a myth fabricated for the creation of Israel. The hardening of Iran's opposition to Israel was fully in line with the Leader's continued championship of the Palestinians to bolster his own bid to be the Leader of the world's Muslims.

Ahmadinejad's failed attempt to follow the example of the Prophet Muhammad in the "Year of the Prophet, "2006 to convert the world leaders was due to his idiosyncratic initiative and cannot be considered a hardliner policy. Nor did it enjoy the support of the hardliners. It was otherwise with his nuclear policy, however. The hawks in the Bush administration, after advertising a series of "covert" CIA operations against the IRI, officially announced their doctrine of regime change in 2002, hinting at times at Iran as the next in line in the months between the "axis of evil" speech and the invasion of Iraq.[16] (The call for regime change in Iran was routinely repeated in 2003 after the Iraqi invasion as well.) Then came President George W. Bush's baseless linking of terrorism and weapons of mass destruction in his open-ended war on terrorism, and the justification of the invasion of Iraq based on the threat posed by Saddam Hussein's nonexistent weapons of mass destruction. It had at least one unnoted but disastrous consequence. The Iranians, in a state of heightened alert for their national security, drew the only conclusion that was rational: The United States invaded Iraq because it knew Saddam did *not* have any weapons of mass destruction and therefore seemed an easy target. For its own preservation, Iran had to have the nuclear bomb. Indeed, as the American National Intelligence Council had warned the administration in early 2003, as a consequence of regime change in Iraq, "the Iranian regime, like the North Korean regime, would probably judge that their best option would be to acquire nuclear weapons as fast as possible because the possession of nuclear weapons offers protection."[17]

The Shah had embarked on an ambitious nuclear program with the approval of the United States in the mid-1970s, which, according to his Foreign Minister Ardeshir Zahedi's affirmation some three decades later, would develop Iran's nuclear capability so that "Iran should be in a position to develop and test a nuclear device within 18 months."[18] He established the Atomic Organization of Iran in 1974, and signed a contract for the building of two water reactors with a French company. A $15 billion agreement for the construction of eight nuclear reactors with the United States followed in 1975, and contracts for six reactors, including two in Bushehr, with German companies in 1976. Programs for training of Iranian nuclear scientists in Germany and at the Massachusetts Institute of Technology were set up in the same years. The U.S.–Iran Nuclear Energy Agreement was signed in Tehran on the eve of the Islamic revolution on July 10, 1978.[19] The Shah's program inspired an American fiction best seller in which he initiates the nuclear Armageddon.[20]

The original impetus to revive the Shah's program after the revolution came in the mid-1980s. With Iran's military reversals and stalemate and Iraq's use of chemical weapon the search intensified, but Hashemi-Rafsanjani found that the Germans and other Europeans were not helpful. In 1987, he signed a nuclear cooperation agreement with Pakistan to train 39 Iranian scientists, signed a similar agreement with Argentina, and approached A.Q. Khan of Pakistan in the nuclear black market to acquire drawings for a P-1 centrifuge and gas centrifuge; R&D began in 1988.[21] The Chinese agreed to supply Iran with two nuclear reactors in 1991, but withdrew the offer in 1995. In that year, earlier discussions with Russia bore fruit and Russia agreed to rebuild the Bushehr reactor.[22] By then, a subcartel had emerged at Iran's Atomic Energy Institute, with Revolutionary Guards and physicists at the Sharif Technological University, and the nuclear development project began in 1999—this time without informing the International Atomic Energy Agency (IAEA) in compliance with the Nuclear Non-Proliferation Treaty of which Iran was a signatory. When the exiled opposition group Mojahedin-e Khalq revealed the operation of a centrifuge uranium enrichment plant in Natanz and a heavy water plant in Arak in August 2002, thereby causing an international crisis, the matter was taken over by Iran's Supreme National Security Council.[23] The IAEA inspected both sites before it issued its first report in June 2003, followed by a U.S.-sponsored UN ultimatum to Iran in September 2003 that set a close deadline (October 31) for Iran's cooperation and implicitly threatened to refer the matter to the UN Security Council if it failed to do so. The seriousness of the crisis was evident, and the Leader and President agreed to put the Secretary of the Supreme National Security Council, Hojjat al-Eslam Dr. Hasan Ruhani, in charge of negotiations with the IAEA and the EU in October 2003.[24]

Ruhani, who was also the Leader's representative in the Supreme National Security Council, was a pragmatist and an effective negotiator. He decided to cooperate with the IAEA, sign the Additional Protocol as required by the IAEA Director El-Baradei, and prepare Iran's legal dossier to prevent UN Security Council sanctions in any eventuality.[25] For over a year after Bush's "axis of evil" State of the Union address, it was not clear whether the target of invasion would be Iraq or Iran, but in either event the United States had planned to secure the backing of the UN Security Council. To avoid being invaded as well, Ruhani adopted the strategy of exploiting the dissatisfaction of France and Germany with the American invasion of Iraq in that year by negotiating with EU-3. Muhammad El-Baradei as well as the Russians had impressed upon him that only a Big Deal with the Europeans would prevent the United States' drive to refer Iran's case to the Security Council. He invited the foreign ministers of France, Germany, and England to Tehran to begin negotiations. On October 21, 2003, Ruhani reached an agreement with the EU-3 ministers and Iran announced that it would voluntarily suspend uranium enrichment and sign the nuclear nonproliferation treaty (NPT)'s Additional Protocol on international inspection.[26] The signing of the Additional Protocol became a public bone of contention between the radicals and the pragmatists, with the former branding it treason and the latter wanting it ratified by the Majles as a matter of urgency. As Ruhani put it later in his final report to President Khatami, at that time there were two sharply opposed positions. The hardliner position, or "North Korean" strategy, was to push ahead with nuclear development at full speed, ignore the IAEA and NPT, and force the United States to make major concessions similar to those it was making for North Korea. The pragmatic, conciliatory position, or the "Libyan" strategy, was that of capitulating and turning in all the nuclear equipment.[27] Ruhani's position was close to the latter, and he was remarkably successful in concluding, in just over a year, the Big Deal with EU-3 in the form of the Paris agreement of November 15, 2004.

The Paris agreement, though not definitive, offered a provision for uranium enrichment for peaceful purposes to Iran in exchange for unimpeded IAEA inspection, and included two incidental features considered highly desirable by Iran: European support for Iran's application to join the World Trade Organization (WTO), and an antiterrorist cooperation measure that put al-Qaeda and the Mojahedin-e Khalq on the same footing as terrorist organizations.[28] President Bush, heady with his reelection against predicted odds and his misperception of "mission accomplished" in Iraq, put his full force behind wrecking this agreement. In February 2005, Secretary Rice rejected the deal with the EU-3, thereby humiliating the "old European" allies, and

President Bush hammered the final nails into its coffin during his visit to Europe shortly thereafter.[29] The second Bush administration thus began by bestowing a valuable and presumably unintended gift on the hardliners in Iran. In the Bush administration's final year in office, Secretary Rice finally felt compelled to add her signature to a very similar offer made to Iran by the EU Foreign Minister Javier Solana on behalf of the permanent members of the UN Security Council on June 12, 2008. But by then she was three years too late.

Hardliners in the Iranian military and security apparatus had always argued that Iran needed the bomb for national security, and unsuccessfully pushed for the "North Korean" strategy in 2003. In the last year of the Khatami administration, the hardliner-dominated Majles had unanimously passed a bill to resume uranium enrichment on October 31, 2004.[30] The portrayal of Iran being bullied by an America armed to the teeth with nuclear weapons, made convincing by Bush's "axis of evil" speech, the repeated talk of regime change, the threats of invasion, and the affirmations that Iran was in America's crosshair—although obstructing its development of nuclear energy according to international norms and the NPT—have been quite effective in arousing popular indignation and demands for the assertion of Iran's national rights and dignity. A few months before Ahmadinejad unexpectedly came to power, the IRI issued a stamp celebrating its nuclear energy program. Even earlier, 250 scientists had signed an open letter at the end of October 2003 protesting Iran's acceptance of the Additional Protocol, and 1,375 professors signed a similar letter calling for the resumption of enrichment activities in October 2004.[31] This privileged and influential segment of the Iranian educated middle class, whose professional interests are served by the policy of nuclear development, significantly broadens the social base of the President's support beyond the revolutionary veterans and the urban poor.[32]

Once Khatami was toppled by Ahmadinejad in the presidential elections of 2005, the hardliners firmly regained the upper hand in nuclear policy. In April 2006 Ahmadinejad celebrated the enrichment of a small amount of uranium to the low threshold level of 3.5 percent. Unlike his obsession with the return of the Mahdi, which does not strike a popular chord, Ahmadinejad's insistence on Iran's nuclear "rights" is popular with the Iranian masses and the middle class alike. His championship of Iran's national right to nuclear energy (for peaceful purposes) was carefully promoted by government-controlled television and other media, and he had both the hardliner Majles and the Leader and Supreme Jurist behind him.[33] Nor did he fail to elicit chants of "Nuclear energy is our legitimate right!" from the crowds he drew in his provincial tours.[34] The publicity campaign for nuclear development culminated in the issue of a new 50,000-Rial bill (the highest denomination) in March 2007. It carries a picture of nuclear isotopes with a *hadith* as its purported scriptural backing on the back, and Khomeini's picture, implying his endorsement of nuclear development, on the front (figure 10.1).

Ahmadinejad thus dragged Iran's nuclear policy from the insulated confines of Iran's Supreme National Security Council to the public arena, making use of the tempting opportunity for demagoguery by appealing to long frustrated nationalist sentiment at a time of widespread disillusionment with Islam, revolution, and reform. The policy also has the advantage of diverting attention from the regime's violations of human rights and civil liberties.[35] In April 2008, on the second anniversary of the 2006 enrichment, Ahmadinejad announced in defiance of the UN Security Council that Iran would add 6000 more centrifuge machines for enrichment, thereby tripling their number. The

FIGURE 10.1 Iran's new 50,000-Rial note. Khomeini's picture is on the front and a nuclear isotope at the center of the map of Iran is on the back, with a *hadith* that reads "Even if knowledge is in the Pleiades, men from Persia will find it." The Greatest Prophet (Peace Be Upon Him). (Supplied by SAA)

number of working centrifuges reached 3,800 in November 2008 and 5,600 in February 2009.[36] By 2009, however, the novelty of the assertion of the right to nuclear energy has worn off and the greatest external stimulus to it in the form of the American Vice-President Cheney's regime change bluff ceased. During the June election campaign Mir-Hossein Musavi saw no cost in criticizing it and declared that he would negotiate with the West on the nuclear issue if elected.

With all the steam behind him, Ahmadinejad was slowed down by the Leader. On January 18, 2006, Ayatollah Khamenei reiterated a declaration of 22 March 2005, presumably in support of the package Ruhani was then about to offer EU-3, that Iran would not produce atomic weapons because they are not allowed by Islam: "The West knows very well that we are not seeking to build nuclear weapons," which are "against our political and economic interests and Islamic beliefs." In August 2005, when Ahmadinejad took office, Ruhani was replaced as the Secretary of the Supreme National Security Council by 'Ali Larijani, very much a Leader's man, even though Article 176 of the Constitution names the President as the Council's chairman. Larijani resumed negotiations with EU-3, and with the rise of insurgency and the desperate situation in Iraq, Secretary Rice now joined the EU-3, Russia, and China in reoffering the package deal she had arrogantly rejected in November 2004. But this time, she was dealing not only with a negotiator insulated from domestic politics but also with Ahmadinejad, who had greatly heated up its air. Ahmadinejad did not say no, but failed to respond within the deadline; Iran was referred back to the Security Council, which demanded suspension of enrichment with a threat of sanctions on July 3, 2006. In December 2006, the UN Security Council finally imposed sanctions on Iran.

In May 2007, Ahmadinejad ordered the arrest of Sayyed Hossein Musavian, Ruhani's spokesman in the nuclear negotiations and a protégé of Hashemi-Rafsanjani, ostensibly on charges of treason, but in reality because he had been severely critical, in January, of Ahmadinejad's nuclear policy and his failure to secure the fundamental goal of avoiding UN Security Council sanctions against Iran. On October 20, 2007, President Ahmadinejad unexpectedly asserted his constitutional prerogative and replaced Larijani by one of his own new men, Sa'id Jalili. This was his boldest challenge to the Leader, who was forced to fall back on his more modest constitutional power and immediately appointed Larijani as one of his two representatives on the Supreme National Security Council, so as to enable the latter to appear side by side with Jalili at the nuclear negotiations with the EU Foreign Minister,

Javier Solana, on October 24, and to show up the new man as an incompetent negotiator.[37] Meanwhile, Musavian had been acquitted in November 2007, but Ahmadinejad prevailed upon the Tehran public prosecutor to order a retrial, during which he blatantly intervened in the court proceeding by calling the critics of his nuclear policy traitors and threatening to disclose intelligence gathered by the Ministry of Information and Security. The intimidation partially worked, and Musavian was given a two-year suspended sentence in April 2008 for the least grave of the three charges against him.[38]

The Leader appeared to be reining Ahmadinejad in even further. In June 2008, Foreign Minister Mottaki wrote a conciliatory letter to the UN Secretary General proposing comprehensive talks and received a prompt answer and offer signed by the foreign ministers of the five permanent members of the UN Security Council and Germany (5+1). In the first days of July 2008, Iran's Foreign Minister Mottaki accepted the 5+1 proposal, while going out of his way to affirm the historicity of the Holocaust. At the same time, the Leader's Foreign Affairs advisor, 'Ali Akbar Velayati, issued a statement emphasizing the Supreme Leader's constitutional authority to decide on matters of strategic importance and affirming the latter's position that a compromise on the "common preoccupations of Iran and the United States" could be reached on the basis of the NPT and respect for Iran's peaceful development of nuclear energy.[39] The Revolutionary Guards' cartel could not be kept out of policy-making indefinitely, however. Presumably considering both the Leader and the President beholden after the June 2009 electoral putsch, the chief of staff of the armed forces, General Firuzabadi, announced on July 1 that the EU had lost its chance for negotiating over the nuclear issue by siding with the "rioters" and thus showing itself to be the enemy of the Iranian people![40]

Overview of Post-revolutionary Foreign Policy

A long established "realist" tradition of foreign policy analysis, probably the dominant one, ignores domestic politics of sovereign states and considers them international actors with determinate geopolitical interests. It would be foolish to deny the importance of the geopolitical constellation and the contingency introduced by shifts within it. Nevertheless, the case of Iran's foreign policy surveyed in this chapter demonstrates that the foreign policy of post-revolution regimes cannot be primarily attributed to their geopolitical interests. The reason is the high degree of dependence of their foreign policy on domestic politics and revolutionary power structures. The general post-revolutionary tendency toward recentralization of power noted by Tocqueville does apply to foreign policy in the long run but with some important quali-fications. Control of foreign policy by the central government proceeds more slowly than centralization of the state, and may remain incomplete for two reasons: (1) the initial impulse to export the revolution creates fifth columns in foreign countries, and these fifth columns create special demands and exigen-cies beyond the control of the post-revolutionary government; and (2) the eventual rationalization of the hydra-headed revolutionary structures of power would tend to accommodate special interest cartels and may stop short of unifying the foreign policy-making mechanism. In Iran, foreign policy decisions can be made by the Leader, by the President through the Ministry of Foreign Affairs and the Supreme National Security Council, and by the IRGC intelligence network, apparently without consulting the Leader.

A long-term perspective on the consequences of revolutions shows a zigzag pattern concerning their export and aggressive foreign policy. To consider a parallel long-term unfolding of revolutionary tendencies, in the Soviet Union, the hardliner ascendancy and the most aggressive phase of Soviet foreign policy and export of socialist revolution came long after the so-called hedgehog policy of "socialism in one country" in the 1920s and 1930s.[41] Internally, Stalin decided to tilt the balance against the pragmatic techno-crats under Malenkov, who had been gaining influence steadily until 1945, by promoting the hardliners' "party revival" and return to ideological orthodoxy championed by Zhdanov, and after his death in 1948 by Soslov. The peak of Soviet expansionism and aggressive foreign policy thus came in 1947–1948—a full three decades after the Bolshevik revolution. Externally, victory in World War II enormously enhanced the international position of the Soviet Union, and its aggressive foreign policy paid off handsomely. An era of the most spectacular export of the Marxist–Leninist revolution to Eastern Europe and Asia was thus inaugurated in Stalin's last years. Moderate expansionism was pushed by increased cartelization long after Stalin's death and under favorable international conditions created by the Third World liberation movements, and did not come to an end until the death of hardliner Soslov in 1982. The return of the hardliners and Ahmadinejad almost three decades after the Islamic revolution in Iran offers a striking parallel. Nevertheless, there are also major differences.

If Ahmadinejad's push to return to an aggressive policy of export of revo-lution has failed despite the immense facilitation from the Bush-Cheney administration, it is because of the fractured nature of the *Pasdārān*-dominated foreign policy cartels and their loose integration by Ayatollah Khamenei. This is in sharp contrast to Stalin's iron fist during the seven-year export of the Marxist–Leninist revolution that followed World War II. Ahmadinejad's aggressive posturing in foreign policy is not sustained by an external pull factor either. Iran's most significant fifth columns, unlike the post–World War II Communist parties, are not pushing for the export of revolution. Many of Iran's Afghan and Iraqi clients are in the U.S.-backed governments of Afghanistan and Iraq, and the Hezbollah confirmed its decision to play the democratic card as a codominant force in Lebanon with the Doha agreement in May 2008, despite the great temptation to take the opposite path since its military success against Israel in 2006. All this, needless to say, is historically contingent and may change at any time.

Geopolitical contingency also plays a great part in facilitating or hindering the emergence of pragmatism in the foreign policy of revolutionary regimes by structuring their external opportunities. Pragmatism did appear as a sequel to revolution and war in foreign policy in Iran. It became the hallmark of President Hashemi-Rafsanjani's foreign policy. It was highly successful regionally—that is, in the Middle East to the south and the Caucasus and Central Asia to the north, but was effectively sabotaged by special interest cartels in Europe. Rafsanjani's push for pragmatism in relations with the United States in the 1990s, by contrast, was defeated externally, being countered by "dual containment" and the sanctions against Iran during President Clinton's first administration. The abrupt reversal of this policy by Secretary Albright in 2000, the last year of the second Clinton administration, presented Iran with a good opportunity, but President Khatami and Foreign Minister Kharrazi were too nervous to take advantage of it, knowing their backs were not covered against the hardliners.

From our long-term perspective on the process of revolution and post-revolutionary reconstruction, pragmatism itself appears as a transitory stage. The eventual assertion of control by the central government and institutionalization of decision making may have the paradoxical consequence of making foreign policy more aggressive rather than more moderate. The establishment of routine channels for input from the Revolutionary Guards and the intelligence services under Ahmadinejad has certainly not made for moderation but, on the contrary, for a push for regional hegemony. This push by the hardliners is not inconsistent with Iran's geopolitical interests, especially as the United States offered Iran little incentive for pragmatism at critical junctures.

Should this change under the Obama administration, pragmatic pursuit of Iran's national geopolitical interests, presumably by the Leader, may diverge from doctrinaire revolutionary expansionism by the military-intelligence second stratum of hardliners, who captured the presidency in 2005 and have kept it in 2009 for four more years. Pragmatism had won the day in nuclear negotiations with the November 2004 Paris agreement between Iran and the EU, but President Bush wrecked it early in 2005 at the beginning of his second term. Unless the situation drastically changes under President Barak Obama, who has displayed the wisdom of putting the EU in the forefront of negotiations, the possible endorsement of a similar offer by a new American administration in 2009 may come too late to be acceptable to Iran's dominant hardliners and require the Leader to step in.

Conclusion

◆▬◆▬▬✓

WE ARE VERY MUCH IN THE MIDST OF THE POST-REVOLUTIONARY TRANSFOR-
MATION OF IRAN, and any summary would impose an arbitrary closure on
a continuous and open development. Events to date could have turned out
differently from the way they did, even though it would still be possible to
detect a pattern to them ex post facto. Khomeini had signed the draft constitution that did not mention the Mandate of the Jurist, and if he had died without
appointing the commission to amend the Constitution on the seven points he
considered causes of the constitutional crisis of the 1980s, the political testament and last will he had left with Hashemi-Rafsanjani would have had little
effect on the constitutional structure of the Islamic Republic of Iran (IRI).

The post-Khomeini power struggle, too, could possibly have had different
winners and losers. Khamanei could have been less astute, or Hashemi-
Rafsanjani more forceful. Khatami and the reformers could conceivably
have been winners had they much stronger political will, less anxiety about
being labeled traitors to the revolution, and more openness toward building
coalitions with the forces they did not regard as *khodi* (one-of-us) or fellow
children of the revolution, and last but not least, if they had had fewer illusions
about the rule of law within the existing constitutional frame. Counterfac-
tual considerations are equally relevant to external factors. Had the United
States welcomed Hashemi-Rafsanjani's overtures in the mid-1990s, he might
have been able to rein in the loose cannons within the intelligence–foreign

policy cartel, increased the central government's control over foreign policy permanently, and possibly even made pragmatism in foreign affairs irreversible.

Khatami not only had illusions about the rule of law in the IRI, but also put his faith naively in a curious form of historical or sociological determinism. His postpresidential reflections were a profession of faith in determinism triggered by a single stroke of social engineering. If he just allowed civic associations to come into existence, he thought, they would strike roots and create a vibrant civil society. This would obviate the need for confrontation with the Leader and the clerical hardliners. As Tolstoy showed long ago, however, taking refuge in historical and sociological determinism is an easy way to avoid responsibility for your actions.[1] Ethical responsibility in politics requires the exercise of the political will and not just faith in determination by impersonal social forces. The moment for decisive political change to democratize the regime of the IRI in a definitive way came between March and August 2000. The first date marks the attempted assassination of Sa'id Hajjarian, the main architect of the stunning electoral victory of the reformists, which gave them control of the Majles; the second date marks the stark failure of the same reformists and of President Khatami to stand up to the Leader when he ordered them to stop discussing a bill to liberalize the press law. That was the one chance for the reform movement to score significant gains by risking suppression and violence, and it was missed.

In concluding *The Turban for the Crown: The Islamic Revolution in Iran,* I described the distinctiveness of the Islamic revolution as follows: "Rather than creating a new substitute for religion, as did the Communists and the Nazis, the Islamic militants have fortified an already vigorous religion with the ideological armor necessary for battle in the arena of mass politics. In doing so, they have made their distinctive contribution to world history."[2] The modern Shi'ite theocratic republic created by that revolution in Iran is unique in world history, and yet it shares certain features with other historical and contemporary regimes.

The Islamic revolution can be said to have been not the first but the second Shi'ite revolution in world history. The first was the establishment of the Safavid empire under the charismatic leadership of Shah Esma'il in 1501. Charismatic leadership could be institutionalized either into traditional authority as hereditary monarchy, by being transformed into the charisma of royal lineage, or into rational-legal authority in modern times. After 1501, Esma'il's charisma was transformed into that of the Safavid lineage as putative descendants of the holy Imams and lieutenants of the twelfth one, the Hidden Imam. In 1979, Khomeini's charisma was transformed into the constitutional authority of the Leader of the IRI. In sharp contrast to the conversion of Iran from Sunni to Shi'ite Islam by Shah Esma'il, Khomeini's revolution resulted in the considerable Sunnitization of Shi'ism with the creation of the Maslahat Council in the last year of his life. The Islamic regime established by the latter developed into a system of collective rule by clerical councils while transforming traditional Shi'ite clericalism into as elective theocratic monarchy. As an elective theocratic monarchy (*saltanat*), the regime has some affinity with the nontheocratic Sunni Muslim elective monarchies, most notably the Mamluk Sultanate in Egypt from 1260 to 1517. This can justify the recent trend among the Iranian dissidents of describing the regime as Sultanism.[3] The major difference, however, is that the Mamluk slave soldiers were the ruling elite who elected a Sultan among themselves, whereas in the IRI, the military-security men constitute the second stratum, and it is the first stratum, the clerical estate, that has the privilege of electing the Supreme Jurist as a theocratic monarch.

In *The Turban for the Crown,* I also suggested a parallel between Khomeini's transformation of the Shi'ite hierocracy and the movement that began with the assertion of the superiority of the Catholic hierocracy over monarchy by Pope Gregory VII, which culminated in the papal monarchy of the later Middle Ages.[4] The obvious difference here is that the popes had to contend with the emperors and the kings they considered their subordinates, and eventually lost the long-drawn constitutional struggle against them. Partly for this reason, the conciliar movement that developed within the Catholic Church against the background of the fragmentation of papal and imperial power was in fact protodemocratic.[5] Khomeini destroyed the Shah's monarchy for good, and the conciliar system he set up was much more akin to the modern institutionalization of the revolutionary leadership of Lenin and Mao into politbureaus within a monistic or totalitarian structure of post-revolutionary power. I have therefore suggested that its clericalism notwithstanding, we treat the post-Khomeini system as a typical system of collective rule that develops in the modern transition to post-revolutionary regimes.

The system of rule by clerical councils in the IRI, reformed and consolidated with the constitutional amendments of 1989, overshadowed the "Republican" features of Khomeini's constitutional settlement of the Islamic revolution. It also contains a strong element of patrimonialism through the Leader's assignment of rent-producing opportunities through the networks spread around the *bonyād*-military-industrial complex whose nodes he controls. Never-theless, the IRI regime also shares elements of modern democracy through them. However, as this latter term is hopelessly overloaded and badly abused, I prefer to describe the democratic features of the IRI as participatory and mobilizational. The Majles, the main organ of participation in representa-tive government, was systematically weakened by the clerical councils when controlled by the reformers under Khatami and is now treated with contempt by Ahmadinejad, a strong President, even though the majority of its members are hardliners. Since 1999, the local, municipal, and provincial councils have provided a new avenue for political participation under favorable conditions created by the integrative dimension of the Islamic revolution. The scope for political participation through the councils, however, is limited and increas-ingly restricted, not so much by the clerical councils and Friday prayer leaders as by the heavy hand of President Ahmadinejad as head of the executive branch of a developmental state and its centralizing bias.

Channels for democratic participation in the IRI are also deeply affected by the revolutionary heritage of mass mobilization. Under the guidance of the Revolutionary Guards, a new political function for the Basij militia emerged and seemed to be consolidated in the current decade: that of bringing people to the ballot box, as political parties do in other countries. This function has its roots in the Islamic revolution. Just as the Revolutionary Institutional Party after the Mexican revolution became a machine for maintaining a narrow political elite in power for decades through the ballot box, so too has the Basij militia taken on and perfected the periodic task of managing the elections in Iran until June 2009. It seems unclear, however, if the Basij can resume this function after its brutal suppression of protests following the 2009 putsch.

As for the future, it is difficult to foresee a return of the reformists to power, despite the highly favorable social preconditions created by the continued unfolding of the integrative revolution. Early in 2009 Khatami indicated that he would run again if the people know the limitations under which he would be operating, but dropped out of the presidential race in March. His fond-ness for Tocqueville's praise of the harmonious combination of religion and politics in American democracy will be of little help to Khatami, however, if he does not take a leaf out of Napoleon's book of opening political and administrative careers to talent and reaching beyond the *khodi* circle of erst-while revolutionaries to the younger generation and women. The growth of Khamenei's personal power, on the other hand, introduces a strong element of unpredictability because systems resting on personal power are fragile.

Institutional trends can be projected into the future, but not so contingencies such as the ruler's death or incapacitation. The Shah's neo-patrimonial regime was fragile because it was a system of personal power in which he made all the decisions, and it collapsed once he was mentally paralyzed. The growth of Khamenei's personal power similarly increases the fragility of the regime, especially after the alienation of many prominent clerics after the June 2009 electoral putsch. It is true that the ruling clerical elite and the military-security second stratum are interdependent. They are economically interdependent through the interlocking of the *bonyāds* and the IRGC economic empire. Politically, they both derive their legitimacy from the Mandate of the Jurist, and have developed an interesting complementarity between the supervisory control of the Guardian Council and the mobilizational role of the Basij militia in managing the elections and supressing protest.

Nevertheless, it remains an entirely open question as to whether the two can coexist in roughly the same form after the summer of 2009, not to say under a new Leader who does not enjoy the same accumulation of personal power as Khamenei. If not, it seems reasonable to project the current trend in the rise of the military-security second stratum into the future. The removal of Khamenei by the Assembly of Leadership Experts no longer seems completely improbable. Nor can a post-Khamenei coup by the IRGC be ruled out, nor can the possibility that the future of Iran may be with the last and rudest children of Khomeini's revolution—the Revolutionary Guards, who have every design for regional hegemony in the Middle East.

APPENDIX: TWO MODELS
OF REVOLUTION

Two ideal-types or models of revolution developed in a comparative study[1] have been drawn upon in this book to analyze the transition from Khomeini's revolutionary leadership to the present regime of the Islamic Republic of Iran (IRI). The two models focus on the long-term consequences of revolutions and are briefly sketched in this Appendix for those interested in the theoretical logic of this analysis.

The Integrative Revolution

Aristotle's idea of revolution as the enlargement of the political community in oligarchies and aristocracies can serve as the starting point for this model. According to Aristotle, oligarchies and aristocracies are prone to revolution because of those they *exclude* from the political society. Impoverished members of the governing class in oligarchies become revolutionary leaders; the regime is undermined by persons who are wealthy but are excluded from office[2]; and sedition in aristocracies arises when the circle of government is too narrow and "the masses of a people consists of men animated by the conviction that they are as good as their masters in quality."[3] From these considerations it would follow that the type of revolution to which oligarchies and aristocracies are prone is what we shall call *integrative revolution,* that is, revolution that enlarges the political community and broadens the franchise and/or other political rights, notably the access to power.

Among the moderns, Pareto's theory of revolution comes closest to Aristotle's idea. Put simply, his theory is as follows: If access to the political class, the ruling elite, is blocked to energetic and resolute individuals—lions—from the lower classes, and if the ruling elite becomes weak and incapable of stern repression because of an increase in the proportion of foxes over lions in its composition, a revolution is likely to occur.[4] In this situation, socially upwardly mobile individuals who are excluded from power develop into a revolutionary counterelite that eventually seizes power and makes history the graveyard of yet another aristocracy.[5]

Oligarchies are not the only kinds of political regimes whose capacity for incorporation is limited. Other personalistic, nonmobilizational regimes have the same characteristic. In the twentieth century, we find a startling difference in the fragility of political regimes and their susceptibility to revolutions. Mobilization, partial and total, and pluralism, even when "limited," act as powerful antidotes to revolution. By contrast, those regimes that remain personalistic despite some bureaucratization of administration—in terms of Juan Linz's classifications of regimes,[6] the "Caudillistic" (or "caciquistic") regimes of prerevolutionary Mexico and Nicaragua or the "Sultanistic" ("neopatrimonial" in my terminology[7]) regimes such as the Shah's—are most prone to revolution.

The model of integrative revolution so far elicited from Aristotle and Pareto can be applied to medieval and modern revolutions as well, with some modifications and extensions. The condition for a revolution is that the counterelite mobilizes a significant segment of society; if it seizes power without doing so, we would have a circulation of elites without revolution. The most important demand the counterelites need to satisfy in order to mobilize their constituencies is the desire for incorporation into the political community, for citizenship, when the term applies. If they can do so, they generate a political motive for opposing the regime. This political motive can be combined with moral motives into an ideology. The oppositional ideology then reinforces the moral motive for denying the legitimacy of the established political order and for seeking to overthrow it. Once an oppositional ideology spreads, the moral motive would make cooptation difficult even if the regime is willing to broaden access to power during crisis.

Pareto, wanting to outdo the Marxists, often discounted ideology as a mere mask for the counterelite's lust for power. But this misses the point. Religious propaganda, nationalism, and ideology are important because they constitute the crucial link between the revolutionary counterelite and the constituencies they succeed in mobilizing. According to Pareto, ideologies are variables—"derivatives"—corresponding to certain constants—"residues"—that are the true social forces. He writes: "a derivative is accepted not so much because it convinces anybody as because it expresses clearly ideas that people already have in a confused sort of way—the latter fact is usually the main element in the situation."[8] The insurgent elite create an emotional bond with its supporters by articulating derivatives that correspond to the residues of deep sentiment. The Khaldunian 'asabiyya, mechanical group solidarity typical of tribes, is clearly one such residue. The derivatives concentrate the sentiments and intensify the residues associated with them, and in doing so they serve as a potent tool for mobilization. Religion and nationalism are important in part because the strongest sentiments that can bind the revolutionary counterelite and its supporters derive from collective identity. Religion emphasizes the identity of the counterelite and its constituency as members of a community of faith; nationalism, of a putative primordial community of blood. This explains the fact, noted by Tocqueville,[9] and even by Pareto himself,[10] that the integrative dimension of modern revolutions makes them akin to the great religious movements of the past.

The ideal-type of integrative revolution needs further modification with regard to the long-term consequences of revolution. A contrary tendency toward closure sets in with the gradual formation of a new political class after the revolution. As mobilization is increasingly controlled with post-revolutionary institution building and the rationalization of revolutionary structures, political participation is rolled back gradually but firmly, and new political opportunities and positions of power are exclusively appropriated by those revolutionaries who form a new political class during the post-revolutionary transition. The limits to and reversal of the expansion of the political community with the closure of access to the new political class can best be understood with the help of Gaetano Mosca. A contemporary of Pareto, Mosca offers a comparative panorama on the formation of ruling classes in different societies on the basis of their respective "political formulae," a term that roughly corresponds to what Max Weber called the "principles of legitimacy" of the political order. This broadens the concept of circulation of elite to cover the formation of a new ruling class on the basis of the new political formula established by the revolution. As the ruling elite cannot govern alone, the political class included an important second stratum that performs the administrative and military functions of the state.[11] As the social basis of the regime is widened, social mobility increases, and there is a considerable circulation of the elite within the second stratum of the new political class. Nevertheless, there is a strong tendency for access to power and entry into the new political class to remain restricted to the children of the revolution who have proven their loyalty.

In short, according to our ideal-type, the integrative revolution enlarges the political community and broadens the franchise and/or other political rights, notably access to power. It also generates a new ruling class on the basis of the new principles of legitimacy established by the revolution that is served by a more broadly recruited second stratum in charge of administrative, military and security functions.

The Tocquevillian Type: Revolution and Centralization of Power

This is the ideal-type of revolution most familiar to us. In this modern type of revolution, a centralized state is already in place. In fact, revolution takes the form of the disintegration of the authority of the state and the collapse of the established political order at the center. It corresponds to Samuel Huntington's "Western" type of revolution, and is the model implicitly adopted by Theda Skocpol.[12] Most integrative revolutions have centralization as a consequence of the termination of revolutionary power struggle. What is distinctive about this type of revolution is that centralization also appears as a *cause* of revolution.

Hannah Arendt inferred, from the "amazing ease" with which those who make revolutions "pick up the power of a regime in plain disintegration," that revolutions "are the consequences but never the causes of the downfall of political authority."[13] She adduced Tocqueville's observation in 1848 that the regime fell "before rather than beneath the blows of the victors, who were astonished at their triumph as were the vanquished at their defeat."[14] The progressive sapping of authority of the old regime is central not only to Tocqueville's analysis of the French revolution, but also, on close reading, to Trotsky's analysis of the Russian revolution.[15] I used the model to explain the Islamic revolution of 1979 in Iran.[16] Tocqueville was also the first to point to the central paradoxic of the French revolution, namely that it made the absolutist state it wanted to destroy all the stronger. Weber predicted the same paradoxic result for the Bolshevik revolution, and Bertrand de Jouvenel highlighted the concentration of power and growth of centralized government as the general consequence of all revolutions in history.[17] Centralization of the structure of authority was thus both the cause and the consequence of the revolution for Tocqueville.

However, the Tocquevillian model should be modified with respect to the causes as well as the consequences of revolution. With regard to causes, it should take account of the consequences of the concentration of power in the state upon its social foundations, namely the social groups that are included in the political community. Tocqueville does mention the reaction of the French nobility against the growing power of the state, which manifested itself in the aristocratic prerevolution of the *parlements*. But he does not have a systematic treatment of the revolutionary role of the groups that are dispossessed by the growing state. The considerable revolutionary role of *declining* classes, and of cohesive social groups with strong solidarity that are dispossessed by centralizing states or threatened by socioeconomic change, is generally neglected. My own analysis of the impact of the state formation on Iranian society as a cause of the Islamic revolution focused on the role of the adversely affected and dispossessed elites and social groups, most notably the clerical estate.

The modification required for the Tocquevillian ideal-type with respect to the consequences of revolution is even more significant. The centralization of power that results from the capture of the prerevolutionary bureaucratic state can be countered by two possible centrifugal tendencies: the transformation of the charismatic leadership of the revolution into institutions that sustain collective rule by the successors, and the institutionalization and rationalization of the structures of revolutionary mobilization, notably militias, revolutionary committees, and revolutionary courts. The relative strength of these centrifugal and centripetal tendencies varies from revolution to revolution.[18]

NOTES

Introduction

1. See Arjomand 1992: 39–40. Constitutional politics is different from and superimposed on the routine politics of give and take, of horse trading, of stealing, and of being robbed. It is a struggle for the definition of order. Constitutional politics should not be confused with constitutionalism or democracy, as the struggle can be over the definition of a nondemocratic order.
2. Arjomand 1986, 1988.
3. Weber 269. The neglect of charismatic leadership in the sociology of revolution may be due to the fact that the great French revolution, which provided the revolutionaries and analysts of the subsequent centuries alike with a model of revolution, was quite atypical in that a charismatic leader capable of holding and consolidating power and exporting the revolution did not emerge until 1799, a decade later. In comparative hindsight, Napoleon was not just the child of the revolution but also its one and only effective charismatic leader.
4. See the Appendix.
5. The work most frequently cited in this connection is Crane Brinton's famous *Anatomy of Revolution* (1938). An earlier formulation of this pattern can, however, be found in Edwards 1927.
6. The anatomy of revolution paradigm ousted the view of some earlier historians who considered Napoleon the child of the revolution, the exporter of its values abroad, and their institutional consolidator at home. Not only did it sever the French Revolution's link to Napoleon, but it also gave it the extremely short life-span of 5 years, as required by the anatomical analogy for revolution as a fever that breaks quickly.
7. The more literal reading of the metaphor suggested the end of the violent elimination of the leftist partners in the revolutionary coalition and Khomeini's declaration of the rule of law at the end of 1982 as the Iranian Thermidor.

8. See Goldstone 1982.
9. On Sorush and Ganji, see chapter 4.
10. *New York Times*, 6/8/09: A4.
11. Needless to say, in reality the lines between these analytical categories are blurred; the groups overlap and membership within each of them changes.
12. Al-Azmeh 30–31, 64–69; Arjomand 2006: 152.
13. Shils 1975: 121, 345–53.
14. See the Appendix.
15. Mosca 1966 [1895]: 80–122.
16. Comparative parallels for the stability of the ruling elite surviving the revolutionary power struggle while the government bureaucracy and its military–industrial complex expand enormously are not difficult to find: Stalin's politbureau (*politboro*) began to die off with Andropov when the ruling generation had turned octogenarian, and the Takriti elite of the Ba'thist revolution dominated the Iraqi regime until the overthrow of Saddam by the invading Americans.
17. Although there is some justification for calling the clerical hardliners "conservative" to indicate their traditionalism, there is none for using the same label for Ahmadinejad and the hardliner military-intelligence second stratum of the Islamic Republic of Iran.
18. The same is true of the theory of revolution more generally. The first necessary modification is to shift the focus from the causes to the consequences of revolution. As in all other revolutions, the Islamic revolution of 1979 in Iran had historical and structural causes and preconditions, as well as more immediate sociopolitical triggers (Arjomand 1986, 1988). But we still need a completely different analytical framework for understanding the direction of post-revolutionary change of the kind offered in this book.
19. The appropriateness of a long-term perspective for the analysis of the Mexican revolution in particular is well brought out in Knight (2002).

Chapter 1

1. This is the literal meaning of "*āyatollāh al-'ozma,* " the honorific title of the foremost authorities in Shi'ite law who are followed by the laity as "sources of imitation" (*marāje'-e taqlid*).
2. Cited in Arjomand 1981: 298, n.12.
3. Arjomand 1988: 148–49.
4. Cited in Bayat 249.
5. Algar 1988.
6. Rajaee 60–67.
7. Khomeini [1944] 192–202.
8. Ibid. 56.
9. Ibid. 30–31, 79–82, 132–33, 173–74.

10. Ibid. 221–305.
11. Ibid. 236.
12. Ibid. 225–30.
13. Ibid. 289.
14. Ibid. 292, 186, 222, respectively.
15. Weber 2: 1195.
16. Rajaee 123–26.
17. Ruhani 1982: 42–50.
18. Khomeini Centennial 9: 15–17.
19. The concept had traditionally been defined narrowly as the authority in matters of *hisba,* devolving on the jurist by default—that is, in cases in which the principal agent was lacking or deficient. Khomeini expanded it into a theory of theocratic government based on the mandate of the jurist to rule (Arjomand 1988: 178).
20. R. Khomeini, *Ketāb al-bay'*(Qom, n.d. [1971]) 2: 461–90. At this time, he was still prepared to grant Islamic legitimacy to a regime not based on direct clerical rule: "The preservation of order and defense of the borders of the Muslims [requires] the establishment of a just Islamic government.... In case the just jurists are lacking or incapable of rising to do so, this is incumbent on the just [lay] Muslims, but they require the permission of the jurist, if available" (Ibid. 2: 497–98). For a critical discussion, see Kadivar (1998): 22–26.
21. Arjomand 1993: 104.
22. Khomeini [1944] 211.
23. *Sahifa-ye Nur* 3: 236, 251–52.
24. The term derived from the traditional notion of "general deputyship" (*niyābat-e 'āmma*) of the Hidden Imam has not remained current, and has been replaced in the discourse of the IRI by near-equivalent terms, *val-yi amr* or *vali-ye faqih,* which I have translated as "clerical monarch."
25. Schirazi 62–71, 97.
26. Cited in Ramazani 1990: 49.
27. Abrahamian 1989.
28. Arjomand 1988: ch. 8.
29. Khomeini Centennial 6: 199–200.
30. The names and dates of execution of 3201 people during the summer of 1988 were published by the Mojahedin. The massacre did not officially end until Khomeini's amnesty on the tenth anniversary of the revolution in February 1989 (Afshari 113, 116).
31. Buchta 2005b: 20.
32. This order showed total disregard for judiciary independence and undermined the authority of the clerical judges by making the intelligence officers their partners on the bench.
33. He was Mostafa Purmohammadi, the future hardliner Minister of the Interior.

34. Cited in Buchta 2005b: 18.
35. Gieling 1999: 31.
36. Cited in Ramazani 49.
37. A play on Khomeini's first name, Ruhollāh.
38. Professor Hamid Algar also confided as much to me when I was in Neauphle-le-Chateau to interview Ayatollah Khomeini in the early days of January 1979: the ultimate goal of the movement was the establishment of an "Islamic Government" and the "Islamic Republic" that was being proposed was for the period of transition.
39. Beheshti 15. *Umma* means the community of believers and imamate is its divine leadership. The argument that the Imam considered the "Islamic Republic" a transitory stage leading to the ultimate "Islamic Government" circulated among the clerical elite since the beginning, and was made explicit and publicized by the supporters of the hardliner Ayatollah Mesbah-Yazdi at the beginning of 2006 (*Iran Emrooz*, 1/2 and 4/06), probably to pave the way for his unsuccessful bid for the Presidency of the Assembly of Leadership Experts at the end of that year.
40. Cited in Algar 1986: 40.
41. Khomeini 1999, 10:29.
42. 'Abdol-Karim Lahidji, member of the drafting committee, thought that Khomeini wanted a constitution quickly because he was worried about a repetition of the August 1953 coup, organized by the CIA and the MI6, that overthrew Mosaddeq and brought the Shah back (interview on 10/18/96).
43. Hāshemi-Rafsanjāni 1997b.
44. Ghamari-Tabrizi 49.
45. Cited in Bakhash 1984: 78.
46. Khomeini [1944]: 185.
47. Cited in Bakhash 1984: 74–75.
48. Arjomand 2001: 303–4.
49. All quotations are as cited in Ghamari-Tabrizi: 52–53, with the translation slightly modified.
50. *1979 Proceedings* 2: 115–16; trans. Ghamari-Tabrizi 68–69.
51. Beheshti 15.
52. Ibid. 16.
53. Ibid. 20.
54. This regime of "the *umma* and Imamate" was incorporated into Article 5, and yet again in Article 57 of the Constitution as "the Mandate to rule (*velāyat-e amr*) and the Imamate of the *umma*" (Arjomand 1988: 150–51). Seeking to refute the accusations of clerical fascism and dictatorship from the Left in that lecture, Beheshti disingenuously argued that the democratic aspect of the rule of the people was minimally affected by their conversion to the *umma* under the Imamate. Official spokesmen for the regime similarly claimed a democratic character for clerical rule by arguing sophistically that

the Leader is indirectly elected by the clerics of the Assembly of Leadership Experts, who are directly elected by the people. The elderly member of the 1979 Assembly of Experts, Ayatollah Khademi, was much more honest and logical in his evaluation of the Majles, the main democratic organ of the regime, in relation to the Mandate of the Jurist. Here is his statement at the Assembly (and he had said as much to me when I interviewed him in Isfahan in the summer of 1977): "The Majles (National Consultative Assembly) is party to consultation by the Jurist. This does not mean obeying its enactments for the people is obligatory. [Its] enactments [matter] because it is a consultative body to the Jurist, and it is obedience to the Jurist's ordinance that is obligatory for the people. The [jurists'] endorsement is required for obedience to the law to become obligatory for the people.... As for the rumors in people's mouths about 'government of the people by the people,' nobody has given such a government to the people...government is only God's" (*1979 Proceedings* 2: 944).

55. "Ideological constitution" is defined in Arjomand 1992: 46.
56. The Appendix has, however, not been reprinted with any of the subsequent editions of the Constitution of the Islamic Republic that I have seen. Can we therefore conclude that it is no longer considered part of the constitutional law of Iran?
57. This was not accidental but was the result of following the *conseil constitutionnel* of the 1958 French Constitution, which was in turn influenced by Hans Kelsen's idea of a constitutional court as "the Guardian of the Constitution" in the late 1920s.
58. Khomeini Centennial 6: 211–12.
59. Brumberg 2001.
60. Mehrpur 1992, 1: 73.
61. Cited in Ghamari-Tabrizi 95.
62. Mehrpur 1992, 1: 80.
63. Khomeini Centennial 6: 227.
64. Schirazi 191–98.
65. Ghamari-Tabrizi 49, 281, n. 23.
66. Ibid. 60.
67. Buchta 2000: 36.
68. Khomeini Centennial 6: 302–06; Arjomand 1988: 161.
69. See chapter 8.
70. Buchta 2005.
71. Khomeini 11: 329–30.
72. Hāshemi 2: 70.
73. For all the citations and dates, see Arjomand, "Shi'ite jurisprudence," pp. 96–98.
74. Schirazi 236–37.
75. *1989 Proceedings* 1: 164.

Chapter 2

1. Hāshemi-Rafsanjani 1997b.
2. The turnout was 56% of the electorate, the median for the IRI presidential elections.
3. Buchta 2000: 49, 165.
4. He was assassinated in 1980.
5. *1989 Proceedings* 1: 181, 185.
6. The fact that not only the *marja'iyyat* but also the qualification of "*ejtehād motlaq*" was at the last minute omitted for the Leader is surely indicative of the incompatibility of the old and the new Shi'ite theories of authority. See *1989 Proceedings* 2: 642–54, 707.
7. Interview with Ayatollah Ebrahim Amini, 5/4/97. In the original 1979 Constitution, the Leadership Council had been conceived as a regular alternative to a single Leader (Beheshti: 27).
8. Such matters, without further specification, had been excluded from the executive authority of the President and the Prime Minister by the old Article 60.
9. Hāshemi 2: 88. The Leadership Committee of the Council for the Review of the Constitution had asked for a far more sweeping extension of the Leader's power, including the dissolution of the Majles—one of the constitutional gaps that remained unfilled—but presumably because of the death of the charismatic revolutionary leader, some of them lapsed. See *1989 Proceedings* 2: 642–700.
10. *1989 Proceedings* 3: 1374–81, 1629–39. Even so, Ayatollah Yazdi and others who had wanted the precise wording "Absolute Mandate of the Jurist" were disappointed. *1989 Proceedings* 3: 1639.
11. Hāshemi 2: 59–60.
12. *1989 Proceedings* 1: 211.
13. The core element of this Sunnitization has been the attempt to find Islamic legitimacy for the new category of "governmental ordinances" hand in hand with the adoption of *maslahat* (public interest) as the criterion for the legitimacy of the nonjuristic rulings of the Supreme Jurist/Leader of the Islamic Republic. The close connection between *maslahat* and "governmental ordinances" is the subject of the seventh volume of the Khomeini Centennial, as indicated by its title: *Ahkām- hokumati va maslahat.* Khomeini's followers drew extensively on Sunni sources to repair the deficiency of the discussion of public law in Shi'ism, including such Sunni concepts as *bay'a[t]* or allegiance to the Caliph (Khomeini Centennial 7: esp. 211–27, 322–23).
14. Bakhash 1995.
15. Buchta 1995; Gieling 1997.
16. See Buchta 2000: 49 for the organizational chart.
17. To be more precise, the Guardian Council also incorporated the idea of a committee of *mojtahed*s with veto power over legislation incompatible with

the Sacred Law from the old Iranian constitution (of 1906–1907) into the model of a *Conseil Constitutionnel* adopted in Bazargan's draft constitution from the 1958 Constitution of the French Fifth Republic.

18. Madani 274–76; Moslem 157.

19. Cited in Madani 509 and 'Alinaqi 8.

20. Hāshemi 2: 315.

21. During the first presidential elections that took place a month after the ratification of the Constitution, and with no clear guidelines for the supervision of elections, the Guardian Council approved the candidacy of 106 men and rejected only 18, mostly Leftists. The Guardian jurists must have regretted this lenience, which allowed Bani-Sadr to become Iran's first President. In the next presidential elections in July 1981, they were stricter in determining when a candidate was among "the religious and political figures (*rejāl*)" and a "believer in the bases of the Islamic Republic of Iran," with such vaguely defined qualities as management capability, trustworthiness, and piety (Article 115). From then on in each presidential election only a handful of men would meet the Guardian Council's unspecified criteria: 4 out of 238 in 1997, 10 out of over 800 in 2001, and 7 out of 3010 in 2005.22. Malekahmadi 1999.

23. The proof was still fresh from late January 1999, when a parliamentary committee charged with supervising the election of the local and municipal councils had disqualified 50 reformers because of insufficient loyalty to the Mandate of the Jurist; however, Khatami's Interior Minister in charge of the elections, Musavi-Lari, defiantly said he would put them on the ballot anyway and a compromise was reached allowing the candidates to run with the approval of the (Khatami-appointed) provincial governors (Buchta 2000: 181).

24. G2K, thread 2, 3/13/08 and *Resālat* 3/12/08. Karrubi claimed that *all* disqualified candidates were reformists "who had been at the Imam's service!"

25. Cited in Schirazi 89.

26. Hāshemi 2: 53–54. The Guardian Council took advantage of this transfer to strengthen its power of supervision in the national elections as well (Mo'men 1998: 150). On the examination of the 1990 candidates under the supervision of Ayatollah Mo'men, see Mo'men 1998.

27. These early opinions were edited and published by one of its lay members, Dr. Hossein Mahrpour (Guardian Council 1).

28. *Ettelā'āt* 7/20/2000.

29. Arjomand 2005: 513.

30. *New York Times* 5/9/04.

31. Interview with the Commission's Chairman 2001.

32. Arjomand 2007.

33. Guardian Council 2: 232–36; Hāshemi 2: 659.

34. Cited in Buchta 2000: 61.

35. Hāshemi 2: 467, 648–59. See Maslahat Council Enactments for other enactments by the Council between 1988 and 1995.

36. Javadi-Āmoli 1998: 12.
37. Amini 1998: 108.
38. Ibid. 118–20.
39. Arjomand 2001: 324.
40. *Ettelā'āt* 9/7/2001.
41. Cited in *The Guardian* 9/5/2007.
42. Ayatollah Ahmad Jannati led a vicious campaign against Hashemi-Rafsanjani in 2007 and got 34 votes as against the latter's 41 (*The Guardian* 9/5/2007). Jannati did not run in 2009, and instead supported former Head of the Judiciary Mohammad Yazdi.
43. The peak of the Supreme Judiciary Council's activities was the period 1984–1989/1363–1368, though its momentum continued for a couple of years after Musavi Ardabili into 1991/1370 and declined thereafter (Qorbani 2003: esp. 345–541).
44. *Ettelā'āt* 11/23/1999. The chronic shortage of judges with the requisite training in Shi'ite jurisprudence, however, made any further Islamicization unlikely. There were only 5000 judges for 10,000 positions, while recognized institutions produced only 600 graduates a year (*Ettelā'āt* 11/30/1999). Only a small proportion of these comes from the *madrasa*s or can become *mojtahed*s.
45. See the following section.
46. *Ettelā'āt* 6/28/2000.
47. Barātiniyā 2002: 68; Zākeri 2002: 21.
48. *Manshur-e tawse'a* 2: 22.
49. Ibid. 2: 15–16.
50. It is based on an expansive interpretation of the above-mentioned Article 156, of Articles 161, 167, and 170, concerning the legality of Islamic standards and uniform judicial process, and finally of Articles 173 and 174, which set up, respectively, a High Administrative Court and a National Inspectorate under the supervision of the Head of the Judiciary.
51. *Manshur-e tawse'a* 2: 30–40.
52. Ibid. 2: 35.
53. Ibid. 2: 28–29; 3: 40–43.
54. *Ettelā'āt* 10/12/2000. To perform the same function, he also proposed the Judiciary Police set up by the late Ayatollah Beheshti, from the general police force with which it was later amalgamated.
55. *Ettelā'āt* 4/3/01.
56. *Ettelā'āt* 7/10/2000; *Manshur-e tawse'a* 3: 52.
57. *Ettelā'āt* 4/26/02.
58. Mo'avenat 2002–2003.
59. ISNA (www.isna.ir) 4/11/08.
60. Instances of stoning have nevertheless occurred despite his disapproval.
61. *Manshur-e tawse'a* 2: 37–38, 55.
62. Daryābāri 2004: 35, 97, 201–2, 223–24.

63. Ibid. 238–40.
64. International Commission of Jurists 198.
65. Unverified figures by a London-based organization of dissident clerics claimed there were 3000 clerics in the Court's prisons in 1998, and improbably put the number executed at 600 (Buchta 2000: 98).
66. Mir-Hosseini and Tapper 87–92.
67. Cited in Ghamari-Tabrizi 254.
68. Bayat 108–9.
69. Kadivar 1998: 13.
70. Ibid. 102–3, 124, 132–33.
71. Arjomand 1988: 117–18.
72. Kadivar 1998: 71, 75.
73. Hajjāriān 2000: 194–204, 256–58.
74. Ibid. 203.
75. Ibid. 541–45.
76. As in the Preamble and Article 5 of the Constitution.
77. To see the extent of the departure from the Shi'ite tradition, just compare it to Ayatollah Mesbah Yazdi's categorical assertion (1996: 91) that "*bay'at* plays no role in the legitimacy of the *velāyat-e faqih,* as it played no role in the legitimacy of the government of the Immaculate Imam." He goes on to say that *bay'at* is merely instrumental in bringing about the government of the jurists as it leaves them with no excuse to shun taking over the management of society.

Chapter 3

1. 'Azimi 52–53, 89, 117–18.
2. Hāshemi-Rafsānjāni 1997a: 1: 269–90.
3. Moslem 194.
4. Amuzgar 2007: 62.
5. Its measure rose from 0.15 for 1981–1988 to 0.32 for 1993–1996, and again to 0.45 for 1997–2000, but it still remained well below the 0.63 for the pre-revolution years (Keshavarzian 2007: 164).
6. As shown in decile dispersion ratios. The rise is less sharp in the Gini coefficient (Salehi-Isfahani 2009).
7. Anecdotally, I should mention that I met two government contractors in Vancouver who had made their millions in this period and moved to Canada at the end of the decade.
8. Cordesman 38.
9. Moslem 192.
10. Ehteshami 172–74.
11. Cordesman Tables 1.1 and 1.3.
12. Moslem 217.
13. *New York Times* 11/2/94.
14. Moslem 219–20.

15. Cordesman 37.
16. International Crisis Group 2007: 13.
17. Ehteshami 183. The term "military-industrial complex" was used by President Eisenhower and popularized by the left in the 1960s. Here, I have adopted the term to denote, more narrowly, the industrial and economic enterprises directly managed and controlled by the armed forces, especially the Revolutionary Guards, and have added the adjective "commercial" to indicate the latter's extensive involvement in the import trade and informal trade, including smuggling and arms deals.
18. Akhavi-Pour and Azodanloo 80.
19. Amuzegar 1997; Buchta 2000: 73.
20. Keshavarzian 2007: 210–11.
21. The term was apparently coined by the secretary-general of the pro-Khatami Hambastegi (solidarity) Party, M.R. Rahchamani (Ettelā'āt 5/2/01).
22. Keshavarzian 2007: 100–113.
23. The openness of the trial caused great indignation among the Friday Prayer Leaders, one of whom thought it had put the foundations of the regime under question (Irān 26 January 02/6 Bahman 1380).
24. Article 90 of the Constitution gives the Majles the power to deal with complaints against the Judiciary (one of the rare instances of leverage over it), and the Judiciary Investigations Committee was set up pursuant to that Article.
25. Nazenin Ansari, G2K communication (Thread 2), 6/8/08.
26. See chapter 7.
27. Gheissari and Nasr 115.
28. See table 4 in chapter 6.
29. Madani 113.
30. Jahanbakhsh 141–43.
31. Moslem 171, 174.
32. Bayat 56.
33. Buchta 2000: 27.
34. Mortaji 55; see also Moslem 103.
35. Mortaji 39; Moslem 136–38.
36. Cited in Moslem 100.
37. Ibid. 102.
38. Ibid. 139.
39. Ibid. 136–38.
40. Cited in Bayat 114.
41. Cited in Moslem 136.
42. Cited in Bāqi 2000: 250.
43. Mortaji 28.
44. Ibid. 44–49.
45. Bayat 116, 122.
46. Ibid. 114, 124.

47. Cited in Moselm 117.
48. Cited in Mortaji 81.
49. Moslem 184.
50. Khomeini Centennial 9: 163–64.
51. Cited in Moselm 117–19.
52. Cited in Mortaji 20–23, 81, 84.
53. Hajjāriān 180.
54. Bayat 67–70.
55. Hajjāriān 175–77.
56. Ibid. 126.
57. Cited in Moselm 235.
58. Mortaji 40–41, 183–94.
59. Moslem 132–33.
60. Moslem 234, 238.
61. Moslem 246, 249.
62. Buchta 2000: 26–27.

Chapter 4

1. Jalal Sadiq al-'Azm, a Syrian philosopher and specialist in Kant, argued that Middle Easterners were guilty of reifying the West in exactly the same way as the literary critic Edward Said charged the Europeans regarding the Orient. As Said (1978) had famously called this reification "Orientalism," al-'Azm (1981) called its counterpart "Orientalism in reverse." Boroujerdi (1996) used the term "Occidentalism" in the same sense, as do Buruma and Margalit more recently (2004).
2. As the title "Sayyed" indicates, the first two were both putative descendants of the Prophet (Boroujerdi 1996: 54–63).
3. Āl-e Ahmad 1984.
4. Cited in Ghamari-Tabrizi 182.
5. Arjomand 1982.
6. Arjomand 1982; Vahdat 1999.
7. Dabashi 1993: 75.
8. Ibid. 395, 406.
9. Taleqani 1982.
10. Rajaee 2007: 141.
11. Ghamari-Tabarizi 193.
12. See chapter 1, section 1.
13. Arjomand 1984.
14. Cited in Arjomand 1989: 118.
15. Cited in Mir-Hosseini and Tapper 65.
16. Matin-asghari 1997: 104; Jahanbakhsh 2001: 151–53.
17. Cited in Mir-Hosseini and Tapper 71.
18. Jahanbakhsh 152.
19. Cited in Brumberg 210.

20. Cited in Rajaee 166.
21. Ghamari-Tabrizi 102–4.
22. Cited in Ghamari-Tabrizi 121.
23. It first appeared in 1990 and was expanded into a book a year later.
24. Cited in Brumberg 2001: 204.
25. Sorush 1995: 5–7.
26. Jahanbakhsh 165.
27. The replacement of the philosophy of science by hermeneutics enabled him to shift the discussion of truth from causal and rational arguments to the level of meaning: "We must not integrate truth [of propositions] with either reasons or causes, but must rather attribute it to meanings and interpretation" (Sorush 1998: 116).
28. Sorush 1999: 21.
29. Ibid. 55, 80.
30. Sorush 1998: 1, 49.
31. Sorush 2000a: 215, 220.
32. The subject was broached in a lecture to the Philosophical Society of Tehran in 1993/1372, if not earlier.
33. The confrontation of tradition and modernity in Islam, he argued, can be confined to the "anthropological viewpoint," and need not assume the form of confrontation between religion and atheism (Mojtahed-Shabestari 1997: 100).
34. Ibid. ch. 8.
35. The title first appeared in an interview with the literary magazine, *Rah-e Naw,* in August 1998/Shahrivar 1377.
36. Mojtahed-Shabestari 2000: 13–15, 21.
37. Ibid. ch. 1.
38. Ibid. ch. 2.
39. Ibid. 34–36.
40. Ibid. 30–34, 37–46.
41. Ibid. 194.
42. Cited in Ghamari-Tabrizi 252. This is in contrast with Sorush's deduction of tolerance from the acceptance of religious pluralism in Islam.
43. Ibid. 184.
44. Mojtahed-Shabestari 1997: 73. When this view is accepted, however, the crucial issue that arises is whether the determination of the compatibility of the political regime with Islamic values is the exclusive prerogative of religious jurists and whether ordinary people are bound to follow them in political matters (Mojtahed-Shabestari 1997: 75–76).
45. Mojtahed-Shabestari 1996: 46–66.
46. Mojtahed-Shabestari 2000: 12.
47. Both these statements were made in September 1999 and are cited in Ganji 2000b: 116, 153.
48. Cited in Bayat 113–14.

49. *Ettelā'āt* 4/14/01.
50. The appellate court reduced his sentence by a total of 3 years in September 2000/28 Shahrivar 1379.
51. Bāqi 2002: 35–57.
52. Ganji 2000b: 186, 199.
53. Ibid. 238, 253.
54. Ibid. 76, 158, 261.
55. The title, *The Fascist Interpretation of Religion and Government: Pathology of Transition to the Democratic and Development-Oriented State,* was daring, and its preface juxtaposed rationalist and mystical reading of Islam to "the reduction of religion to its husk and to dry customs, and the violent imposition of the jurisprudential reading on humankind" (Ibid. 7).
56. Excerpts from the *Manifest-e jomhurikh^wāhi* were translated under "Documents on Democracy" in the *Journal of Democracy* 14.1 (2003): 183–84.
57. I had dealt with the modernity/tradition dichotomy as a graduate student at the University of Chicago under the heading of "An Obituary" in my first published paper (Arjomand 1977).
58. Arjomand 2003: 245.
59. Tabātabā'i 1988.
60. Zibā-Kalām 19. The bulk of the book consists of a simplified sketch of the socio-political history of medieval Iran in which three factors, "Oriental despotism," the tribal social structure, and "the extinction of the light of science" are presented as the major obstacles to development.
61. Matin-Asghari 2004. Nevertheless, the three books had different models of modernization in mind. 'Ali Reza-Qoli, whose *Sociology of Elite-Killing* (1999) quickly overran 10 reprintings, in sharp contrast to the reformists such as Akbar Ganji, lionized Hashemi-Rafsanjani as "Iran's Richelieu" and thus a modernizer typically disowned and destroyed by ungrateful Iranians. By contrast, Ahmad Sayf, whose *Preface to Despotism in Iran* (2000) also had a wide immediate circulation, was more in line with Khatami, and saw the rule of law and civil society as the antidote to Iran's "culture of despotism" (Ibid. 78, 80, 87).
62. Davari 1999.
63. Boroujerdi 1996: 63–76, 159–65.
64. Tabātabāi 1998: 18–20.
65. *Naqd va Nazar* 5.1–2 (Winter and Spring 1377–78): *Sonnat va tajaddod.*
66. Āshuri 20–21.
67. *New York Times* 5/26/01. He added further that "if we try to impose on a changing society issues which do not belong to our time, we will end up harming religion."
68. Hajjāriān 201, as translated by Rajaee 234.
69. Cited in Mir-Hosseini and Tapper 61.
70. Sorush 1995: 11.
71. Khātami 1999: 13, 73–80.

72. Tabātabā'i 1998.
73. Khātami 111.
74. Arjomand 2001a.
75. Khātami 183–213.
76. This facile imputation of decline to "forceful domination" is similar to Ziba-Kalam's resort to "Oriental despotism." In both cases, however, the antipathy to absolute power is significant and contrasts sharply with the hegemonic attitude of the proponents of theocratic government, one of whom is cited by Kadivar as saying: "According to our monotheistic (*tawhidi*) belief, it is not correct to say the concentration of power is corrupting. On the contrary, we maintain that power does not produce corruption....." (Kadivar 1997: 111).
77. Cited in Matin-asghari 1997: 111.
78. Jahanbakhsh 156–57.
79. Sorush 2000b: 143.
80. Mojtahed-Shabestari 2000: 18.
81. Sorush 2000: 376–77.
82. Eisenstadt 1999.
83. Bayat 11.
84. Ibid. 12.
85. Ghamari-Tabrizi 268, 270.
86. Cited in Bayat 90.
87. Hajjarian, for instance, entitled his collection of editorials published in 2000 *Republicanism (jomhuriyyat)*.
88. Nuri 262. Nuri adduced a number of Qur'anic verses and *hadith*s from the Prophet and Imam 'Ali in his trial by the Special Court for Clerics in 1999 to establish religious tolerance and political pluralism.
89. Nuri 228 as translated in Mir-Hosseini and Tapper 142.
90. Nuri 255, adducing the Quor'anic verse, Q.11.118.
91. Bayat 96–97.
92. Ibid. 10.

Chapter 5

1. Arjomand 2005: 502.
2. Even as late as May 2008, he would warn the students at the University of Gilan of the danger of distorting the Imam's thought, confirming that "we consider it an honor to be moving in the line of the Imam, and are defending the values he expounded which manifested themselves in the course of the Islamic revolution and are realized in our Constitution." (Text of the speech to the Association of Islamic Students of the University of Gilan as reported in the press on 13 Ordibehesht 1387.)
3. Lewin 1991.
4. Karrubi's interview with the Fars News Agency, 9/24/07 (2 Mehr 1386).

5. Although he never disputed the principle of clerical supremacy as inscribed in the Constitution, the invidious contrast between the popular mandate of the President and the Mandate of the Jurist became evident. Once a legal matter becomes a contested issue in constitutional politics, the gates are wide open for debate over the fundamental principles of order. This is precisely what happened, shortly after the presidential elections, in November 1997, when Ayatollah Hossein-'Ali Montazeri and some other disgruntled senior clerics, who had been pushed aside by the Supreme Jurist after a very long association with the regime, openly challenged the Mandate of the Jurist. At this point, it was clerical dissent and the rift within the ruling clerical elite that gave secular political forces the chance to express their opposition to clericalism openly.

6. Bayat 109.

7. Ibid. 108.

8. Bayat 119–200.

9. Arjomand 2000a: 286.

10. Afshari 211–15.

11. See chapter 1, section 1.

12. Parsi 2007: 211.

13. The actual effect of the order was to save Hashemi-Rafsanjani some further embarrassment and to knock two reformists off the list to make room for two candidates favored by the hardliners.

14. According to the UN sources used by Schirazi (130–31), the Freedom Movement of Iran (FMI) had applied for a license to the Ministry of the Interior, but its application to operate as a political organization was turned down in August 1992. But according to Bazargan in my interview with him on 1/24/1993, the Ministry of the Interior did send a letter informing them that the FMI's application for a license had been rejected, but he had not applied as he maintained that the FMI was already a party and refused to acknowledge the constitutionality of the committee set up in the Ministry of the Interior for vetting political parties. It appears that the FMI, whose offices had been taken over in June 1988, when four of the leaders were arrested, approved the newly formed committee for vetting political parties and groups in 1988 in the hope of being recognized, but evidently nothing came of it (Afshari 235).

15. As a medical student, Sami had been one of the organizers of the Islamic Association of Physicians. He belonged to a small group of so-called theistic socialists, was the founder of the Liberation Front of the People of Iran, JAMA (*Jebha-ye Āzādibakhsh-e Mardom-e Irān*) (Chehabi 1990: 211), and ran against Bani-Sadr in the first IRI presidential election in 1980.

16. International Commission of Jurists 200–1.

17. Afshari 245.

18. Ten of these were later released on bail (*Ettelā'āt* 4/4/01).

19. *New York Times* 4/9/01.

20. Cited in Mortaji 92–93.
21. *Ettelā'āt* 4/19/99.
22. Tajbakhsh 2000: 380, 390–92.
23. Hajjāriān 2000: 736.
24. Cited in Arjomand 2001b: 329, with added emphasis.
25. Mehrpur 2001: 50–51.
26. Article 13.
27. Mehrpur 2005: 11–12.
28. See chapter 4, section 2.
29. Mehrpur 2005: 24.
30. *New York Times* 1/9/02.
31. Compare Khatami's statement during the constitutional crisis caused by the rejection of the Majles budget in February 2001: "We must all submit to the vote of the people and the Fundamental Law," with Montazeri's statement: "There is no way except for the amendment of the Fundamental Law!" (*Ettelā'āt* 2/12 and 13/2001). As for the reformists in the Majles, one had to hear about their "murmurs of the amendment of the Fundamental Law and a referendum" from the clericalist newspaper *Resālat.* (cited in *Ettelā'āt* 2/6/2001).
32. He issued the warning according to the terms of Article 113.
33. Arjomand 2005: 510–11.
34. ISNA website, isnagency.com, 8/30/02.
35. I had urged the Office of the President, through Deputy-President Abtahi, and a number of reformist members of the Majles, to do so. In its internal communications and drafts, the Commission had also sought to draw on the President's oath of office, which makes him the guard (*pāsdār*) of "the Islamic order and the Constitution. (Article 121). Taking the terms "guard" (*pāsdār*) and "guardian" (*negahbān*) as synonymous, the President could conceivably have strengthened his responsibility for the implementation of the Constitution in Article 113, and staked a bolder claim to constitutional interpretation at the expense of the Guardian Council than the more assertive Head of the Judiciary did. The Judiciary's counterargument, however, was that the Law of 1986 had been superseded by the constitutional amendments of 1989 (Mehrpur 2005: 20).
36. Mehrpur 2005: 87–88.
37. *Financial Times* 11/2/02.
38. *The Economist* 11/16/02: 42.
39. *The New York Times* 12/11/02.
40. The Supreme Court subsequently returned the case to the original judge in Hamadan to reconsider, and the latter confirmed the death sentence in May 2004. Aghajari still refused to appeal, but the Leader pardoned him.
41. *Emrooz* website 2/12/03.
42. *Nawruz* 5/29/02. When interpreting Article 112 of the Constitution in October 1993 to mean that no legislative organ could rescind any enactment of the Maslahat Council (discussed in chapter 2, above), the Guardian

Council had also stated with regard to Article 110.8 of the Constitution now cited that the Maslahat Council could choose to refer a difficult issue (*mo'zal*) singled out by the Leader to the Majles with the latter's approval. (Guardian Council 2: 236) It would be natural for the Maslahat Council to infer that it was under no obligation whatsoever to do so.

43. Berkeley and Siamdoust 2004.
44. Ganji 2003: 183–84.
45. Bayat 96, 130.
46. Cited in Bayat 132.
47. Keshavarzian 2005: 82, 86.
48. RFPE/RL, *Iran Report* 6.15: 4/7/03.
49. *Financial Times* 3/17/03.
50. RFE/RL, *Iran Report* 6.49: 12/27/03.
51. Former Majles Speaker Mehdi Karrubi, who belonged to the clerical wing of the reformist movement, came third in the first round partly by magnifying a leaf out of President Bush's book and promising every Iranian a substantial, monthly negative tax paycheck, and justifiably complained of electoral fraud. But the fact remains that the total hardliner vote in the first round was larger than the total reformist vote.
52. When Mo'in took over the chancellorship of the (formerly Pahlavi) University of Shiraz during the Cultural Revolution, he told the faculty in earnest that he regretted not having the authority to shoot all professors trained in the United States. (G2K communication of 6/27/05 from Gholamreza Vatandust.)
53. RFE/RL, *Iran Report* 7.8: 2/23/04.
54. *The Economist* 2/28/04: 10.
55. This was to be done by making being a Muslim in good standing to run attestable by neighbors and acquaintances according to custom (*'orf*), rather that requiring the determination of the Guardian Council.
56. BBC Persian website, 2/15/04.
57. The turnout, however, was not as heavy as in 1997. It was 67% of the eligible voters (aged over 16 years) as compared to 88% in May 23, 1997, when Khatami received 69% of the popular vote.

Chapter 6

1. See the Appendix for an explanation of the model of integrative revolution.
2. Hunt 1984.
3. The increasingly rare lawyer or engineer is put with them in the category of "Medical and Other Professionals."
4. This minority is even smaller than our figures suggest because considering the Friday prayer leaders in the IRI as religious (as distinct from political) functionaries may be overindulgent.
5. Cited in International Crisis Group 2007: 4.
6. Ibid.

7. Naji 227, 231–32.
8. This is similar to what some immigration officers reportedly did at Ellis Island with the names of the immigrants coming into the United States in the same period and earlier.
9. Hāshemi-Rafsanjāni 1997, 1: 436, 441. He appears as Akbar Hashemi-Rafsanjani in the book on Palestine he translated in 1964.
10. Nader Entessar, G2K communication 5/24/05.
11. Sorush's actual first name is Hossein.
12. Naji 4–5, 215.
13. From 0.4552 in 1960, the Gini coefficient reached to around 0.5 in 1974. (The rural coefficient was over 0.1 lower, but a different estimate puts the overall coefficient over 0.6 for 1970.) But the Gini coefficient was standing again at 0.45 in 1984–1985 and was the same in 2000–2002 (Looney 248–50; Plan and Budget Organization 28). See Salehi-Isfahani (2009) for a more detailed discussion. We unfortunately have no coefficients (and no data) for the distribution of wealth, which could show much sharper fluctuations.
14. Amuzegar 2003: 53–55.
15. Slavin 197.
16. Parsa 1989.
17. Kashavarzian 2007.
18. *The Guardian* 11/3/08.
19. *Sālmāna-ye āmāri (Statistical Yearbook)* 1385: 108.
20. Eshani 2009.
21. From 668,000 in 1976 to 1,464,000 in 1986 [*Sālmāna-ye āmāri (Statistical Yearbook), 1385:* 108].
22. Ehsani 2009: 46, Table 2.1.
23. Shaditalab 2003.
24. *Sālmāna-ye āmāri 1385:* 124. Men's average marriage age in the same period increased by roughly half as much to 25.5 and 26.5 for the rural and urban areas, respectively.
25. The number of female MPs in the first three parliaments had been constant at four.
26. Her advocacy of women's sports and riding of bicycles and motorbikes alarmed the hardliners who considered her seditious and harassed her in her 1996 campaign by pairing her in a rigmarole with 'Ayesha, Muhammad's wife, and the mortal enemy of the first Imam, 'Ali, who went to the battlefield against him on her camel: " *'Āyesha bā shotor, Fā'eza bā motor!*" ('Ayesha on the camel, Faeza on the motorbike!) (Mir-Hosseini 2001: 9).
27. Ibid. The number of female MPs had remained constant through the 1980s at four. See table 6.1.
28. Bayat 2007: 109.
29. Eshani, Keshavarzian, and Moruzzi 7. Reports of their activities were posted on the feminist website, Meydaan: http://www.meydaan.com.
30. Chehabi 1997: 241.

31. Ibid. 242–43.
32. Ibid. 246.
33. Ehsani 2007.
34. Cited in Sadeghi 2007a: 45.
35. Ibid. 46.
36. See chapter 5.
37. The list of detainees includes most of the important activists promoting women's rights in Iran, and is given in G2K communication by Hadi Ghaemi, 3/5/07.
38. See the website of the Kanun-e Zanan-e Iran: http://www.irwomen.info/spip.php?article5727.
39. The numbers actually elected in 1999 were 4,879 urban and 104,709 rural councilors (Tajbakhsh 2006: 23).
40. Tajbakhsh 2003: 2.
41. Naji 213–21.
42. Tajbakhsh 2003: 2.
43. Tajbakhsh 2006: 32.
44. Sadeghi 2007b.
45. Shambayati 2004.

Chapter 7

1. For greater detail and citation of sources for this section, see Arjomand 1991.
2. Skocpol 1988.
3. Walt 1966: 18–19.
4. In March 1980, on the occasion of Nawruz (Persian New Year 1359) shortly after the ratification of the Constitution, Khomeini reaffirmed: "We should try hard to export our revolution to the world" (cited in Ramazani 50).
5. Cited in Mortaji 59–60.
6. Slavin 2007: 17.
7. Ramazani 1990: 44–45.
8. Sick 2002: 360.
9. Cited in Gieling 1999: 121–22.
10. Slavin 2007: 88.
11. Ramazani 1990: 53.
12. Gieling 1999: 125–26.
13. Sick 1991.
14. Parsi 2007:107.
15. Bill 1990: 166, 177; Walt 1996: 227.
16. Sick 2002: 356–57 for both citations.
17. Cited in Ramazani 1990: 54.
18. Cited in Moslem 2002: 176.
19. Ramazani 1992: 399.
20. Snyder 1991: 237–38.
21. Ramazani 1992.

22. Rundle 2002: 18.
23. Ramazani 1992: 397.
24. *International Herald Tribune* 3/21/91.
25. Parsi 2007: 143.
26. See chapter 1.
27. *The Independent* 2/3/91 as cited in Alfoneh 2008.
28. One example is particularly instructive. The serious predicament of the Shi'ite population in the wake of the postwar uprisings in Hilla, Najaf, and Karbala induced the aged, traditionalist, and remarkably apolitical Shi'ite leader resident in Iraq, Grand Ayatollah Abu'l-Qasem Kho'i, to issue an edict appointing a Shi'ite shadow cabinet for Iraq. This decree was made public on 18 March 1991 by the Lebanese Shi'ite leader, Shaikh Mohammad Fadlallah. On the same day, Ayatollah Khamenei expressed the hope that "an Islamic and truly popular government based on the wishes of the innocent people of Iraq" would come to power. The coincidence is significant. Kho'i, the highest Shi'ite religious leader (*marja' al-taqlid*) in Iraq, had been Khomeini's chief rival; pictures of Kho'i were burned during the Iranian revolution. In postwar propaganda the Iranian pragmatic ruling elite did not want to be outdone by Kho'i any more than by Saddam's declaration of holy war in August 1990, or by the Iranian radical clerics throughout the crisis. Ayatollah Khamenei's statement, however, did not affect Iranian policy: President Hashemi-Rafsanjani would categorically deny that Iran provided troops or military assistance to the Shi'ite rebels in Iraq. He said that the Iraqis could do their own work.
29. Sick 2002: 362.
30. Early in March 1991, Iran was excluded from the meeting of the Gulf Cooperation Council states Egypt and Syria, and their agreement, the Damascus Declaration, in March 1991, even though Deputy-President Habibi and Foreign Minister Velayati were already in Damascus for talks with the Syrian President.
31. Council on Foreign Relations 2004: 35.
32. Naji 2008: 152–55. On the development of Ahmadinejad's idea, see chapter 7.
33. Ramazani 1992: 401–02.
34. Interview with 'Ata'ollah Mohajerani, 1/18/1993.
35. Bayat and Baktiari 2002: 317.
36. Ehteshami 1995: 148–59.
37. Ramazani 1992: 403–8.
38. Radio Free Europe 10/16/08.
39. Parsi 2007: chs. 13–15.
40. Cited in Slavin 2007: 179; see also Parsi 2007: 153.
41. It would take Nabavi a decade to come around, in November 2001, to the view that "normalizing ties with the U.S. does not contradict our values—the conditions today require different policies" (cited in Takeyh 120). By then, however, September 11 had ushered in the Bush-Cheney era of

preemptive war and regime change that made Nabavi's new goal impossible to attain.

42. Moslem 124.

43. Parsi 2008: 155. These were developed after the Oslo agreement.

44. *Ettelā'āt* 11/7/93.

45. *The Wall Street Journal* 6/28/1994; Gary Sick, G2K Communication 5/7/2008.

46. Parsi 2008: 157–65.

47. Ibid. 187–88.

48. Ibid. 200–201.

49. *New York Times* 7/27/01.

50. Parsi 2008: 212.

51. Ibid. 204.

52. See the section immediately below.

53. CNN interview with Khatami 1/7/98, also cited in Slavin 184.

54. Slavin 2007: 186–87.

55. Sick 2002: 368–69.

56. Khatami, for instance, did not attend a major musical event at Asia Society modeled after one that had led to Nixon's overture to China.

57. Slavin 2007: 217–20. The rejection was hardly surprising in view of Secretary Rice's statement a year earlier that had singled out "the fundamental character of regimes" as what mattered most in this new world in which the "goal of our statecraft is to help create a world of democratic, well-governed states" (cited in Takeyh 125). Larijani, needless to say, had not proposed regime change from within but matters of mutual interest to the two countries.

58. Barry Schweid, G2K communication 10/8/ 2008.

59. Parsi 2007: 229–31.

60. *Washington Post* 2/12/07.

61. The drafts are reproduced in Parsi 2007: 341–46.

62. Ibid. 243–47; Slavin 2007: 199–204, 229–31.

63. Secretary Powell's chief of staff, Colonel Lawrence Wilkerson, as cited in Parsi 2007: 249.

64. Ibid. ch. 15.

Chapter 8

1. Naji 36–39.

2. Ibid. 49–50.

3. Ibid. 53.

4. Cited ibid. 57, 70.

5. Ibid. 32; *New York Times* 7/2/09.

6. See the fascinating and well-documented account of this electoral highjacking in Naji 72–88.

7. Ibid. 77–78.

8. Ahmadinejad's often repeated promise prompted a group of workers with a sense of humor to write to him in March 2007 that they do not want the oil money for dinner, but just wanted to keep their jobs to provide for a meager meal at their dinner tables (Naji 235).

9. 4 Azar 1387/November 25, 2008. The vast majority of the Basijis are, however, not hardcore militia members but had joined up for scholarship opportunities, discounted tour packages, and other perks.

10. Aryan 2008.

11. Naji 53–54.

12. Lazrak 2006.

13. International Crisis Group 2007: 12–13.

14. Ibid. 10.

15. Cited in Ganji 2008.

16. Alfoneh 2008.

17. Tehran, Agence Presse France (APF), 9 February 2008, 14:26:17–0500 (EST).

18. Fars News Agency interview with Asghari's wife: http://www.farsnews.com/newstext.php?nn=8512210191.

19. BBC News: http://news.bbc.co.uk/2/hi/middle_east/7350165.stm.

20. The association's name derives from *hojja,* meaning proof, as the Hidden Imam is called the Proof of God (*hojjat allāh*), and is in full the Charitable Association of the Proof [of God] and the Mahdi (*anjoman-e khayriya-ye hojjatiyya-ye mahdaviyya*).

21. His election was highly improbably because of the division of the hardliners in the first round of presidential elections, which made an influential hardliner columnist despair: "it's over...we have no chance." (Cited in International Crisis Group 2005: 4.)

22. *E'temād-e Melli,* 7/1/08, as cited in Ahdiyyih 2008.

23. The prayer with which he ended his address to the same General Assembly in September of the following year was more earnest and included the yearning to be among the Mahdi's martyrs. See Amanat 2009: 241.

24. Far more common is the belief that the Lord of the Age disappeared down a well or an underground water reservoir in Samarra in present-day Iraq.

25. Both citations in Naji 92–93.

26. Peterson 2005.

27. Naji 94.

28. Ahdiyyih 2008.

29. *Washington Post* 5/8/08.

30. *New York Times* 5/20/08.

31. Naji 140.

32. Ibid. 156.

33. Ibid. 164–83.

34. Cited ibid.: 91.

35. Ibid. 195–97.

36. Amanat 2009: 243–44.

37. Ibid. ch. 10.

38. The year after Ahmadinejad's election, a Mahdist association published a series of some 40 booklets in Persian and seven in English in runs of 5000

(also available at www.ejlasmahdi.com/paygah.aspx) in the spring and summer of 2006. The first title in the series was 'Ali-Akbar Velayati's *Imam Mahdi and the Blooming (shokufā'i) of Islamic Culture and Civilization in the World,* and it displayed evidence of political modernism such as the title of Publication #10: *The Blooming of Citizenship Rights (hoquq-e shahrvandi) in the Age of Advent.*

39. http://www.rsf-persan.org/spip.php?article16694.

40. Naji 244.

41. I am grateful to Dr. Majid Mohammadi for this estimate of the number purged in 2006.

42. Copenhagen University Middle East and Islam Network: http://cuminet. blogs.ku.dk/2009/02/23/assault-on-tehran-university/.

43. Ibid. 85, 220.

44. International Crisis Group 2007: 22.

45. Ibid. 211.

46. Amuzgar 2007: 68–71.

47. Both citations in Naji 98, 104.

48. *New York Times* 4/19/07.

49. Naji 265.

50. Transcript of a talk given by the former Deputy-Minister of Interior, Mostafa Tajzadeh, at the Faculty of Social Sciences of the University of Tehran in November 2008.

51. Naji 264–65.

52. Ibid. 225–26, 232.

53. Farideh Farhi, G2K communication, 1/22/08.

54. Naji 55.

55. Ibid. 175.

56. *New York Times* 7/26, 27 & 28/09.

57. Juan Cole, *Informed Comment* (http://www.juancole.com) 7/25/09; Qaemi G2K communication 7/27/09.

58. *Los Angeles Times* 7/21/09.

59. RFL/RL Radio, 5/19/09. He also increased pensions but rolled them back after the election in July. *New York Times* 7/27/09.

60. Keshavarzian, G2K communication 6/15/09. The first was the Islamic revolution of February 1979; the second, the takeover of the American embassy almost 9 months later.

61. Hadi Semati, G2K communication, 6/13/09; *The Economist* 6/20/09: 25–27.

62. *The Guardian* 7/9/09. This leading role reportedly caused tension with the Revolutionary Guards.

63. Electoral fraud was subsequently documented by Musavi's monitors and those of the other candidates. The results were announced before the polling stations had completed and signed the appropriate forms certifying the totals; some fifteen million or more ballots in excess of the electorate were not accounted for, and the 14,000 mobile voting booths introduced for the first time had returned high numbers suspiciously at variance with

the regular stations in the areas they covered. More critically, in 78 urban districts comprising 11 million votes the aggregate figures did not match those of the polling stations, and in 60 urban districts and 192 sub-districts the number of votes exceeded 100% of the electorate (up to 211%). The number of votes for some boxes was given in multiples of 100 (the number of ballots in the batches distributed); and in 307 boxes more than 99% of the votes were for one of the four candidates. (Guess which!)

(Committee for the Protection [*siyānat*] of Musavi's Vote, Announcement # 15 and the letter of 6/29/09 to the Guardian Council by Hojjat al-Eslam Mohtashamipur, and by the former Interior Minister who had conducted the elections under President Khatami, Hojjat al-Eslam Musavi-Lari as electronically distributed.) The Guardian Council admitted irregularities in 50 cities involving 3 million votes and instances of votes in excess of electorates, but refused any random recounting and certified the election whose result was declared final by the Leader on 6/24/09.

Mohammad 'Asgari, a Musavi supporter working at the computer center in the Ministry of the Interior had reportedly tipped off the latter who declared victory an hour or so after the polls were closed. 'Asgari was mysteriously killed in a car accident a few days later.

64. *Kalemeh-ye Sabz,* 1.22 (6/14/09): 2. (www.kalemeh.ir)
65. Ibid. 1.
66. Youtube video.
67. *New York Times* 6/16/09: A10.
68. Hadi Ghaemi G2K communication of 6/15/09.
69. Shahram Kholdi in a G2K communication of 6/14/09.
70. Human Rights Activists, translated by Shahram Kholdi in a G2K communication of 6/17/09.
71. Hadi Ghaemi G2K communication of 6/16/09 for a partial list.
72. According to *Seda-ye 'Adālat* (voice of justice), 6/20/09.
73. *Islamic Republic of Iran News Network Television (IRINN),* June 19, 2009.
74. At least 8 Basij militiamen were killed in June. The number of deaths posted at the website of the 2005 reformist presidential candidate, Mostafa Moin, on July 16 was 168 (http://drmoeen.ir/archives/88/4/25.php). On August 2, 2009, Musavi's advisor and the late Ayatollah Beheshti's son, 'Alireza Beheshti, who directs a center for monitoring casualties with another reformist, Morteza Alviri, mentioned an incomplete list of the names of some 1,700 detainees and said that number of deaths could be as high as 365 (http://www.roozonline.com/persian/news/newsitem/article/2009/august/02//365.html).
75. Unfortunately for them, the reformists could not resist the temptation of competing with the hardliners in using the old political rhetoric and occasional charges of conspiracy with foreigners against Ahmadinejad and the hardliners. Just before he was arrested, in a message distributed on 7/23/09, the prominent reformist 'Abdollah Ramazanzadeh alleged that the

hardliners had "carried out the coup [as a step] toward compromise with the West and selling the country!"

76. *New York Times* 8/2 and 3/09; *Wall Street Journal* 8/3/09. 'Atrianfar's confession was available in different recordings on Youtube on 7/3/09.

Chapter 9

1. Limited institutional pluralism is underlined in Chehabi 2001. For the regime's characterization as fragmented authoritarianism, see Keshavarzian 2005: 65. A "limited polyarchy" and "institutionally balkanized" state have also alternatively been used to describe the regime in Keshavarzian 2005: 73–74, and by Kamrava and Hassan-Yari 2004. In my opinion, these characterizations exaggerate fragmentation, which has been declining as a result both of state centralization and the growth of the personal, neo-patrimonial power of the Leader.

2. Max Weber formulated the concept of patrimonialism as the ideal-type of a system of personal authority in which the country is considered the patrimony of the ruler and is administered as an extension of his household. Many sociologists and political scientists have subsequently argued that the personal authority persists in many political regimes despite the formal adoption of modern impersonal systems that legally recognize the authority of offices rather than persons. I used the term neo-patrimonialism to describe this aspect of the last Shah's rule before the Islamic revolution (Arjomand 1988).

3. Cited in Bakhash 1995: 111.

4. Some *mojtahed*s allow the "imitation of the dead."

5. Arjomand 2001: 320–21.

6. Gieling 1997: 780–82.

7. Buchta 1995: 459–60. Khamenei's statement (cited in Buchta 1995: 470) that he had reached this decision because there were many qualified *marāje'* in Iran but not outside of Iran, thus making him indispensable, was patently incorrect, as demonstrated by the acclamation of Ayatollah Sayyed 'Ali Sistani and three other Grand Ayatollah in Iraq. It also ignored the failed attempt by his supporters to delegitimize *marja'iyyat* after the establishment of the Mandate of the Jurist. It is also worth noting that the clerical promoters of Khamenei in Iran who presented lists of *marāje'* in the first days of December 1994 (Society of Militant Clergy and the Qom Seminary Professors) did not have the civility to mention Sistani or any other Grand Ayatollah outside of Iran.

8. I owe this significant information to Dr. Houchang Chehabi.

9. Khalji 2006: 28–31.

10. Ibid. 34–35.

11. Rajaee 167–68.

12. Ibid. 167 for both citations.

13. Cited in Rajaee 169.

14. Cited in Sadjadpour 2008: 18.
15. Ibid. 17.
16. Ibid. 18.
17. Ibid. 21–22.
18. Ganji was sure the future was with him and reform, and considered the alienation of Rafsanjani a negligible cost the reformists could easily spare. "He is no cost (*hazineh*)," Ganji told my friend 'Ezzatollah Fouladvand at the time.
19. Ganji 2000a: 97.
20. See Table 6.2.
21. The traditionalist hardliners from the clerical elite, needless to say, constitute the majority of the members of the Maslahat Council, alongside two token reformists. (G2K communication by Majid Mohammadi, 2/28/07.)
22. International Crisis Group 2007: 3, 12.
23. Amuzgar 2007: 73.
24. International Crisis Group 2007: 19.
25. See Centre for Iranian Studies 2007 for details.
26. *New York Times,* 4/11/08.
27. Statement made on 1/3/08 as cited in Sadjadpour 17.
28. Farideh Farhi, G2K communication, 1/8/09.
29. See p. 179, above.
30. All he could claim at the Friday sermon on July 17, 2009, was that he had passed the proposal he was about to make by certain members of the two councils.
31. See pp. 154–55, above.
32. See *New York Times* 7/18/09 for a summary of the major points of the sermon in English. Contrary to usual practice, Hashemi-Rafsanjani's Friday sermon was not broadcast live at noon but only in the evening, slightly doctored.
33. Mohammadi 2009. However, only two Grand Ayatollahs expressly defended Ahmadinejad.
34. K.G. Niknejad G2K communication 6/18/09; the *fatwās* were posted on Mohsen Kadivar's website (http://www.kadivar.com/DocId=2329&DT=dpv) on July 14, 2009.
35. Moslem 94.
36. See p. 34, above.
37. Youtube video (www.youtube.com/watch?v=ngkO-vY-t10k)
38. See Chapter 6.
39. According to Article 57 of the amended 1989 Constitution.
40. Karimi and Najibullah (2008). The Majles had never exercised its right to supervise the extensive activities and expenditure of any of the branches of the Leadership Office. Feeble attempts were made to do so in the reformist Majles between 2000 and 2004, but to no effect.
41. Ganji 2008.
42. E-mail circulated on 6/15/09.

43. *Islamic Republic of Iran News Network Television (IRINN)*, June 19, 2009.
44. See Arjomand 1988: ch. 10 on the fragility of neopatrimonial regimes, including that of the Shah, which makes them prone to coups d'etat and revolution. It is interesting to note that the Shah's regime has also been characterized as "Sultanistic" (Chehabi and Linz 1998).

Chapter 10

1. Snyder 1991: ch. 6. We have seen this development in revolutionary Iran in chapter 3.
2. Buchta 2000: 76–77.
3. Cordesman 2004: 35–37.
4. Slavin 2007: 180.
5. Sick 2002: 357.
6. *New York Times* 11/12/1992.
7. Buchta 2000: 6.
8. Slavin 2007: 92.
9. Nasr 2000.
10. Nasr 2002.
11. Council on Foreign Relations 29, 35.
12. Slavin 2007: 202–4.
13. She maintains that Iranian officials remained helpful on al-Qada. (Barry Schweid, G2K communication, 10/8/2008.)
14. The possibility of a hoax cannot be overruled as the whole episode, from the Israeli point of view, seems too good to be true. See Parsi 2007: 234–35.
15. Peterson and LaFranchi 2008.
16. Gerecht 2002.
17. Robert Hutchings as cited in Slavin 2007: 25.
18. Cited by Takeyh 2006: 136.
19. Kibaroglu 213–15.
20. Paul E. Erdman, *The Crash of '79*, published in 1976, selects 1979, the year destined for the Islamic revolution, for the apocalyptic thermonuclear war.
21. Cordesman 2004: 74–75.
22. Kibaroglu 2006: 216–17.
23. Bali 2006: 13.
24. Ruhani A; B: 12.
25. Ruhani (B: 13) stated that he had the backing of Iran's Supreme National Security Council for making the October 21 concessions unilaterally, if no agreement was reached with the EU-3 foreign ministers by the ultimatum deadline, to avoid being referred to the UN Security Council.
26. Ruhani B: 29. The ministers paid a courtesy visit to President Khatami only after the agreement was announced (Bellaigue 31).
27. Ruhani A.
28. Ibid.
29. Bali 2006: 17.

30. *New York Times* 11/1/04.
31. Takeyh 2006: 155–57.
32. Kibaroglu 2006: 221.
33. Naji 130–31.
34. Ibid. 209.
35. Ayatollah Montazeri had this advantage in mind when making his astute remark that no one denied the right of the Iranian people to peaceful nuclear development. "But let me ask the President if he thinks the people of Iran also have other rights, and ones that are much less costly and easier to grant."
36. *New York Times* 2/20/09.
37. Centre for Iranian Studies (Durham).
38. Associated Press 4/8/08.
39. *Libération* 7/2/08.
40. *New York Times* 7/2/09.
41. See Snyder 1991: 244–52.

Conclusion

1. Berlin 1979.
2. Arjomand 1988: 210.
3. For example, Ganji 2008.
4. Arjomand 1988: 75–76.
5. Tierney 1955.

Appendix

1. See Arjomand, forthcoming.
2. *Politics* 219.
3. Ibid. 221.
4. Pareto 1968 [1917–1919]: #2227.
5. Ibid. 1304–1305, #2053–2057.
6. Linz 1975: 259–64.
7. Arjomand 1988.
8. Pareto 1968 [1917–1919]: 1086, #1747.
9. Tocqueville 1955.
10. Pareto 1968 [1917–1919]: 1301–3, #2048–2050.
11. Mosca 1966 [1895]: 80–122.
12. Huntington 1968; Skocpol 1979.
13. Arendt 1963: 116.
14. Ibid. 260.
15. Stinchcombe 1978.
16. Arjomand 1988.
17. Jouvenel 1949.
18. For brief sketches of the other types, "Constitutive Revolution" and the Khaldunian subtype of "Integrative Revolution," see Arjomand 2006: 151–52.

REFERENCES

Documents

Āshenā'i bā Majles-e shurā-ye eslāmi, Tehran: Majles Public Relations Office, 1982/
1361, 3 vols.

International Commission of Jurists, *Iran: Attacks on Justice,* August 27, 2002
(http://www.icj.org/IMG/pdf/iran.pdf).

Guardian Council 1

Mehrpur, H. 1992/1371. *Majmu'a-ye Nazariyyāt-e shurā-ye negahbān,* 3 vols., Tehran:
Keyhān.

Guardian Council 2

Markaz-e Tahqiqāt-e Shurā-ye Negahbān, *Majmu'a-ye Nazariyyāt-e shurā-ye
negahbān, tafsiri va mashvarati dar khosus-s qānun-e asāsi, 1359–1380.*

Maslahat Council Enactments

Majma'-e Tashkhis-e Maslahat-e Nezām. 1995/1374. *Majmu'a-ye mosavvabāt-e
Majma'-e Tashkhis-e Maslahat-e Nezām az tārikh-e 3/12/1366 tā 31/4/1374.*

Markaz-e Tahqiqāt-e Feqhi-ye Qovva-ye Qazāiyya. 2002/1381a. *Majmu'a-ya Ārā-ye
Feqhi-ye Qazdā'i dar Omur-e Kayfari,* Qom.

———. 2002/1381b. *Majmu'a-ya Ārā-ye Feqhi-ye Qazā'i dar Omur-e Hoquqi,*
Qom.

———. 2002/1381c. *Majmu'a-ye Nazariyyāt-e Moshvarati-ye Feqhi dar Omur-e
Kayfari,* Qom.

———. 2002/1381d. *Majmu'a-ye Nazariyyāt-e Moshvarati-ye Feqhi dar Omur-e
Qazā'i,* Qom.

Mo'arefi-ye nemāyandegan-e Majles-e shurā-ye eslāmi, Tehran, 2000/1378 (for the first
five sessions), 2003/1382 (sixth session), 2007/1386 (seventh session), 2009/1387
(eighth session).

Mo'avenat-e Āmuzesh va Tahqiq-e Qovva-ye Qazā'iyya. 2002–3/1381. *Majmu'a-ye Neshastha-ye Qazā'i*, 6 vols., Qom.

1979 Proceedings

Surat-e mashruh-e mozākerāt-e majles-e barrasi-ye nahā'i-ye qānun-e asāsi-ye jomhuri-ye eslāmi-ye Irān (Tehran, 1985/1364), 4 vols.

1989 Proceedings

Surat-e mashruh-e mozākerāt-e shurā-ye bāznegari-ye qānun-e asāsi-ye jomhuri-ye eslāmi-ye Irān (Tehran, 1990/1369), 4 vols.

Ruhani A

Ruhāni, H. 2005a. "*Farāsu-ye chāleshha-ye Irān va āgānce dar parvada-ye hasta'i*," *Goftemān*, 37 (Fall 2005/1384), pp. 7–38.

Ruhani B

Ruhāni, H. 2005b. "Matn-e goshāresh-e kāmel-r Dr. Ruhāni beh ra'is-e jomhur," *ISNA*, 05/09/1384.

Sālmāna-ye āmāri (Statistical Yearbook), published annually by the Iran Statistical Bureau and available at their website: www.sci.org.ir.

Books and Articles

Abrahamian, E. 1989. *Radical Islam: The Iranian Mojahedin*, London: I.B. Tauris.

Afshari, R. 2001. *Human Rights in Iran. The Abuse of Cultural Relativism*, Philadelphia: University of Pennsylvania Press.

Ahdiyyih, M. 2008. "Ahmadinejad and the Mahdi," *Middle East Quarterly*, Fall 2008, pp. 27–36.

Akhavi-Pour, H., and Azodanloo, H. 1998. "Economic Bases of Political Factions in Iran," *Critique: Critical Middle Eastern Studies*, 7(13): 69–82.

Al-Azmeh, A. *Ibn Khaldun*. 2003. *An Essay in Interpretation*, Budapest: Central European University Press.

Al-e Ahmad, J. 1984. *Occidentosis: A Plague from the West*, R. Campbell, trans., and H. Algar, ed., Berkeley: Mizan Press.

Alfoneh, A. 2008. "The Revolutionary Guards' Role in Iranian Politics," *Middle East Quarterly*, Fall 2008, pp. 3–14.

Algar, H. 1986. "Social Justice in the Ideology and Legislation of the Islamic Revolution in Iran," in L. Michalak and J. Salacuse, eds., *Social Legislation in the Contemporary Middle East*, Berkeley: University of California Press.

———. 1988. "Imam Khomeini: The Pre-revolutionary Years," in E. Burke, III and I.M. Lapidus, eds., *Islam, Politics and Social Movements*, Berkeley: University of California Press.

'Alinaqi, A. H. 1999/1378. *Nezārat-e bar entekhābāt va tashkhis-e salāhiyyat-e dāvtalabān*, Tehran: Nashr-e Nay.

Amanat, A. 2009. *Apocalyptic Islam and Iranian Shi'ism,* London: I.B. Tauris.

Amini, E. 1998/1377. "Moqarrarāt va 'Amalkard-e Majles-e Khobragān," *Hokumat-e Eslāmi,* 8: 103–21.

Amuzegar, J. 1997. *Iran's Economy under the Islamic Republic,* London: I.B. Tauris.

———. 2003. "Iran's Crumbling Revolution," *Foreign Affairs,* 84(1) (January/ February): 44–57.

———. 2007. "Islamic Social Justice, Iranian Style," *Middle East Policy,* 14(3): 60–78.

Arendt, H. 1963. *On Revolution,* New York: Viking Press.

Aristotle 1962. *Politics,* E. Barker, ed. and trans., New York: Oxford University Press.

Arjomand, S.A. 1977. "Modernity and Modernization as Analytical Concepts: An Obituary," *Communications and Development Review,* 1–2: 16–20.

———. 1981. "Shi'ite Islam and the Revolution in Iran," *Government and Opposition,* 16(3): 293–316.

———. 1982. "A la recherche de la conscience collective: The Ideological Impact of Durkheim in Turkey and Iran," *The American Sociologist,* 17(2): 94–102.

Arjomand, S.A. 1984. "Traditionalism in Twentieth Century Iran," in S.A. Arjomand, ed., *From Nationalism to Revolutionary Islam,* London: Macmillan and Albany: State University of New York Press.

———. 1986. "Iran's Islamic Revolution in Comparative Perspective," *World Politics,* 38(3): 383–414.

———. 1988. *The Turban for the Crown. The Islamic Revolution in Iran,* New York: Oxford University Press.

———. 1989. "History, Structure and Revolution in Shi'ite Tradition in Contemporary Iran," *International Political Science Review,* 10(2): 109–17.

———. 1991. "A Victory for the Pragmatists: the Islamic Fundamentalist Reaction in Iran," in J. Piscatori, ed., *Islamic Fundamentalisms and the Gulf Crisis,* Cambridge, MA: American Academy of Arts and Sciences, pp. 52–69.

———. 1992. "Constitutions and the Struggle for Political Order: A Study in the Modernization of Political Traditions," *European Journal of Sociology,* 33(4): 39–82.

———. 1993. "Shi'ite Jurisprudence and Constitution-Making in the Islamic Republic of Iran," in M. Marty and R.S. Appleby, eds., *Fundamentalisms and the State. Remaking Polities, Economies, and Militance,* Chicago: University of Chicago Press, pp. 88–109.

———. 2000. "Civil Society and the Rule of Law in the Constitutional Politics of Iran under Khatami," *Social Research,* 76(2): 283–301.

———. 2001. "Authority in Shi'ism and Constitutional Developments in the Islamic Republic of Iran," in W. Ende and R. Brunner, eds., *The Twelver Shia in Modern Times: Religious Culture & Political History,* Leiden: Brill, pp. 301–32.

Arjomand, S.A. 2003. "Modernity, Tradition and the Shi'ite Reformation in Contemporary Iran," in G. Skapska, ed., *The Moral Fabric in Contemporary Societies,* Leiden: Brill, pp. 241–61.

———. 2005. "The Rise and Fall of President Khātami and the Reform Movement in Iran," *Constellations,* 12(4): 504–22.

————. 2006. "Revolution in Early Islam: The Rise of Islam as a Constitutive Revolution," *Yearbook of the Sociology of Islam*, 7: 125–57.

————. 2007. "Shari'a and Constitution in Iran: A Historical Perspective," in A. Amanat and F. Griffel, eds., *Islamic Law in the Contemporary Context. Shari'a*, Stanford, CA: Stanford University Press, pp. 156–64.

————. 2010. *Revolution in World History*, Chicago: University of Chicago Press. (Forthcoming)

Aryan, Hossein. 2008. "Iran's Basij Force—The Mainstay of Domestic Security," RadioFree Europe, 12/7/2008 (www.rferl.org/articleprintview/1357081.html).

'Āshuri, D. 1998/1377. "*Goftemānhā-ye rawshanfekri: gharbzadehgi, rawshanfekri- ye dini va...*," Rāh-e Naw, 1(9) (30 Khordād): 18–24. (Interview.)

'Azimi (Ārāni), H. 1991/1370. *Madārhā-ye tawse'a-nayāftegi dar eqtesād-e irān*, Tehran: Nashr-e Ney.

al-'Azm, J. S. 1981. "Orientalism and Orientalism in Reverse," *Khamsin*, 8: 2–26.

Bakhash, Shaul. 1984. *The Reign of the Ayatollahs. Iran and the Islamic Revolution*, New York: Basic Books.

————. 1995. "Iran: The Crisis of Legitimacy," *Middle Eastern Lectures*, 1: 99–118.

Bâli, Asli Ü. 2006. "The US and the Iranian Nuclear Impasse," *Middle East Report*, 241 (Winter 2006) (*http://www.merip.org/mer/mer241/bali.html*).

Bāqi, 'E. 2000/1379. *Trāzhedi-ye demokrasi dar Irān*, Tehran: Nashr-e Nay.

————. 2002/1381. *E'dām va qesās. Chāleshhā-ye fekr-e dini dar irān-e emruz*, Tehran: Sarā'i.

Barātiniyā, M. 2002/1381. "Barrasi-ye chāleshha va rāhkārha-ye asāsi barāye vosul be-tawse'a-ye qazā'i," in *Majmu'a-ye maqālāt-e tawse'a- ye qazā'i*, Tehran: Mo'avenat-e 'Ejtemā'i-ye Qovva-ye Qazāiyya, pp. 59–72.

Bayat, A. 2007. *Making Islam Democratic*, Stanford, CA: Stanford University Press.

Bayat, A., and Baktiari, B. 2002. "Revolutionary Iran and Egypt: Exporting Inspirations and Anxieties," in N.R. Keddie and R. Matthee, eds., *Iran and the Surrounding World. Interactions in Culture and Cultural Politics*, N.R. Keddie and R. Matthee, eds., Seattle: Washington University Press, pp. 305–26.

Beheshti, M. Hosayni. 1999/1378. *Mabāni-ye nazari-ye qānun-e asāsi*, Tehran: Bonyād-e Āthār-e shahid Beheshti.

Berkeley, Bill, and Siamdoust, Nahid. 2004. "The Hostage-takers' Second Act," *Columbia Journalism Review* 6 (2004): 42–50.

Berlin, I. 1979. "The Hedgehog and the Fox," in *Russian Thinkers*, New York: Penguin Books, pp. 22–81.

Bill, J. A. 1990. "The U.S. Overture to Iran, 1985–86: An Analysis," in Nikki R. Keddie and Mark J. Gasiorowski, eds., *Neither East nor West: Iran, the Soviet Union, and the United States*, New Haven: Yale University Press, pp. 166–79.

Boroujerdi, M. 1996. *Iranian Intellectuals and the West. The Tormented Triumph of Nativism*, Syracuse: Syracuse University Press.

Brown, N. J. 1997. "Shari'a and the State in the Modern Middle East," *IJMES*, 29.3: 359–76.

————. 2002. *Constitutions in a Nonconstitutional World. Arab Basic Laws and the Prospects for Accountable Government,* Albany, NY: SUNY Press.

Brinton, C. 1938. *The Anatomy of Revolution,* New York: W.W. Norton.

Brumberg, D. 2001. *Reinventing Khomeini. The Struggle for Reform in Iran,* Chicago: University of Chicago Press.

Buchta, W. 1995. "Die Islamische Republik Iran und die religiös-politische Kontroverse um die *marja'iyat," Orient,* 36(3): 449–74.

————. 2000. *Who Rules Iran? The Structure of Power in the Islamic Republic,* Washington, D.C.: The Washington Institute for Near East Policy.

————. 2005. "Mehdi Hashemi's Fall: An Episode of the Iranian Intra Elite Struggle for Power under Khomeini," in M. Hamid Ansari, ed., *Iran Today. Twenty-five Years After the Islamic Revolution,* New Delhi: Rupa, pp. 197–226.

Buruma, I., and Margalit, A. 2004. *Occidentalism: The West in the Eyes of Its Enemies,* New York: Penguin Press.

Centre for Iranian Studies, University of Durham. "Only Personal? The Larijani Crisis Revisited," Policy Brief #3, November 2007.

Chehabi, H. E. 1990. *Iranian Politics and Religious Modernism: The Liberation Movement of Iran under the Shah and Khomeini,* Ithaca: Cornell University Press.

————. 1997. "Ardabil Becomes a Province: Center-Periphery Relations in Iran," *International Journal of Middle East Studies,* 29(2): 235–53.

————. 2001. "The Political Regime of the Islamic Republic of Iran in Comparative Perspective," *Government and Opposition,* 16(1): 48–70.

Chehabi, H. E., and Linz, J. E. 1998. *Sultanistic Regimes,* Baltimore: Johns Hopkins University Press.

Cordesman, A. 2004. *Iran's Developing Military Capabilities,* Washington, D.C.: Center for Strategic and International Studies.

Council on Foreign Relations. 2004. *Iran: Time for a New Approach,* New York: Council on Foreign Relations.

Dabashi, H. 1993. *Theology of Discontent,* New York: New York University Press.

Daryābāri, S. M. 2004. *Dādsarā va dādgāh-e vizha-ye ruhāniyyat,* Tehran: Markaz-e Asnād-e Enqelāb-e Eslāmi.

Dāvari, R. 1999/1377–78. "Din va tajaddod," *Naqd va Nazar,* 5(1–2): 58–71.

Edwards, L. P. 1927. *The Natural History of Revolution,* Chicago: The University of Chicago Press.

Ehsani, K. 2004. "Round 12 for Iran's Reformists," *Middle East Report Online,* 1/29/2004. Online at http://www.merip.org/mero/mero012904.html.

————. 2006. "Iran: The Populist Threat to Democracy," *Middle East Report,* 241: 4–9.

————. 2007. "Survival through Dispossession: Privatizations of Public Goods in the Islamic Republic" presented at the Symposium on "Building Linkages between Civil Society and Constitutional Democracy in Iran" at Stony Brook-Manhattan on November 15, 2007.

Ehsani, K. 2009. "The Urban Provincial Periphery in Iran: Revolution and War in Ramhormoz," in A. Gheissari, ed., *Contemporary Iran. Economy, Society, Politics,* New York: Oxford University Press, pp. 38–76.

Eshani, K., Keshavarzian, A., and Moruzzi, N. C. 2009. "Tehran, June 2009,"
Middle East Report Online (http://www.merip.org/mero/mero062809.html).

Ehteshami, A. 1995. *After Khomeini. The Iranian Second Republic,* London:
Routledge.

Eisenstadt, S. N. 1999. *Fundamentalism, Sectarianism and Revolution. The Jacobin
Dimension of Modernity,* New York: Cambridge University Press.

Erdman, P. E. 1979. *The Crash of '79,* New York: Simon & Schuster.

Ganji, A. 2000a/1379. *'Ālijenāb-e sorkhpush va 'ālijenābān-e khākestari,* Tehran:
Tarh-e Naw.

————. 2000b/1379. *Talaqqi-ye fāshisti az din va hokumat. āsibshenāsi-ye gozār
bedawlat-e demokrātik-e tawse'a-gerā,* Tehran: Tarh-e Naw.

————. 2003. "Documents on Democracy," *Journal of Democracy* 14.1: 183–84.

————. 2008. "The Latter-Day Sultan," *Foreign Affairs,* 87.6 (November/December).

Gerecht, R. M. 2002. "Regime Change in Iran?" *The Weekly Standard,* 7(45)
(8/5/02).

Ghamari-Tabrizi, B. 2008. *Islam and dissent in postrevolutionary Iran : Abdolkarim
Soroush, religious politics and democratic reform,* London: I.B. Tauris.

Gheissari A., and Nasr, V. 2006. *Democracy in Iran. History and the Quest for
Liberty,* New York: Oxford University Press.

Gieling, S. 1997. "The Marja'iya in Iran and the Nomination of Khamanei in
December 1994," *Middle Eastern Studies,* 33(4): 777–87.

————. 1999. *Religion and War in Revolutionary Iran,* London: I.B. Tauris.

Goldstone, J. 1982. "The Comparative and Historical Study of Revolutions,"
Annual Review of Sociology, 8: 187–207.

Hairi, A. 1977. *Shi'ism and Constitutionalism in Iran,* Leiden: E.J. Brill.

Hajjārian, S. 2000/1379. *Jomhuriyyat. Afsunzodā'i az qodrat,* Tehran: Tarh-e Naw.

Hāshemi, M. 1996/1375. *Hoquq-e asāsi-ye jomhuri-ye eslāmi-ye Irān,* 2 vols., Tehran:
Mojtame'-e 'Āli-ye Āmuzesh-e Qom.

Hāshemi-Rafsanjāni, A. 1997a. In *Hāshemi-Rafsanjāni. Dawrān-e mobāreza,*
M. Hāshemi, ed., 2 vols., Tehran: Daftar-e Nashr-e Ma'āref-e Enqelāb.

————. 1997b. "Hāshemi-Rafsanjāni chegunagi-ye entekhāb-e rahbar va jarayān-e
marja'iyyat rā sharh dād," *Ettelā'āt,* 12/1/1997 (10/9/1376): 9.

[Hāshemi Shāhrudi, M.] 2001/1380. *Manshur-e tawse'a-ye qazā'i,* vols. 2 and 3,
Tehran: Mo'avenat-e 'Ejtemā'i-ye Qovva-ye Qazāiyya.

Hunt, L. 1984. *Politics, culture, and class in the French Revolution,* Berkeley:
University of California Press.

Huntington, S. P. 1968. *Political Order in Changing Societies,* New Haven, CT: Yale
University Press.

International Crisis Group. 2005. "Iran: What does Ahmadi-Nejad's Victory
Mean?" Middle East Briefings No. 18, Tehran/Brussels, 4 August 2005.

International Crisis Group. 2007. "Iran: Ahmadi-Nejad's Tumultuous Presidency,"
Middle East Briefings No. 21, Tehran/Brussels, 6 February 2007.

Jahanbakhsh, F. 2001. *Islam, Democracy and Religious Modernism in Iran
(1953–2000),* Leiden: Brill.

Javādi Āmoli, 'A. 1996/1375. "Sayri dar mabāni-ye velāyat-e faqih," *Hokumat-e Eslāmi,* 1: 50–80.

———. 1998/1377. "Jāygāh-e feqhi-hoquqi-ye majles-e khebragān,"*Hokumat-e Eslāmi,* 8: 10–30.

Jouvenel, B. de. 1949. *On Power, Its Nature and the History of Its Growth,* J.F. Huntington, trans., New York: Viking Press.

Kadivar, M. 1997/1376. *Nazariyahā-ye dawlat dar feqh-e shi'a,* Tehran: Nashr-e Nay.

———. 1998/1377. *Hokumat-e velā'i,* Tehran: Nashr-e Nay.

Kamrava, M., and Hasan-Yari, H. 2004. "Suspended Equilibrium in Iran's Political System," *The Muslim World,* 94: 495–524.

Karimi, R., and Najibullah, R. 2008. "More Power to Iran's Most Powerful Leader," RadioFreeEurope, 12/19/ 2008 (www.rferl/articleprintview/1361676.html).

Kazemi Moussavi, A. 1992. "A New Interpretation of the Theory of *Vilayat-i Faqih,*" *Middle Eastern Studies,* 28(1): 101–107.

Keshāvarz, B. 1996/1375. *Majmu'a-ye Mohshā-ye Qānun-e Ta'zirāt-e Mosavvab-e 1375,* Tehran: Ganj-e Dānesh.

Keshavarzian, A. 2005. "Contestation without Democracy: Elite Fragmentation in Iran," in M. P. Posusney and M. P. Angrist, eds., *Authoritarianism in the Middle East. Regimes and Resistance,* Boulder, CO: Lynne Rienner, pp. 63–88.

———. 2007. *Bazaar and State in Iran. The Politics of the Tehran Marketplace,* New York: Cambridge University Press.

Khalji, M. 2006. *The Last Marja: Sistani and the End of Traditional Religious Authority in Shi'ism,* Washington, D.C.: The Washington Institute for Near East Policy, Policy Focus #59.

Khāmane'i, 'A. 1996/1375. *Farhang va tahājom-e farhangi,* Tehran: Vezārat-e Ershād-e Eslāmi.

Khātami, M. 1999/1378. *Ā'in va andisha dar dām-e khodkāmagi. Sayri dar andisha-ye siyāsi-ye mosalmānan dar farāz va forud-e tamaddon-e eslāmi,* Tehran: Tarh-e Naw.

[Khomeini, R.] Anonymous. n.d. [1944]. *Kashf-e asrār,* Qom.

Khomeini, R. n.d. [1971]. *Ketāb al-bay,'* 2 vols., Qom.

———. 1999/1378. *Sahifa-ye nur. Majmu'a-ye rahnamudhā-ye emām Khomeini,* 2nd ed., 11 vols., Tehran: Ministry of Culture and Islamic Guidance.

Khomeini Centennial:

Kongerah-e Imām Khomeini 1999–2000/1378. *Emām Khomeini va hokumat-e eslāmi,* 10 vols. (papers presented at the Congress to mark Khomeini's hundredth birthday), Qom: Tabliqāt-e Eslāmi.

———. 2000/1378. *Emām Khomeini va hokumat-e eslāmi, Vol. 5: Akhām-e hokumati va maslahat,* Qom: Tabliqāt-e Eslāmi.

———. 2000/1378. *Emām Khomeini va hokumat-e eslāmi, Vol. 6: Nahādhā-ye siyāsi va osul-e madani,* Qom: Tabliqāt-e Eslāmi.

———. 2000/1378. *Emām Khomeini va hokumat-e eslāmi, Vol. 9: Ma'khadh-shenāsi,* Qom: Tabliqāt-e Eslāmi.

Kibaroğlu, M. 2006. "Good for the Shah, Banned for the Mullahs: The West and Iran's Quest for Nuclear Power," *Middle East Journal,* 60(2): 207–32.

Knight, A. 2001. "The Modern Mexican State. Theory and Practice," in
M.A. Centeno and F. López-Alves, *The Other Mirror. Grand Theory through the
Lens of Latin America,* Princeton, NJ: Princeton University Press.

Lazrak, J. 2006. "The Pasdaran's Private Empires," *Le Monde diplomtique,*
December 2006.

Lewin, M. 1991. *The Gorbachev Phenomenon: A Historical Interpretation,* Berkeley:
Univeristy of California Press.

Linz, J. 1975. "Totalitarian and Authoritarian Regimes," in F. Greenstein and
N. Polsby, eds., *Handbook of Political Science, Vol. 3: Macropolitical Theory,*
Reading, MA: Addison-Wesley.

Looney, Robert E. 1982. *Economic Origins of the Iranian Revolution,* New York:
Pergamon Press.

Madani, J. 1988–91/1367–69. *Hoquq-e asāsi dar jomhuri-ye eslāmi-ye Irān,* 7 vols.,
Tehran: Sorush.

———. 1995/1374. *Hoquq asāsi va nahādhā-ye siyāsi-ye jomhuri-ye eslāmi-ye Irān,*
Tehran.

Malekahmadi, F. 1999. "The Sociological Intersection of Religion, Law and
Politics in Iran: Judicial Review and Political Control in the Islamic Republic
of Iran," Ph.D. Dissertation, State University of New York at Stony Brook,
Stony Brook, NY.

Matin-Asghari, A. 1997. " 'Abdolkarim Sorush and the Secularization of Islamic
Thought in Iran," *Iranian Studies,* 30(1–2): 95–115.

———. 2004. "The Intellectual Best-sellers of Post-Revolutionary Iran: On
Backwardness, Elite-killing and Western Rationality," *Iranian Studies,* 30(1):
73–88.

Mehrpur, H. 1993/1372. *Didgāhhā-ye jadid sar masā'el-e hoquqi,* Tehran.[a]

———. 2001/1380. *Ra'is-e Jomhur va mas 'uliyyat-e ejrā-ye qānun-e asāsi,* Tehran:
Ettelā'āt, 2001/1380.

———. 2005/1384. *Vazifa-ye doshvār-e nezārat bar ejrā-ye qānun-e asāsi,* Tehran:
Nashr-e Thāleth.

Mesbāh-Yazdi, M.T. 1981/1360. *Pāsdāri az sangarhā-ye ideolozhik,* Qom: Rāh-e
Haqq.

———. 1996/ 1375. "Ekhtiyarat-e vali-ye faqih dar kharej az marzha," *Hokumat-e
Eslami,* 1: 81–95.

———. 1998/1377. *Eslām, Siyāsat va Hokumat,* 2 vols., Tehran: Sazmān-e
Tablighāt-e Eslāmi.

Mir-Hosseini, Z. 2001. "The Rise and Fall of Fa'ezeh Hashemi: Women in Iranian
Elections," *Middle East Report,* 218 (Spring 2001): 8–11.

Mir-Hosseini, Z., and Tapper, R. 2002. *Islam and Democracy in Iran. Eshkevari and
the Quest for Reform,* London: I.B. Tauris.

Mohammadi, M. 1998/1377. *Sar bar āstān-e qodsi, del dar gero-ye 'orfi,* Tehran:
Nashr-e Qatra.

———. 2009. "Pāyān-e eqtedār-e ejtemā'i-ye nahād-e marja'iyyat," IWPR website
(http://www.iwpr.net/?p=irn&s=f&o=354173&apc_state=hfapirn).

Mohtashamipur, 'A.-A. 2000/1379. *Chand sedā'i dar jāme'a-ye ruhāniyyat,* Tehran: Khāna-ye Andisha-ye Javān.

Mojtahed-Shabestari, M. 1996/1375. *Hermeneutic, kitāb va sonnat,* Tehran: Tarh-e Naw.

———. 1997/1376. *Imān va Āzādi,* Tehran: Tarh-e Naw.

———. 2000/1379. *Naqdi bar qerā'at-e rasmi-ye din,* Tehran: Tarh-e Naw.

Mo'men, M. 1997/1375. "Mabāni-ye velāyat-e faqih," *Hokumat-e Eslāmi,* 2: 6–11.

Mo'men, M. 1998/1377. "Shura-ye negahbān va ehrāz-e salāhiyyat-e kāndidāhā-ye khebragān," *Hokumat-e Eslāmi,* 8: 138–52.

Montazeri, H.-'A. 1988/1408Q. *Deràsàt fi velàyat al-faqih,* 2 vols., Qom.

Mortaji, H. 1999/1378. *Jenāhhā-ye siyāsi dar Irān-e emruz,* Tehran: Naqsh va Negār.

Mosca, G. 1966 [1895]. *La classe politica,* Norberto Bobbio, ed., Bari: Editori Laterza.

Moslem, M. 2002. *Factional Politics in post-Khomeini Iran,* Syracuse: Syracuse University Press.

Naji, K. 2008. *Ahmadinejad. The Secret History of Iran's Radical Leader,* Berkeley: University of California Press.

Nasr, S. V. R. 2000. 'The rise of Sunni militancy in Pakistan: The changing role of Islamism and the ulama in society and politics,' *Modern Asian Studies,* 34(1): 139–80.

———. 2002. "The Iranian Revolution and Changes in Islamism in Pakistan, India, and Afghanistan," in N.R. Keddie and R. Matthee, eds., *Iran and the Surrounding World. Interactions in Culture and Cultural Politics,* Seattle: Washington University Press.

Nuri, 'A. 1999/1378. *Shokarān-e eslāh,* Tehran: Tarh-e Naw.

Pareto, V. 1968 [1917–19]. *Oeuvres Complètes,* XII, *Traité de Sociologie Générale,* Geneva: Librairie Droz.

Parsa, M. 1989. *Social origins of the Iranian revolution,* N.J.: Rutgers university Press.

Parsi, T. 2007. *Treacherous alliance : the secret dealings of Israel, Iran, and the United States,* New Haven: Yale University Press.

Peterson, Scott. 2005. "Waiting for the Rapture in Iran," *Christian Science Monitor,* 12/21/05.

Peterson, S., and LaFranchi, H. 2008. "Iran shifts attention to brokering peace in Iraq," *Christian Science Monitor,* 5/14/08.

Plan and Budget Organization. 1999. *Islamic Republic of Iran. Bulletin of Socio-Economic Statistics,* Tehran, December 1999/Azar 1378.

Popper, K. R. 1945. *The Open Society and Its Enemies,* London: G. Routledge & Sons, Ltd.

Qorbāni, F. 2003/1382. *Majmu'a-ye ārā'-e vahdat-e raviya-ye divān-e 'āli-ye keshvar— Jazā'i. 1328–1382,* Tehran: Enteshārār-e Ferdawsi.

Rajaee, F. 2007. *Islamism and Modernism. The Changing Discourse in Iran,* Austin: University of Texas Press.

Ramazani, R. K. 1990. "Iran's Export of the Revolution: Politics, Ends and Means," in John L. Esposito, ed., *The Iranian Revolution: Its Global Impact,* Miami: Florida International University Press.

————. 1992. "Iran's Foreign Policy: Both North and South," *Middle East Journal,* 46(3): 393–412.

Ruhāni, H. 1982. *Enqelāb-I eslāmi: Rishahhā va chālish,* Tehran: Markaz-e Pazhuhesh-e Enqelāb-e Eslāmi.

Rundle, C. 2002. "Reflections on the Iranian Revolution and Iranian-British Relations," Durham Middle East Papers, No. 68.

Sadeghi, F. 2007a. "Siyāsat-zodā'i as jāme'a-ye madani: Tajroba-ye sāzmānhā-ye ghayr-e dawlati dar dawra-ye eslāhāt," *Goftogu,* 47 (January 2007/Dey 1385): 45–59.

————. 2007b. "Bāzgasht be-moshārekat-e sunnati: tahlil-e sevvomin dawra-ye entekhābāt-e shurāhā," *Goft-o-Gu,* 49 (Mordād 1386): 41–59.

Sadjadpour, K. 2008. *Reading Khamenei: The World View of Iran's Most Powerful Leader,* Washington, D.C.: Carnegie Endowment for Peace.

Said, E. W. 1978. *Orientalism,* New York: Pantheon Books.

Salehi-Isfahani, Djavad 2009. "Oil Wealth and Economic Growth in Iran," in A. Gheissari, ed., *Contemporary Iran. Economy, Society, Politics,* New York: Oxford University Press, pp. 3–37.

Schirazi, A. 1997. *The Constitution of Iran. Politics and the State in the Islamic Republic,* J. O'Kane, trans., London: I.B. Tauris.

Shaditalab, J. 2003. "Zanān-e irāni: entezārāt-e erteqā'-yāfta," *Studies on Persianate Societies,* 1: 86–128.

Shambayati, H. 2004. "A Tale of Two Mayors: Courts and Politics in Iran and Turkey," *International Journal of Middle East Studies,* 36(2): 253–275.

Shari'ati, 'A. n.d. [1970]. *Ommat va emāmat,* Tehran: n.p.

————. 1979. *On the Sociology of Islam: Lectures,* H. Algar, trans., Berkeley: Mizan Press.

Shils, E. 1975. *Center and Periphery. Essays in Macro-sociology,* Chicago: University of Chicago Press.

Sick, G. 1991. *October Surprise,* New York: Times Books.

————. 2002. "Iran's Foreign Policy: A Revolution in Transition," in N.R. Keddie and R. Matthee, eds., *Iran and the Surrounding World. Interactions in Culture and Cultural Politics,* Seattle: Washington University Press.

Skocpol, T. 1979. *States and Social Revolutions,* New York: Cambridge University Press.

————. 1988. "Social Revolutions and Mass Military Mobilization," *World Politics,* 40(2) (January 1988): 147–68.

Slavin, B. 2007. *Bitter Friends, Bosom Enemies: Iran, the U.S., and the Twisted Path to Confrontation,* New York: St. Martin's Press.

Snyder, J. 1991. *Myths of Empire. Domestic Politics and International Ambition,* Ithaca, NY: Cornell University Press.

Sorush, A. 1991/1370. *Qabz va bast-e teorik-e shari'at,* Tehran: Serāt.

————. 1995/1374. "Ma'ishat va fazilat," *Kiān,* 25 (June–July/Khordād–Tir).

————. 1998/1377. *Serāthā-ye mostaqim,* Tehran: Serāt.

————. 1999/1378. *Bast-e tajrobah-ye nabavi,* Tehran: Serāt.

————. 2000a/1379. *Siyāsat-nāma,* Tehran: Serāt.

————. 2000b/1379. "Dindāri va ā'in-e shahryāri," in *Dindāri va ā'in-e shahryāri (Siyāsatnāma. II),* Tehran: Serāt.

Stinchcombe, A. L. 1978. *Theoretical Methods in Historical Sociology,* New York: Academic Press.

Tabātabā'i, J. 1988/1367. *Darāmadi falsafi bar andisha-ye siyāsi-ye irān,* Tehran: IPSI.

————. 1998/1377. "Sonnat, modernité, postmodern," *Rah-e Naw,* 1(8) (23 Khordād): 18–24. (Interview.)

Tajbakhsh, K. 2000. "Political Decentralization and the Creation of Local Government in Iran," *Social Research,* 67(2): 377–404.

————. 2003. "Fate of Local Democracy under Khatami," Woodrow Wilson Center Website, Events, 12/16/2003.

————. 2006. "Decentralization, Municipal Management and Local Economic Development in Iran," unpublished paper.

————. 2009. "State-Building and Local Government in the Islamic Republic of Iran," paper presented at the workshop on Constitutionalism, the Rule of Law and the Politics of administration in Egypt and Iran, 28–29 May 2009, Oñati, Spain.

Takeyh, R. 2006. *Hidden Iran. Paradoxes and Power in the Islamic Republic,* New York: Times Books.

Taleqani, M. 1982. *Society and Economics in Islam. Writings and Declarations of Ayatollah Sayyid Mahmud Taleghani,* R. Campbell, trans., and H. Algar, ed., Berkeley: Mizan Press.

Thaqafi, M. 2006. "Āghāz va pāyān-e jāme'a-ye madani," *Goft-o-Gu,* 47 (Day 1385): 85–97.

Tierney, B. 1955. *Foundations of the conciliar theory; the contribution of the medieval canonists from Gratian to the Great Schism,* Cambridge University Press.

Tocqueville, A. de. 1955. *The Old Régime and the French Revolution,* S. Gilbert, trans., New York: Doubleday.

Vahdat, F. 1999. "Metaphysical Foundations of Islamic Revolutionary Discourse in Iran: Vacillations on Human Subjectivity," Critique. *Journal for Critical Studies of the Middle East,* 14: 49–73.

Walt, S. 1996. *Revolution and War,* Ithaca: Cornell University Press.

Weber, M. 1978. *Economy and Society,* G. Roth and C. Wittich, eds., University of California Press.

Zākeri, M. 2002/1381. "Tawse'a-ye qazā'i dar qānun-e asāsi-ye jomhuri-ye eslāmi-ye Irān," in *Majmu'a-ye maqālāt-e tawse'a- ye qazā'i,* Tehran: Mo'avenat-e 'Ejtemā'i-ye Qovva-ye Qazā'iyya, pp. 11–21.

Zibā-Kalām, S. 1999/1377. *Mā cheguna mā shodim,* Tehran: Rawzanah.

Newspapers, Weeklies, and Websites Cited in the Text

RFE/RL Iran Report = Radio Free Europe/Radio Liberty Iran Report (weekly electronic report); reports cited are by Bill Samii.

Agence Presse France

Associated Press
BBC News website
BBC Persian website
CNN Television
Copenhagen University Middle East and Islam Network (http://cuminet.blogs
.ku.dk)
The Economist
Emrooz.com
Ettelā'āt
Fars News Agency
Financial Times
G2K= Gulf/2000 Members Only Website (https://members.gulf2000.columbia
.edu/)
Irān
Iran Emrooz
Iran Report
The Guardian
Informed Comment (http://www.juancole.com)
The Independent
International Herald Tribune
Iran Student News Agency, ISNA (www.isna.ir)
Kalemeh-ye Sabz (www.kalemeh.ir)
Kanun-e Zanan-e Iran website
Libération
Los Angeles Times
Meydaan.com
Nawruz
New York Times
Resālat
Seda-ye 'Adālat
Washington Post
Youtube

INDEX